D1291236

America Online
FOR BUSY PEOPLE

David Einstein

Osborne/**McGraw-Hill**

Berkeley / New York / St. Louis / San Francisco / Auckland / Bogotá
Hamburg / London / Madrid / Mexico City / Milan / Montreal / New Delhi
Panama City / Paris / São Paulo / Singapore / Sydney / Tokyo / Toronto

Osborne/**McGraw-Hill**
2600 Tenth Street
Berkeley, California 94710
U.S.A.

For information on translations or book distributors outside the U.S.A., or to arrange bulk purchase discounts for sales promotions, premiums, or fundraisers, please contact Osborne/**McGraw-Hill** at the above address.

America Online for Busy People

1234567890 DOC 99876

ISBN 0-07-882295-5

Publisher: Brandon A. Nordin
Acquisitions Editor: Joanne Cuthbertson
Project Editor: Emily Rader
Technical Editor: Leigh Yafa
Copy Editors: Katherine Krause, Luann Rouff
Proofreader: Linda Medoff
Indexer: David Heiret
Graphic Artists: Lance Ravella, Richard Whitaker
Computer Designers: Roberta Steele, Leslee Bassin, Peter F. Hancik
Quality Control: Joe Scuderi
Series and Cover Designer: Ted Mader Associates
Series Illustrator: Daniel Barbeau

About the Author

David Einstein is a technology reporter for the *San Francisco Chronicle*, specializing in personal computers. He has also been a reporter for the *Los Angeles Times* and the Associated Press. Dave lives in Petaluma, California, with his wife, two sons, two dogs, and several PCs.

MOM

Contents at a glance

Contents

Part 3

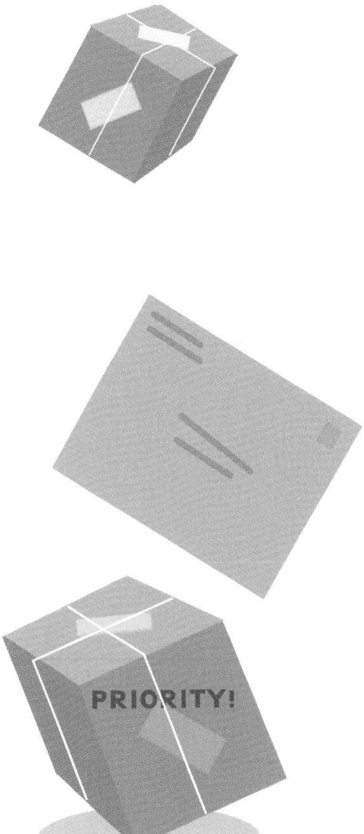
PRIORITY!

INTRODUCTION

The online revolution is in full swing, and America Online is leading the charge. Thanks to explosive growth in subscribership over the past several years, AOL is now the largest commercial online service by far, boasting more than 5 million subscribers as of this spring. AOL has attained its leadership position thanks to a slick look and feel that makes it easy to use, combined with rich content that offers something for everyone. There's news and information on hundreds of topics, as well as access to the Internet and electronic mail. But with this plethora of possibilities also comes complexity. The key to using AOL is knowing how to get the most out of it without getting lost in it.

That's where this book comes in. Like other titles in the Osborne/McGraw-Hill *Busy People* series, *America Online for Busy People* is designed for people who don't have time to learn by trial and error, or by wading through technical jargon. This book is easy to read for people who, to paraphrase Sergeant Joe Friday of Dragnet fame, just want the facts.

I KNOW YOU'RE IN A HURRY, SO...

Let's get down to cases. AOL is the biggest of four major commercial online services, the others being CompuServe, Prodigy, and the Microsoft Network. All the services work the same, charging monthly rates for access time. In the case of AOL, the rate as of this book's release is $9.95 a month for five hours, plus $2.95 for each additional hour.

To use AOL, you're going to need the right equipment. That means a personal computer capable of running Windows, or an Apple

Macintosh, and a modem that lets you hook up to a telephone line. You'll also need AOL's software—which is free. In fact, it is one of the most widely available pieces of software in the world. AOL floppy disks are regularly packaged with computer magazines, and if you buy a new PC, chances are the AOL software is already loaded on it.

Once you've got the hardware and software, the only other thing you need is this book, which will make it easy for you to

- Connect to AOL and sign up
- Customize your account
- Find your way around the service
- Access the Internet
- Send and receive e-mail
- Chat with other AOL members
- Find and download software
- Get the latest news and sports
- Read movie reviews
- Track your stocks
- Further your education
- Shop online

As you can see, there's a lot of territory to cover, but don't worry. You don't have to be a computer genius to take advantage of what AOL has to offer. In fact, all you really have to know is how to turn on your PC. I'll teach you the rest.

KEEPING PACE WITH THE FUTURE

Although services like AOL have experienced tremendous growth, they have found themselves threatened by another sort of online competition—the Internet. Once a government-backed network for scientists and professors, the Internet has blossomed into the greatest conduit of information the world has ever seen. Online services have decided that if they can't beat this new phenomenon, they'll join it. They are doing everything they can to integrate their features with the Internet—especially the graphically rich World Wide Web.

AOL has taken a leading role in this area, offering seamless access to information on the Internet that supplements AOL's own stable of features. AOL even has its own separate Internet access service called GNN, which will be discussed later. The point, I suppose, is that it's impossible to put too much emphasis on the Internet these days, so chapters pertaining to it have been positioned early in the book.

THINGS YOU MIGHT WANT TO KNOW ABOUT THIS BOOK

In the book, various points of interest will appear in margin notes like this one.

Because the whole purpose of the *Busy People* series is to help you work quickly and efficiently, this book is designed to give you answers to your questions, not fill your head with useless information. It's arranged so that if you want to know about a specific topic, you can go right to it, without having to plod through material that doesn't interest you. If you're new to AOL, it's probably best to start at the beginning and get the basics out of the way first. If you're already familiar with the service but aren't yet acclimated to the Internet, the chapter on the World Wide Web would be a good starting point. In any event, feel free to hop around. For the sake of simplicity, I'm writing this with owners of Intel-based PCs in mind. But if you have a Macintosh, don't despair. Most of the features in AOL are identical, or nearly so, no matter which system you're using.

Throughout the book, you'll encounter a number of elements designed to help make your reading experience more enjoyable and informative. Here's a rundown of some of them:

Fast Forwards

Each chapter begins with a Fast Forward section. These sections are just the thing for people who are impatient, are already experienced with the subject, or both. They give step-by-step instructions on major

AOL features in just a few words and provide page references to the more in-depth treatments of those topics contained within the chapter. For some of you, the Fast Forward is all you'll need on a particular topic.

Habits & Strategies

This feature—accompanied by a picture of a man at a chessboard—suggests time-saving tips and techniques that can make your computing experience more efficient and productive. Think of Habits & Strategies as habit-forming notes that let you see the forest for the trees and help you plan ahead.

Shortcuts

If there's one thing busy people need, it's the ability to do things faster. When there's a way to do something that's not as conventional as the normal method described in the text, but is *faster*, I'll tell you about it in the margin. Just look for the man jumping over the fence with his tie flying in the breeze.

Cautions

Whenever you use a PC, there's always the possibility of making a mistake and spending time trying to discover what went wrong. In some instances, you can even mess up your computer system by flailing around. That's why we've included this feature. The guy in the hard hat will warn you of possible pitfalls, and point out how you can avoid them.

Definitions

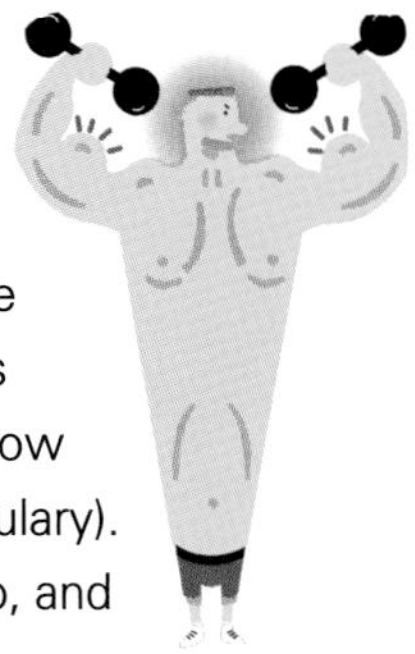

I'll try my best to avoid computer jargon, otherwise known as "technobabble," but when I must use it, I'll usually explain a term the first time it occurs in the text. If a more thorough definition is called for, you'll find it in the margin, beneath a yellow body builder (who's beefing up his technical vocabulary). That way, you can read the definition if you want to, and refer back to it whenever necessary. Or, you can ignore it, which is probably what I'd do most of the time.

LET'S DO IT

Okay, now that you've had your *Busy People* orientation course, it's time to get up and running with America Online, because everybody knows that the place to be in the '90s is online, and the place to be online is on AOL. So hook up your modem and let's dial in.

Part 1

THE BASICS FOR BUSY PEOPLE

CHAPTER 1

The Right Connections

INCLUDES

- Getting ahold of the software
- Checking out your modem
- Creating an account
- Protecting your password
- Adding family members
- Finding answers to your questions

FAST FORWARD

GET THE AOL SOFTWARE ➤ *pp. 6–8*

You can't become an AOL member without the special software that lets you access and use the service. The AOL software, which comes on a floppy disk, is free. The disk comes bundled with computer magazines, and you might even have received one in the mail. If you can't find a disk, call AOL at (800) 827-6364. They'll be glad to send you one.

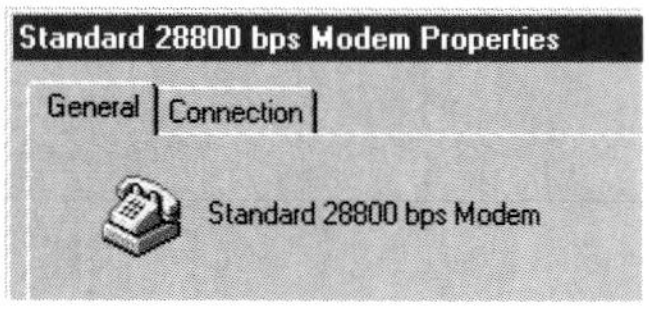

MAKE SURE YOUR MODEM IS UP TO THE JOB ➤ *pp. 8–9*

To efficiently use AOL, you're going to need a modem that runs at 14.4 kbps or faster. To find out what kind of modem you've got inside your PC:

1. Click the Start button on the Windows 95 taskbar.
2. Point to Settings and select Control Panel.
3. Double-click the Modems icon.
4. Choose the tab labeled General to see what brand of modem you have.

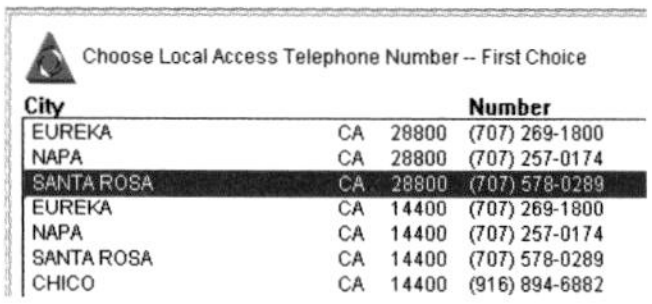

Choose Local Access Telephone Number -- First Choice
City
Number
EUREKA CA 28800 (707) 269-1800
NAPA CA 28800 (707) 257-0174
SANTA ROSA CA 28800 (707) 578-0289
EUREKA CA 14400 (707) 269-1800
NAPA CA 14400 (707) 257-0174
SANTA ROSA CA 14400 (707) 578-0289
CHICO CA 14400 (916) 894-6882

CHOOSE AN ACCESS NUMBER ➤ *p. 11*

As part of the process of starting an account, you'll be asked to choose telephone numbers that your PC will use to connect to AOL. You'll be presented with a list of numbers in your area. Look for numbers that are close to you and that support the fastest rate at which your modem can operate.

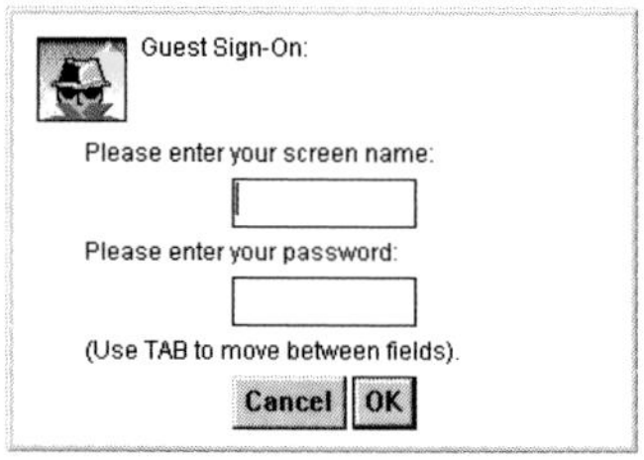

ACCESS AOL FROM ANOTHER PC ➤ *p. 16*

You can connect to your account from any computer that has the AOL software installed on it. Here's how:

1. Start the AOL program and choose Guest from the drop-down list of screen names.
2. Click SIGN ON.
3. Once you are connected, enter your screen name and password, and then press ENTER.

CHANGE YOUR PASSWORD ➤ *pp. 17–18*

The only way to make sure that no one ever has unauthorized access to your account is to keep your password to yourself. Changing your password occasionally is an extra bit of insurance. To change your password:

1. Click the Keyword button on the AOL toolbar (the group of icons that runs across the top of the screen).
2. Enter the word **password** and click Go.
3. Follow the onscreen instructions to change your password.

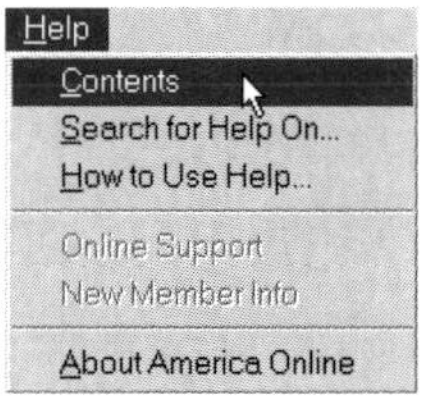

GET HELP EVEN WHEN YOU'RE NOT CONNECTED ➤ *pp. 20–23*

AOL offers myriad ways to get help when you're online. But even when you're not, you can find answers to general questions, including tips on getting connected. To access offline Help, just start AOL and click Help on the menu bar at the top of the screen.

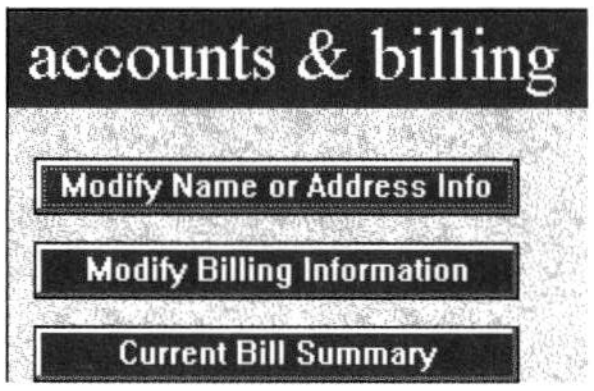

MONITOR YOUR BILLING INFORMATION ➤ *pp. 23–24*

1. Choose Member Services from the Members menu or click the Members Services button on the toolbar, which runs across the top of the screen just beneath the menus. (The Member Services button looks like a question mark.) You'll see a dialog box telling you that you're heading into a free area of the service. Click Yes.
2. Double-click Account Management & Billing.
3. Select Current Bill Summary to see how your account stands.

America Online members liken their service to an electronic community—one populated by millions of members who use the service to gather information and share opinions and ideas. It's a shopping mall, a reference library, a newsstand, an entertainment center, and a gateway to the Internet, all rolled into one. On top of that, it's easy to use, with a slick look and feel that takes advantage of the point-and-click environment of Microsoft Windows. If you have a basic knowledge of Windows, you'll have no trouble at all mastering AOL. But first, you'll have to set yourself up with an AOL account, and that's the subject of this chapter.

AOL SOFTWARE—IT'S EVERYWHERE

To subscribe to AOL, you'll need the appropriate software to access and use the service. Obtaining it should be no trouble at all. AOL puts its Windows-compatible software on floppy disks and distributes them for free by the millions. (Recently AOL has also begun giving out its software on CD-ROMs.) The software comes packaged with computer magazines, and you might even have gotten a disk in the mail. I personally have encountered more than a dozen AOL floppies over the past couple of years. This marketing blitz has been instrumental in vaulting AOL past its competitors to the No. 1 spot among all online services. If you're one of the unlucky few who don't have an AOL disk lying around, here are some ways to obtain one:

- Call AOL at (800) 827-6364. They'll send you a free disk.
- Borrow one from a friend (or have someone copy an AOL disk for you).

Many personal computers come with AOL preinstalled; so before you go looking for an AOL floppy, make sure the software isn't already on your PC. If it is, skip the following section and go right to the part about setting up an account.

- If you have access to the Internet, you can download the free software from AOL's World Wide Web site at **http://www.aol.com**.

Free Trial Period!

Everyone who subscribes to AOL starts out with a free trial period. There's no charge for the first month's membership, plus you get 15 hours of free connect time to start with. The trial period gives you a chance to try out the service without making a financial commitment. When the free trial period is over, you'll have the choice of two rate plans: a basic plan of $9.95 per month, which includes 5 free hours, and an extended-use plan that gives you 20 hours per month for $19.95. (If you use up the allotted time in either plan, each additional hour will cost you $2.95.) The second option, which AOL refers to as its "20/20 Plan," is the less expensive alternative if you spend more than about 8 hours per month online. It's designed especially for Internet users who tend to sit in front of their computers for hours on end.

What You'll Need to Accept the Free Trial Offer

Every AOL disk comes with a certificate number and a temporary password that you must use to create an account. If for some reason you don't have that information—if you're using a borrowed disk, for instance, or if you downloaded the software from the Internet—don't sweat. Just call (800) 827-6364, and the good people at AOL will be happy to supply you with a certificate number and a temporary password. They really want your business.

Your free trial time must be used within the first 30 days of your membership. Likewise, unused time each month doesn't carry over to the next month. Use it or lose it, as they say. But most people like AOL enough to keep it after the free trial.

Installing the Software

AOL version 3.0 for Windows is installed in the same way that any other Windows program is installed. It works with either Windows 95 or its predecessor, Windows 3.1, and basically looks the same in either environment. (In an effort to stay as up to date as possible, I've assumed that you're using Windows 95.) To install the software on a Windows 95–equipped PC, just slip the AOL disk into the floppy disk drive. Click the Start button on the taskbar, and follow that by clicking

Run. Then type **a:\setup** in the Open box, as shown here, and either click OK or press the ENTER key.

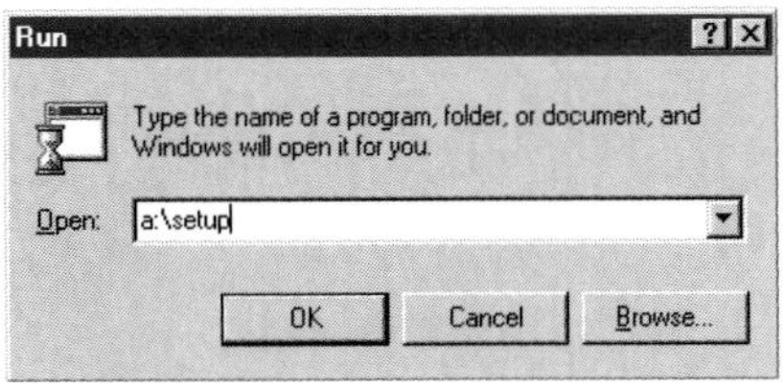

Follow the onscreen instructions, which will lead you through the brief installation process. After that, you'll be ready to connect your PC to AOL and create your new account.

As of this writing, AOL planned to release a version of its software specifically designed for Windows 95 sometime in the second half of 1996. That program will take advantage of Windows 95 goodies, such as long filenames.

THE ALL-IMPORTANT MODEM

To connect to AOL—or to any online service or the Internet, for that matter—you'll need a properly configured modem and a telephone line to hook it up to. Modems transmit computer data over telephone lines. A modem can be either an external device that plugs into the back of your PC or an internal one in the form of a circuit card that fits into a slot inside the PC case. Internal modems are far more common than external ones—all PCs now being sold for the home have internal modems. For the sake of this discussion, let's assume that you have an internal modem.

Before you start the process of creating an AOL account, you should know what kind of modem you have, what its maximum speed is, and which COM port it's using on your PC. This information can be found in the documentation that came with your modem; but if you can't find the manual, here's an easy way to get the lowdown:

1. Click the Start button on the Windows 95 taskbar, point to Settings, and select Control Panel.
2. Double-click the Modems icon.

3. If necessary, select the tab labeled General and then click the button marked Properties, which will bring up a window that looks similar to this:

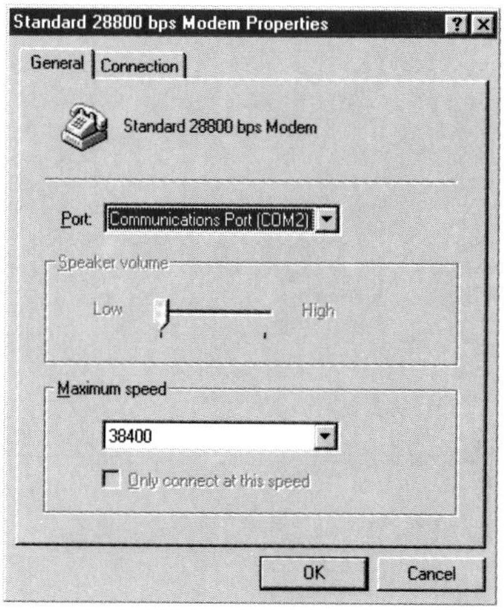

The Faster the Better

Most PCs sold today come with modems capable of processing data at 14.4 or 28.8 kbps. The higher the number, the faster the modem, and the more efficiently you'll be able to use AOL. That's because AOL is a graphically rich service, and graphics take time to send over telephone lines. If you have an older PC with a modem slower than 14.4 kbps, you'd be well advised to buy a new modem. An internal 14.4-kbps modem costs less than $50, and a 28.8-kbps model can be had for less than $150.

SOUNDS AS WELL AS SIGHTS

AOL is a multimedia experience, which means that it offers sounds as well as colorful graphics. For instance, when you sign on, a voice says "Welcome," and when you quit, it says "Good-bye." Okay,

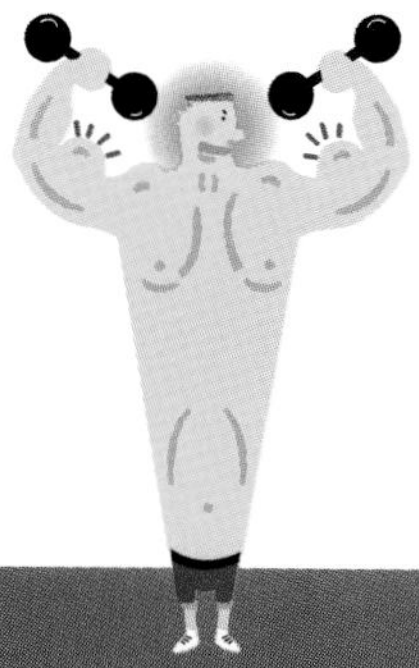

definitions

COM port: *Communications port. Your modem uses a COM port to communicate with the PC. Most PCs have four COM ports, and most modems come pre-configured to work on COM 2. However, you can change the port setting on the modem—check your modem's manual.*

kbps: *Kilobits per second. This is a standard way of measuring the speed of data transmission. A kilobit is 1,000 bits. A bit is the basic unit of digital information. The fastest modems for PCs transmit at 28.8 kbps.*

so that's not very thrilling. But in other cases, this feature can be quite useful. When you have new e-mail, for instance, the voice tells you so. Anyway, to benefit from this, you'll need a sound card—standard equipment on most PCs sold for home use.

BECOMING A MEMBER

Okay, now you're ready to go through the process of joining the AOL community. Don't worry, it's painless (except for the normal pain associated with giving someone your credit card number). First, launch the AOL program. In Windows 95, the easiest way to do this is

1. Click the Start button and point to Programs.
2. Point to the America Online program group and select the America Online program item.

The first time you start AOL, you'll be presented with a series of dialog boxes that lead you through the process of creating your account. (A dialog box is a window that presents you with information and lets you choose an action.) The first box will show you the modem settings that AOL has determined for your PC. If the information is correct, click Yes and go on to the next dialog box. If it's not right, click No and make the necessary changes. You'll be able to modify the configuration using this box:

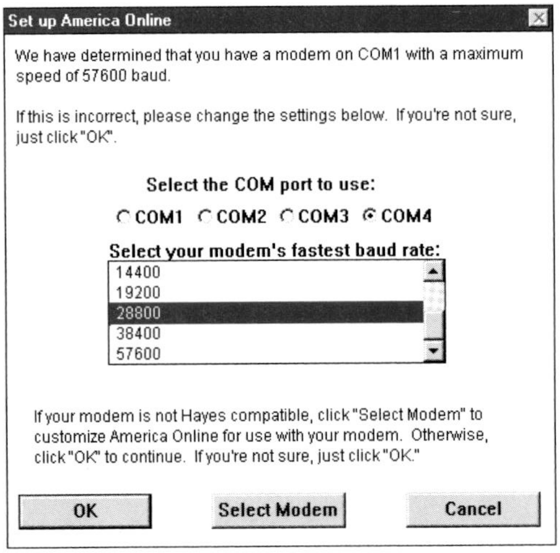

habits & strategies

AOL assumes that your modem is Hayes-compatible. If it isn't, click the Select Modem button in the setup box and follow the directions. Most modems are Hayes-compatible, so the best thing to do is try to connect before you make changes.

Getting Access Numbers

Once you get your modem information straight, click Continue. AOL will then automatically connect you to a toll-free 800 number and ask you to choose the telephone numbers that you'll use to access your AOL account—a primary number and a backup number to use if the first one is busy. After you enter your area code, you'll be presented with a list of access numbers in your area, along with the maximum modem speeds that they can handle, as shown here:

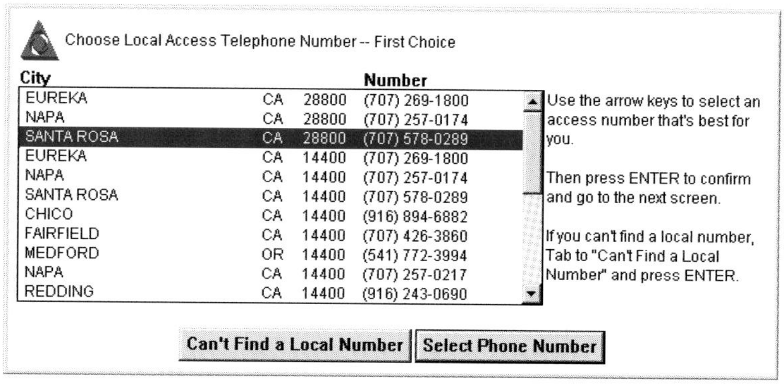
Choose Local Access Telephone Number -- First Choice
City
Number
EUREKA CA 28800 (707) 269-1800
NAPA CA 28800 (707) 257-0174
SANTA ROSA CA 28800 (707) 578-0289
EUREKA CA 14400 (707) 269-1800
NAPA CA 14400 (707) 257-0174
SANTA ROSA CA 14400 (707) 578-0289
CHICO CA 14400 (916) 894-6882
FAIRFIELD CA 14400 (707) 426-3860
MEDFORD OR 14400 (541) 772-3994
NAPA CA 14400 (707) 257-0217
REDDING CA 14400 (916) 243-0690
Use the arrow keys to select an access number that's best for you.
Then press ENTER to confirm and go to the next screen.
If you can't find a local number, Tab to "Can't Find a Local Number" and press ENTER.
Can't Find a Local Number
Select Phone Number

Look for local numbers that support the fastest speed at which your modem can operate. If you don't see a suitable number in your city, pick one from the city closest to you. But be forewarned that if the access number is out of your local calling area, you may have to pay toll charges every time you connect to AOL, and that can really add up fast.

AOL is continually adding new access numbers. But if you're out in the boonies with no local access number, you can always connect using AOL's 800 line. There's just one catch—it will cost $6.00 an hour, which will be billed to your account.

Creating Your Account

After you choose your access numbers, AOL will disconnect you and then dial your new primary access number (thus saving themselves money—from now on, it's your dime, not theirs). Once you're reconnected, you'll be able to create your account online.

First you'll be asked for the certificate number and temporary password that came with your AOL software (or that you got by calling AOL). Enter the information in the following box:

habits & strategies

If you're already an AOL member and are reinstalling or updating to a new version, enter your AOL screen name and password in the boxes. This configures the software so that you can use your account. (But you won't get another free trial.)

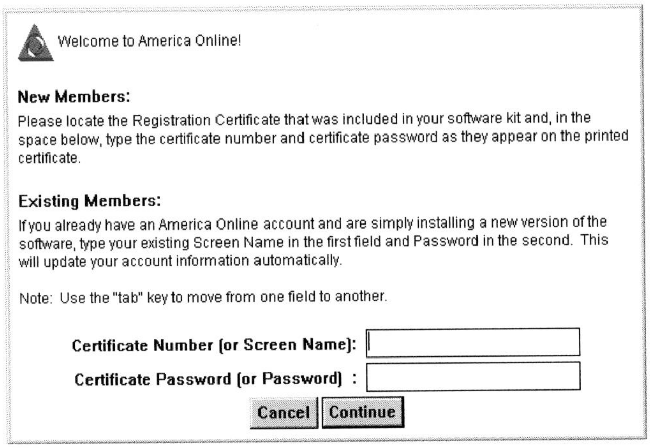

Welcome to America Online!

New Members:

Please locate the Registration Certificate that was included in your software kit and, in the space below, type the certificate number and certificate password as they appear on the printed certificate.

Existing Members:

If you already have an America Online account and are simply installing a new version of the software, type your existing Screen Name in the first field and Password in the second. This will update your account information automatically.

Note: Use the "tab" key to move from one field to another.

Certificate Number (or Screen Name):

Certificate Password (or Password) :

Cancel **Continue**

Filling Out the Forms

The electronic paperwork starts with forms that provide information on yourself, including your name, address, and day and evening phone numbers. Then it's on to the really important stuff—your billing information. Most people have their accounts billed to credit cards. You can also have the monthly charges deducted directly from your checking account, but the credit card route is easier—and it's a better bargain. AOL charges a handling fee of $3.00 a month to debit your checking account. If you choose to use your credit card, you'll enter the vital statistics into this box:

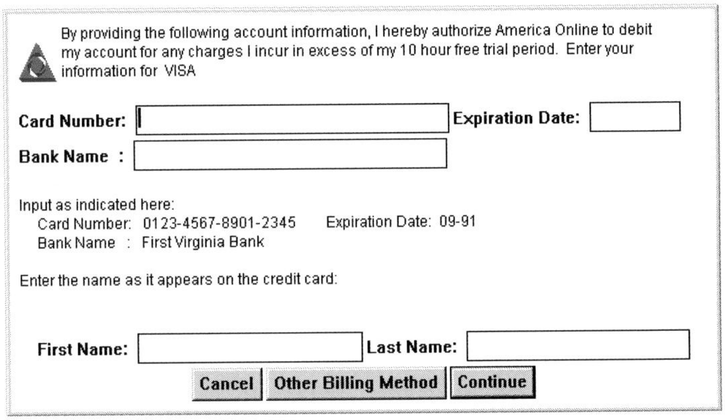

By providing the following account information, I hereby authorize America Online to debit my account for any charges I incur in excess of my 10 hour free trial period. Enter your information for VISA

Card Number: **Expiration Date:**

Bank Name :

Input as indicated here:
Card Number: 0123-4567-8901-2345 Expiration Date: 09-91
Bank Name : First Virginia Bank

Enter the name as it appears on the credit card:

First Name: **Last Name:**

Cancel **Other Billing Method** **Continue**

CAUTION

Be aware that once you pick a screen name for your account, you're stuck with it. Also, your screen name is your AOL e-mail address—another reason to choose an intelligible name if possible.

habits & strategies

If you're the forgetful type, write down your screen name and password and put them in a safe place. Never give your password to a stranger. That's like an open invitation to run up charges on your account.

Choosing an Identity

Every AOL member has a unique *screen name* between three and ten characters long that identifies him or her. But if you're thinking of using your own first or last name, forget it. Unless you have a very unusual name, it's probably already been taken by one of AOL's other members. It's the same sort of situation that you run up against when you're looking for a name to put on a vanity license plate. Go ahead and try your first name, your last name, or even your dog's name. If they're already spoken for, AOL will suggest a name that nobody else has, trying to get as much of your own name into it as possible. Here's the unfortunate name it came up with for me after I tried *Einstein* and then *DEinstein*:

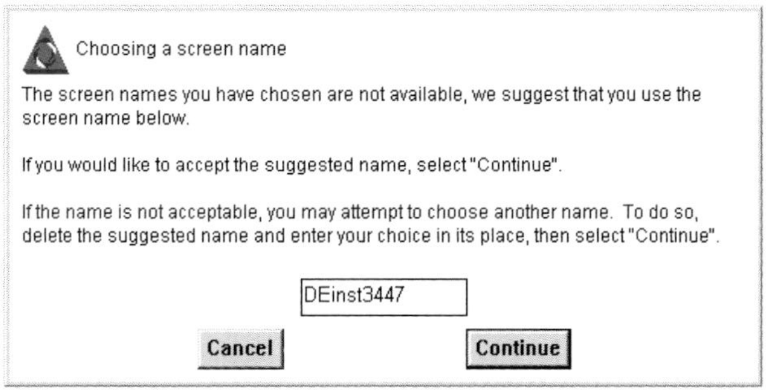

Picking a Password

The last step in establishing your new AOL account is choosing a personal password. This is a whole lot easier than coming up with a screen name, because AOL doesn't care if more than one member has the same password. Your password must be between four and eight characters long, and it can be any combination of letters and numbers. The password won't appear on the screen when you type—it will come out as a string of asterisks. You'll be asked to enter the password twice, just to make sure you typed what you meant to type.

SIGNING ON

Now that you've opened your AOL account, you can sign on any time you like, 24 hours a day, 365 days a year. (AOL never closes.) When you start AOL's new version 3.0 software in Windows 95, the screen shown in Figure 1.1 will appear.

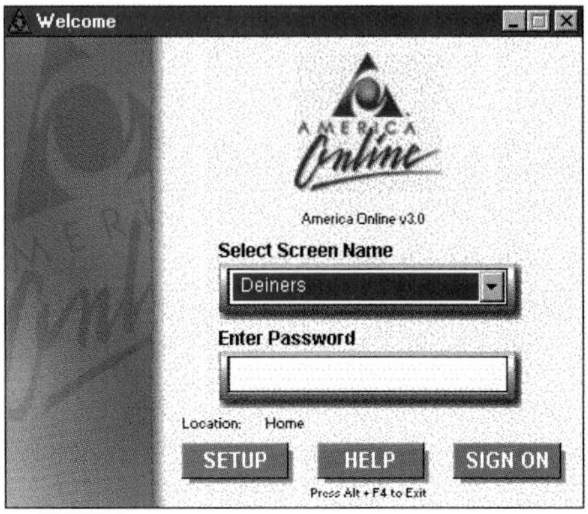

Figure 1.1 The AOL Welcome dialog box

Your screen name will be displayed. Enter your password, and then click the SIGN ON button. The program will then go through three sign-on steps. It will

1. Get your modem's attention
2. Dial your primary access number
3. Connect to AOL's computer system in Virginia, verify your screen name and password, and start your online session

During sign-on, a three-panel display appears on the screen to keep you informed of how the process is going. Each panel changes slightly to show when that step is completed. In the third step, you'll see the speed of your connection, as illustrated here:

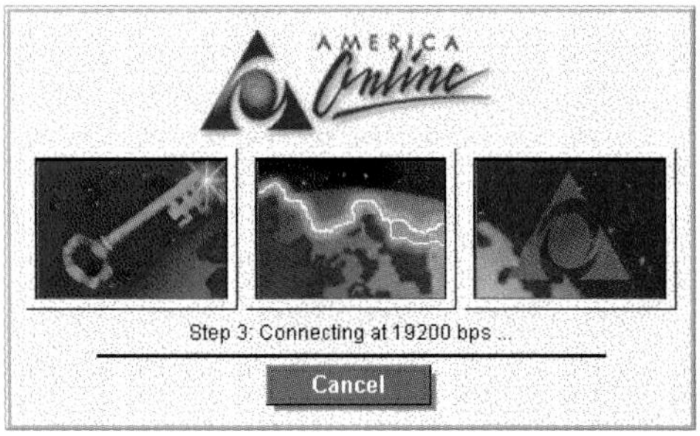

The connection speed will probably vary from session to session, depending on network traffic, your modem, and other factors. It's not unusual for a 28.8-kbps modem to connect at a lower rate. Note that the connection in the illustration is just 19.2 kbps.

And Getting Off

Friends tell me that AOL can be mildly addictive. Nevertheless, there comes a time when every online session must end. To quit, click Exit on the File menu or click the X in the upper-right corner of the AOL window. Either way, the Exit window will be displayed. It gives you two choices: Sign Off or Exit. Signing off disconnects you but keeps the AOL program running on your PC. Exiting disconnects you *and* closes the program. Why would you want to keep the program open after you have disconnected? One reason is so that your PC can use AOL's FlashSession feature to automatically sign on while you're away and check for things like new e-mail (see Chapter 4).

Changing the Setup

Over time, you might get a new PC, upgrade your modem, or move to another city. Or AOL might upgrade its access in your area with a new high-speed number. Don't worry. There's an easy way to deal with such changes. Just click SETUP in the box shown in Figure 1.1. You'll see the following Network & Modem Setup box:

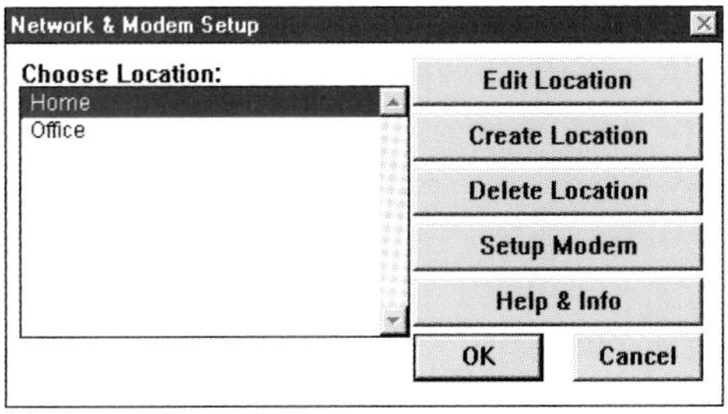

Notice that the word *Location* is all over the place in this box. A Location contains information about access numbers and your modem that your software uses to connect to AOL. When you first created your account, a location called Home was automatically created. By clicking Edit

habits & strategies

Call waiting can cause problems in an online session. If you're connected to AOL and get a call, call waiting will break your online connection. You can disable call waiting for the duration of your AOL session using the Network Setup box.

Location, you can display your Home setup, which looks like the example below. You can modify your Home setup in this dialog box if necessary.

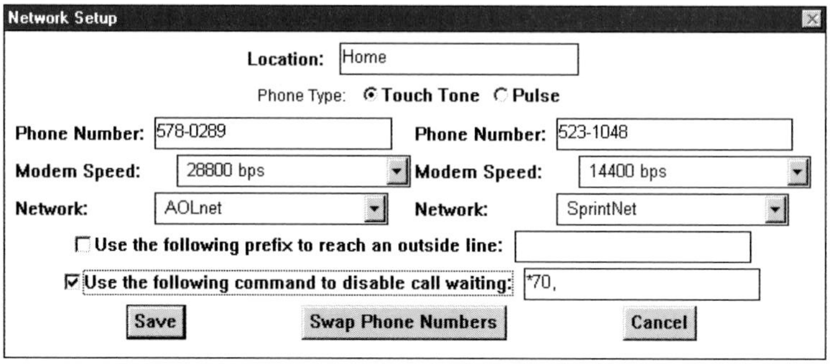

AOL lets you have multiple locations. This is especially useful for busy people who have AOL on their notebook computers. It lets you create separate locations for use at home, at work, or out of town in cities you frequent.

Using Someone Else's Computer

One of the most convenient features of AOL is the ability to sign on from any PC that has AOL installed on it. Say you're visiting a friend, and you want to check your e-mail. Here's how:

1. Start AOL and choose Guest from the drop-down list of screen names.
2. Select SIGN ON.
3. When the connection is made, you'll be prompted to enter your screen name and password.

Once you've signed on this way, the time you spend online will be charged to your AOL account. But your friend will have to pick up any telephone surcharges if the call to AOL isn't a local one. Hey, that's what friends are for.

CUSTOMIZING YOUR ACCOUNT

At this point, I'd like to introduce you to My AOL, shown below, which you can access by clicking the My AOL button on the toolbar.

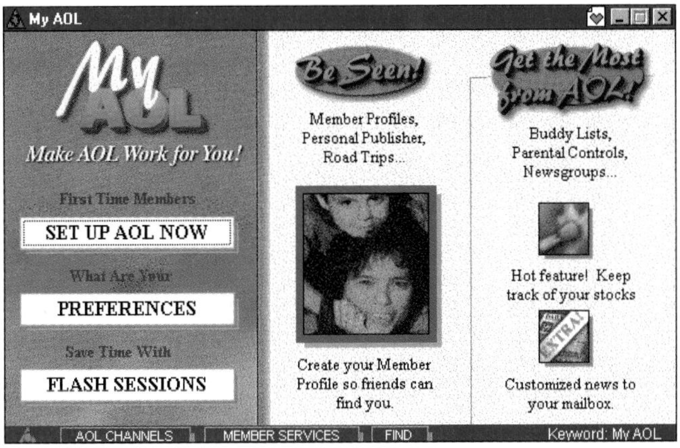

This is the area in which you'll find all the tools necessary to customize AOL to suit your tastes. In subsequent chapters I'll show you how to fine-tune various aspects of the service. Right now, though, let's take a look at some ways you can tweak your brand-new account to get the most out of it.

SHORTCUT

One of the easiest ways to find stuff on AOL is with keywords, which are words that take you directly to an area of interest. There's a keyword for nearly every destination on AOL. You'll read more about this nifty shortcut in the next chapter.

Password Protection

The best way to prevent unauthorized access to your account is to keep your password from falling into the wrong hands. (This is especially a threat if you have any KGB agents in your office.) Seriously, though, it's not a bad idea to change your password every once in a while. As they say, "It couldn't hurt." And it's easy to do using the following steps:

1. Click the Keyword button on the toolbar.
2. Enter the word **password** in the Keyword window and click Go.

3. Select Change Password to display the Change Your Password dialog box shown below. Enter your new password twice, just to make sure you've typed it correctly, and then click Change Password to make the change effective.

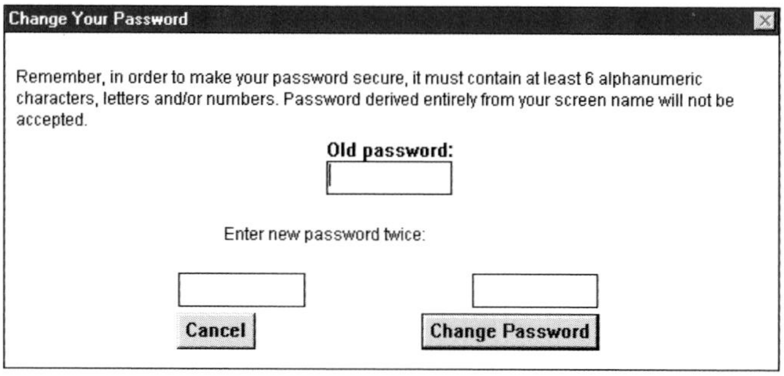

Change Your Password
Remember, in order to make your password secure, it must contain at least 6 alphanumeric characters, letters and/or numbers. Password derived entirely from your screen name will not be accepted.
Old password:
Enter new password twice:
Cancel
Change Password

Storing Your Password

One of the simplest things you can do to streamline your AOL experience is to store your password. That way you won't have to enter it each time you sign on. To store a password, use the following steps:

1. Click the My AOL button on the toolbar, and then click Preferences.
2. Click Your Password, then click Set Up Now.
3. Click Edit Your Stored Password.
4. Enter your password next to your screen name. To "unstore" your password, follow the first three steps above and remove the password from the box.

CAUTION

Storing a password can be risky. Anyone can sign onto an account that has a stored password. The rule of thumb is that you should never store a password for an account on a computer that a stranger might have access to.

Multiple Screen Names

You can have up to five screen names on your account—four in addition to the primary name, which can't be deleted. What would you do with four extra names? Well, if you're wanted in several states, you could use them as aliases. But that's not what AOL had in mind. A better use would be to give them to other family members. Or you could use two of them yourself, one for business and the other for personal stuff. Each screen name comes with its own password and gives the user his or her own e-mail, Personal Filing Cabinet, and, if

habits & strategies

Don't like your original screen name? Just add another one and use it as your primary AOL identity. You'll be like Bernard Schwartz, who changed his name to Tony Curtis.

desired, a Member Profile. (We'll get to Member Profiles in a minute. Filing Cabinets are covered in Chapter 2.)

Creating a Screen Name

Use the following steps to create a new screen name:

1. Click the My AOL button on the toolbar, then click Set Up AOL Now.
2. Click Screen Names, then click Set Up Now.
3. Double-click Create a Screen Name to display the Create or Delete Screen Names dialog box.

If that's too much work for you, just use the keyword *names* to go directly to the dialog box, shown in Figure 1.2.

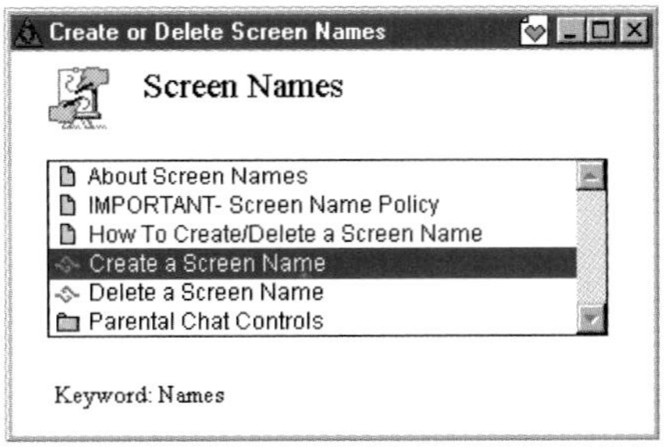

Figure 1.2 The AOL Create or Delete Screen Names dialog box

Double-click Create a Screen Name to start the process, which is identical to the process for creating your own screen name when you opened your account.

Getting Rid of a Screen Name

You can delete any screen name except the one with which you began your account. Just choose Delete a Screen Name from the box shown in Figure 1.2 and follow the instructions.

Setting Up a Member Profile

AOL gives you the opportunity to get into the community spirit by letting other AOL members know all about you. You do this by creating a Member Profile. It isn't mandatory, and if you prefer not to get personal about this online business, just forget it. But if you want other members to be able to find you, do the following:

1. Click the My AOL button on the toolbar, then click the picture of the two people in the center of the window.
2. Double-click Create/Modify Your Member Profile, which will display the following screen:

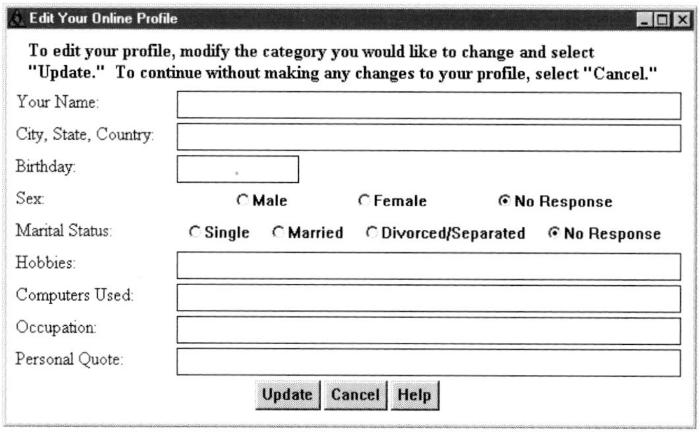

Fill in as many blanks as you want and then click Update. This updates the AOL database and makes your information available to other members. To locate a member using information in a profile, choose Member Directory from the Members menu. From there, you can conduct a search. There's even helpful information on the best way to go about it.

HELP!

After reading this book, you shouldn't need much in the way of help. But just in case, assistance is available both online and offline. When you installed the AOL software, a help file came as part of the package. Because it's always on your PC, you can use the Help feature even when you're not connected. It offers answers to general questions as well as specific help for those having trouble connecting to the service. To access it, start AOL and select the Help menu at the top of

HOW TO SAFEGUARD THE CHILDREN

Although most of AOL's content falls under the "G" rating category, there are certain areas in which the subject matter drifts into territory more suited to adults than children. In addition, AOL has no control over what you see when you venture out onto the Internet. That's where Parental Controls come in handy. This feature lets you limit your kids' access to online material. Specific ways to use these controls will be discussed at appropriate points in this book. At any time, however, you can invoke, disable, or change Parental Controls. Just choose Parental Control from the Members menu.

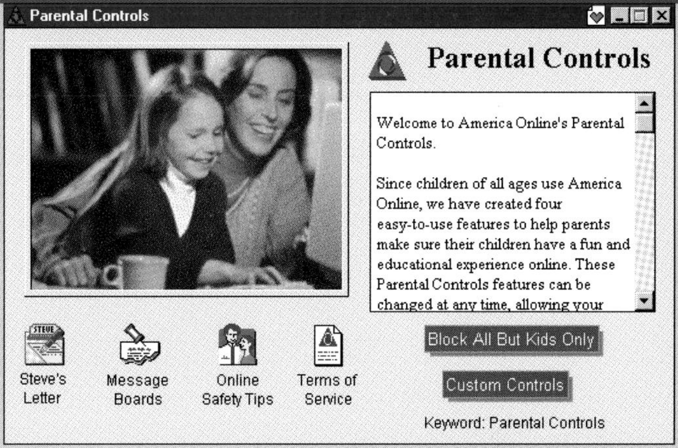

the screen. AOL's Help feature is similar to the Help features in other Windows 95 programs. It lets you search by topic or browse through an index.

If you're really stumped about some aspect of using AOL, you can get live technical support online. Click Tech Support Live in the Member Services window. This service is available free of charge from 8 A.M. to 3:45 A.M. eastern time, seven days a week.

Member Services

For help during an AOL session, take advantage of the online Help feature, which is found under Member Services. This is a free area, which means that while you're in it, you won't be charged for connect time. (You still have to pay any telephone charges, however.) To get to the Member Services window, do one of the following:

- Click the Member Services button (the question mark) in the toolbar.
- Click Member Services at the bottom of AOL's main Channels window.
- Choose Member Services from the Members menu.

In each case, a box will appear telling you that you are about to enter a free area. Click Yes or press ENTER to display the Member Services window, which looks like this:

You'll find answers to just about any question in Member Services. And the best part is that AOL continually updates it with new information. For instance, if you're in the market for a new access number, double-click the Accessing America Online folder, which will let you search for access numbers and get information on AOL's plans for extending its high-speed network to new cities.

habits & strategies

If you find yourself going to Member Services repeatedly with the same question, do yourself a favor and save or print out the answer: with the text of the answer displayed, choose Save As from the File menu to save it, or Print to print it.

More Ways to Get Answers

As you'll see in later chapters, there is always more than one way to find what you're looking for on AOL. When it comes to getting help, there are a lot of options, including one called *One Stop Infoshop*. I know, it sounds like some kind of online mini-mart, but in truth it's a compartmentalized cornucopia of information on a broad range of AOL topics. To access it, go to the Member Services window and click Have Questions? Then select Browse the One Stop Infoshop, which will present the screen shown in Figure 1.3.

If you have a specific question in mind, try using AOL's Member Services Search function. It lets you hunt through the Member Services database, an extensive collection of articles on how to use the service. You can access this feature by clicking Search at the bottom of the Member Services window or Search For Answers in the One Stop Infoshop window.

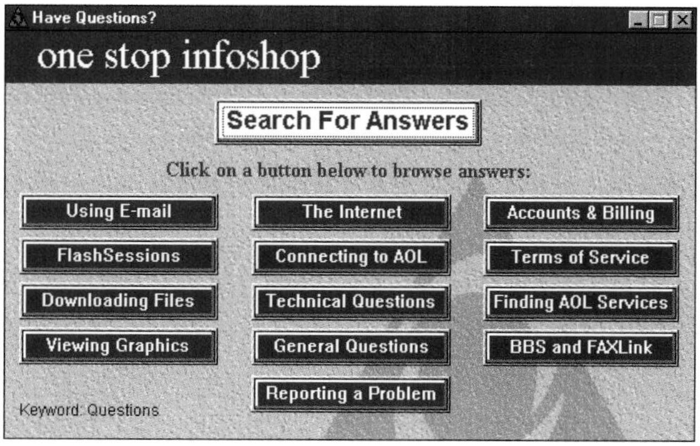

Figure 1.3 The One Stop Infoshop screen

TIME IS MONEY

Your monthly billing date is the day of the month on which you opened your account. Until you have used up your monthly allotment of 5 free hours, your summary will be updated at the end of each session. After that, it is updated every 24 hours.

Want to know how much time you've spent on AOL this month, and how much of a bill you ran up last month? No problem. Go to Member Services and double-click Account Management & Billing. This area (which is also free because it's within Member Services) provides answers to questions about billing, as well as an updated summary of your account activity and your bill.

The Accounts & Billing window also gives you a way to change the name and address on your account, as well as your billing information—to switch from one credit card to another, for example.

Watching the Clock

It's always a good idea to keep track of how long you stay online in any given AOL session. (Time flies when you're having fun, and AOL can be a lot of fun indeed.) To find out how long you've been connected, click the clock button on the AOL toolbar. You'll see a message box like the one below:

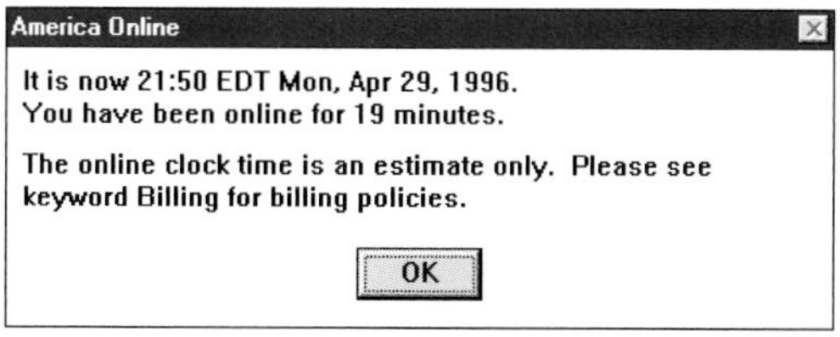

Oops, looks like I'm rolling up my bill. Time to go.

WHAT'S NEXT?

I know you're just itching to get going with your new AOL account, so I won't stop you. In fact, I'm gonna help. In the next chapter, you'll learn all about the latest software—version 3.0—with its flashy new toolbar and expanded content areas. Let's go.

CHAPTER 2

Learning and Using AOL—Don't Worry, It's No Sweat

INCLUDES

- Exploring the AOL channels
- Moving around
- Using the toolbar
- Using keywords and the Find feature
- Saving your Favorite Places
- Customizing your AOL experience

FAST FORWARD

DISPLAY THE CHANNELS WINDOW ➤ *pp. 30–31*

When you first sign on to AOL, the Channels window is hidden behind the Welcome window. To view the channels, do one of the following:

- Click CHANNELS in the Welcome window.
- Click the Channels button on the toolbar.
- Choose Channels from the Go To menu.

USE THE TOOLBAR TO CUT TO THE CHASE ➤ *pp. 43–45*

The AOL toolbar provides one-button access to AOL's key areas and features. Want to go straight to the World Wide Web? Click the button that looks like a globe. In a hurry to read today's headlines? Click the button shaped like a newspaper. With the toolbar you can also read your mail, write messages, find stuff on AOL, and even check stock prices.

USE KEYWORDS TO JUMP AROUND ➤ *pp. 46–47*

The Keyword feature allows you to specify a word or words that will quickly take you to a chosen area within AOL. To use a keyword:

1. Click the Keyword button on the toolbar.
2. Enter the keyword for the area you want to visit.
3. Click Go.

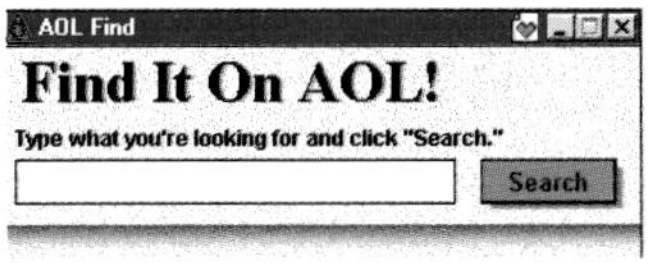

FIND STUFF FAST ➤ *pp. 47–49*

The latest rendition of AOL's software includes a new feature that helps you find people, places, and events quickly. Naturally enough, it's called Find. To use it:

1. Click the Find button on the toolbar.
2. Use the tabbed pages in the directory to find what you're looking for.
3. If you can't find what you're looking for in the directory, use Find's Search function to hunt through AOL's database of services and features.

SAVE YOUR FAVORITE PLACES ➤ *pp. 49–51*

Whenever you find an area on AOL—or on the Internet—that you really like, save it to your Favorite Places folder so that you can have easy access to it in the future. If a window can be saved as a Favorite Place, it will have a small red heart near the right end of its title bar. Just drag the heart to the Favorite Places button on the toolbar. Clicking the Favorite Places button displays a list of your favorite places, and you can go directly to any place on the list by double-clicking it.

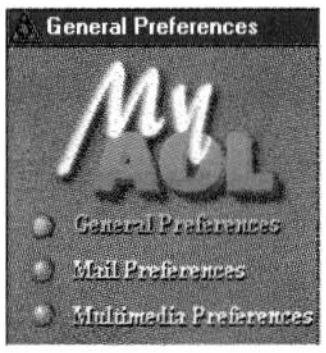

CUSTOM TAILOR YOUR AOL EXPERIENCE ➤ *pp. 52–53*

Various aspects of AOL can be tailored to suit your particular needs. In the General Preferences window, for instance, you can turn off the sounds AOL generates when you're online or change the size of the text as it appears onscreen. To do either:

1. Click the My AOL button on the toolbar.
2. Click Preferences.
3. Click General Preferences to display the dialog box in which you can make the changes.

America Online has always been the best-looking online service. It was the first to embrace Microsoft Windows, and it has continually set the standard for the industry with its easy-to-use, point-and-click interface. The latest rendition of AOL's Windows software, version 3.0, offers a profusion of splashy colors and flashy graphics. It's almost enough to make you think you're on the bridge of the Starship Enterprise rather than sitting in front of a personal computer. AOL is a huge service, and behind its Welcome screen are thousands of places for you to visit. In this chapter, we'll show you how to find your way around in this brave new online world.

WELCOME!

In fact, that's exactly what you'll hear when you sign on to AOL (if you have a multimedia PC, that is). A friendly male voice ushers you in with a glowing "Welcome." And there, in front of you, is the Welcome window inside the main AOL window. Your computer screen will look like Figure 2.1.

The same voice that welcomes you when you sign on will also tell you when you've got mail and bid you goodbye when you sign off. He's nice, but some users find him a bit irritating after a time. Later in this chapter you'll learn how to shut him up.

The Welcome window is your gateway to AOL, providing instant entry to major areas of the service, including the channels, the People Connection (for live chats between members), and the Internet. In addition, any time you have unread mail, the flag on the mailbox in the Welcome window will be up and the MAIL CENTER button will read "You Have Mail."

THE CHANNELS WINDOW

If the Welcome window is your gateway to AOL, your road map is the Channels window. Here you'll find one-button access to the 21 general subject areas—called *channels*—into which the service is organized. When you sign on, the Channels window is there on your

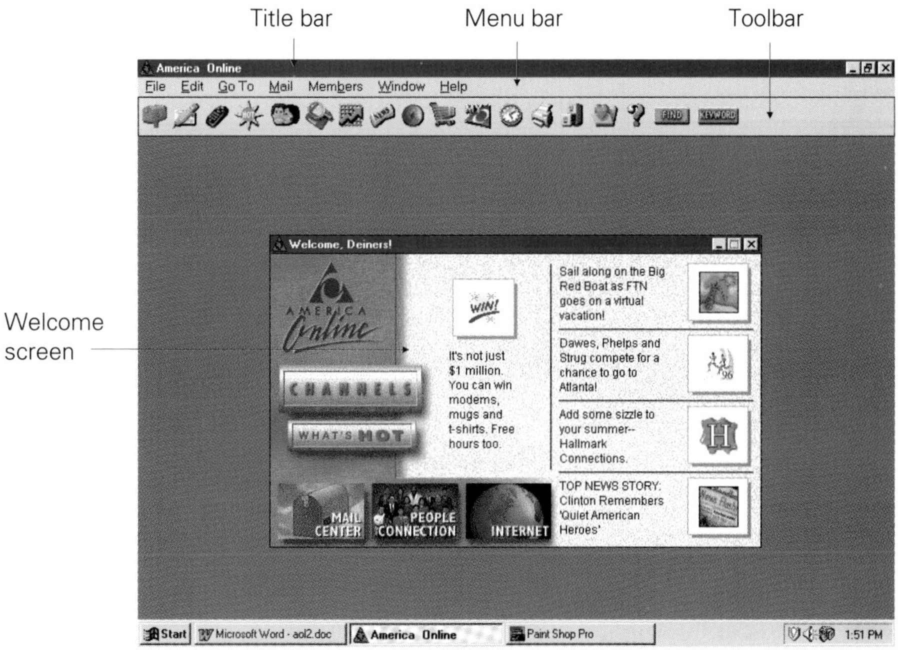

Figure 2.1 The AOL Welcome window

screen, but it's mostly hidden because the Welcome window is sitting on top of it. To view the Channels window, click CHANNELS in the Welcome window, click the Channels button on the toolbar, or choose Channels from the Go To menu. (To display the Welcome window again, click Welcome at the bottom of the Channels window.) The Channels window looks like this:

MAKE SURE YOU HAVE THE LATEST AND GREATEST

If you're not using version 3.0 of the AOL software, this chapter—and, in fact, most of this book—isn't going to make a lot of sense. To find out which version you're using, choose About America Online from the Help menu, which will present you with a window like the one shown here. If you're using an earlier version, such as version 2.5, now's the time to upgrade. Just click the Keyword button on the toolbar, type in the word **upgrade**, and click Go. Then click the Upgrade Now button.

Individualized Looks, but a Common Purpose

Each channel window has its own unique format. However, you'll find some common elements, such as one-click access to key features and a list of available resources, in every window. (Double-click any resource to go to it.) Many of the channels will be covered in depth later in this book. In the meantime, the following sections provide descriptions of the channels that were part of the initial release of AOL version 3.0.

The Computers and Software Channel

This channel has everything for the personal computer user. You can read top PC magazines and get technical support from hardware and software companies in this channel's window (see Figure 2.2), and you can download useful software files from the many thousands of files in AOL's software libraries.

The Digital City Channel

In the Digital City channel window, you can get information about major cities across the country. The channel offers localized news and information on a city's weather, sports, politics, and nightlife, among other things. It's perfect for busy people who do a lot of traveling or for the rest of us who just like to fantasize about being somewhere else.

Figure 2.2 The Computers and Software channel

The Entertainment Channel

Capitalizing on the nation's fascination with television and movies, AOL has loaded this channel with news, features, and behind-the-scenes facts about Hollywood and your favorite TV shows. (Trekkers love AOL.) There's also plenty of stuff for you bookworms out there.

The Games Channel

The PC has become a major platform for video games, and AOL is right there with a variety of shoot-em-ups, sports games, fantasy games, and role-playing adventures. On the Games channel you'll also find hints and strategies for playing your favorite games.

The Health and Fitness Channel

Want to lose weight? Get in shape? Eat better? Check out the latest trends and tips on the Health and Fitness channel (see Figure 2.3). You'll also find general information on health, including medical references about diseases and prescription drugs. In short, this channel is a hypochondriac's dream.

Figure 2.3 The Health and Fitness channel

The Hub

This channel, which is new with AOL version 3.0, is a venture from AOL and New Line Television. The Hub provides an offbeat, irreverent approach to culture and the arts "not likely to be found anywhere else in the real or cyber world."

The International Channel

AOL's influence reaches across the globe. You can use this channel to find out what's happening in Canada, France, Germany, the United Kingdom, Japan, or just about any other country. The International channel (see Figure 2.4) offers, among other things, the latest international news and sports scores, as well as quotes from the world's stock markets.

The Internet Connection

If the Internet Connection (see Figure 2.5) isn't the most popular channel on AOL already, it probably will be soon. It's your jumping-off point for the World Wide Web, and it offers a comprehensive list of resources available in cyberspace.

Figure 2.4 The International channel

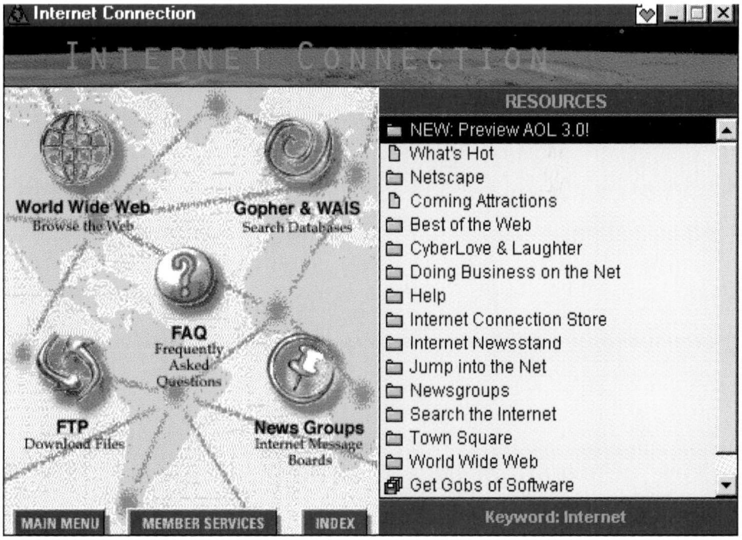

Figure 2.5 The Internet Connection channel

The Kids Only Channel

Want to wean your kids away from TV? This is the way to do it, with the games and online entertainment for the younger set on the Kids Only channel. The channel is also an excellent resource for schoolwork—kids will find the reference materials and the Homework Help feature, a sort of interactive classroom, especially useful.

The Learning and Culture Channel

If you'd like to improve your education—or just use the one you already have—this is the place for you. On this channel (see Figure 2.6) you'll find online courses, career guidance, and links to learning resources. There's also stuff on literature, art, dance, music, and photography.

Figure 2.6 The Learning and Culture channel

The Life, Styles & Interests Channel

This channel pulls together everything normally associated with the nebulous term *lifestyle*. If you own a home, are involved in your community, or like to cook, check out this channel. You'll also find all kinds of forums here—there's even one devoted to Hillary Rodham Clinton.

The Marketplace

If it can be bought, you can probably buy it on AOL. The Marketplace (see Figure 2.7) is like a shopping mall on your computer. You can get flowers for your sweetie, a jacket for yourself, or a new modem for your computer. Just have your credit card handy.

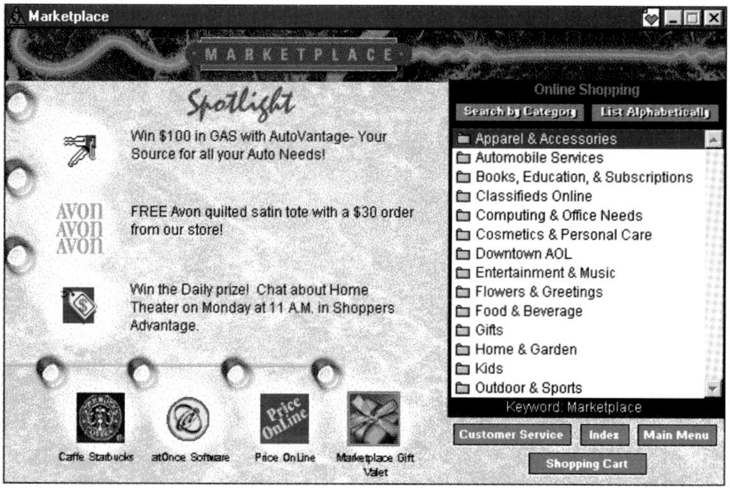

Figure 2.7 The Marketplace channel

The MusicSpace Channel

Because music is such a big part of modern life, AOL created a channel devoted to the subject. Learn about new music CDs, read features about recording artists, and discuss your favorite kind of music with other members on the MusicSpace channel. From Mozart to Metallica, it's all here.

The Newsstand

You can't subscribe to 100 magazines and newspapers all at once. Or can you? In the Newsstand window (see Figure 2.8) you'll find the complete text and selected photos and graphics from more than 100 leading publications, including *Business Week, Atlantic Monthly,* and *Consumer Reports.*

Figure 2.8 The Newsstand channel

The Today's News Channel

Extra, extra, read all about it! Drawing from a dozen sources, this channel brings you up-to-date, breaking news from around the world, plus top stories on sports, entertainment, and business—and you can also find out if it's snowing in Des Moines (see Figure 2.9).

The People Connection

The People Connection is where AOL members come to meet online for live discussions. No matter what you want to talk about, there's probably a *chat room* devoted to it. The People Connection also lets you meet top athletes, politicians, entertainers, and business people in AOL's huge online auditoriums.

The Personal Finance Channel

If you're talking money, you're talking the Personal Finance channel (see Figure 2.10). Here you'll find investment advice and information about hundreds of companies. You can use this channel's features to evaluate mutual funds and learn how your stocks are doing at any time.

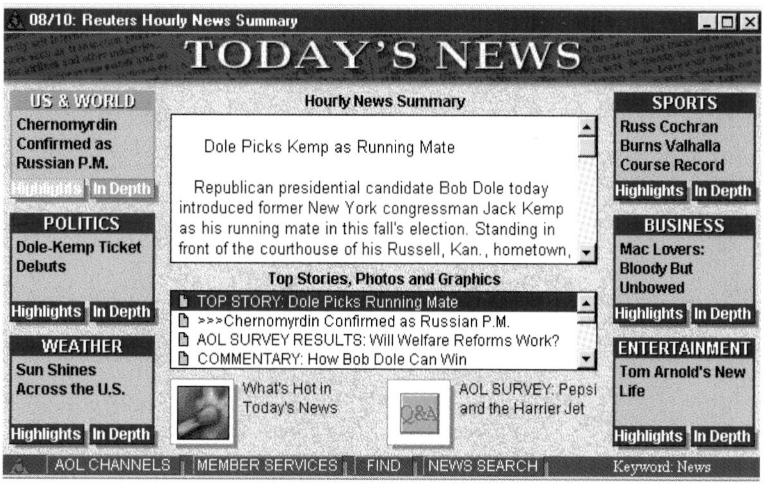

Figure 2.9 The Today's News channel

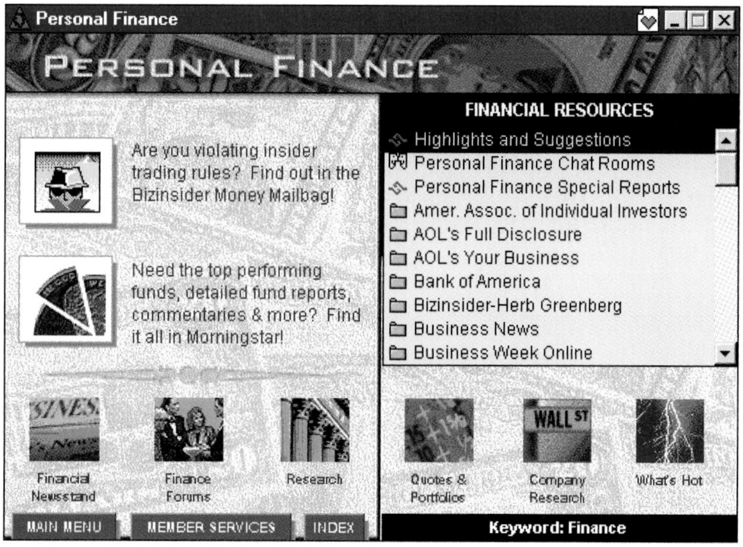

Figure 2.10 The Personal Finance channel

The Reference Desk

The public library is nice, but for real convenience you can't beat the 24-hour availability of AOL's collection of encyclopedias, dictionaries, almanacs, and other reference materials. With AOL's Reference channel, you can even search the Bible if you want to.

The Sports Channel

Forget the sports pages. With AOL, you can find out almost instantaneously who won, who lost, who got injured, and who got a rich new contract. Every major professional and college sport is covered in the Sports channel (see Figure 2.11), along with other sports such as pro wrestling, which newspapers tend to ignore.

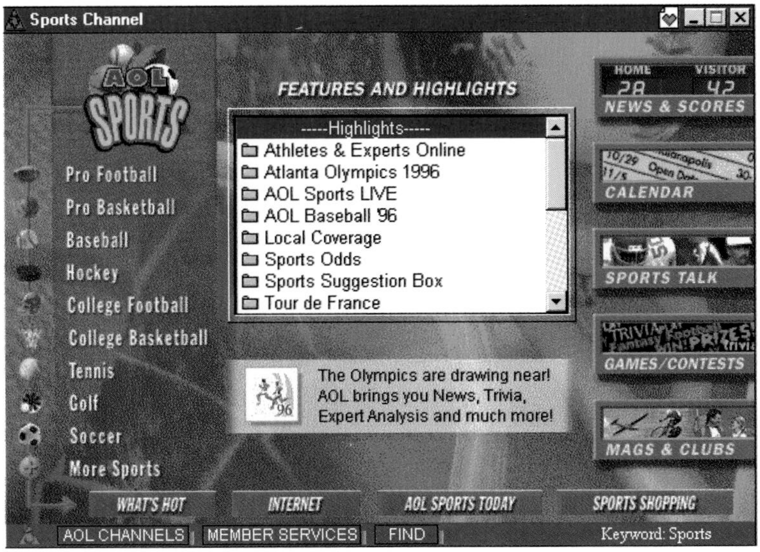

Figure 2.11 The Sports channel

The Style Channel

Fashion news and advice, along with celebrity gossip, make up the main bill of fare for this fun-oriented channel, which was put together by AOL and ABC. Use it to check out the hottest runway looks and get suggestions for your next makeover.

PRESENTING. . .

As time goes on, AOL will add new channels to its lineup in an effort to better organize the service and give users clearer choices. You can preview channels under development by clicking Presenting at the bottom of the Channels window. As you can see, several channels were under construction when I wrote this. Click any channel in the Presenting window to see what the channel will look like.

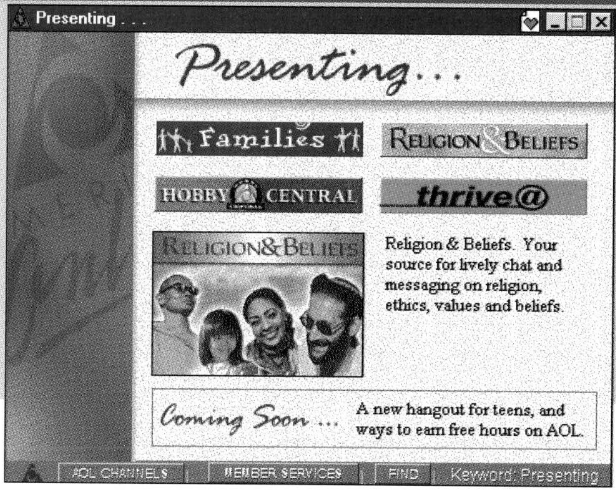

The Travel Channel

Don't leave home without consulting the Travel channel (see Figure 2.12). It offers information on everything from Caribbean cruises to bed-and-breakfasts in New England. On this channel, you can even book your airfare and rental cars online.

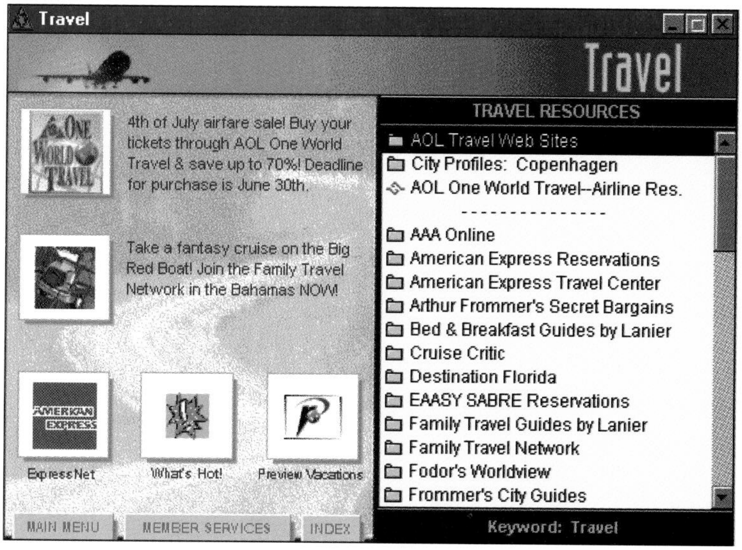

Figure 2.12 The Travel channel

BASIC AOL TECHNIQUES

If you're the least bit familiar with Microsoft Windows, you should have no trouble at all using AOL. The methods you'll use to manipulate files, move and copy text, and use the mouse on AOL are practically carbon copies of the methods used in most Windows-based programs. This section covers some of the basic techniques that will help you get things done quickly and easily.

Moving Between Windows

When you move from place to place in AOL, each new window you open is automatically placed atop the previous one. You can have an unlimited number of windows open at one time. To switch between open windows, click AOL's Window menu at the top of the screen and, from the list at the bottom of the menu, choose the name of the window you want to have displayed.

SHORTCUT

You don't have to manually close every window. You can close them all at once by choosing Close All from the Window menu. And don't bother to close windows when you end your AOL session—clicking Exit automatically closes all windows.

Closing and Minimizing Windows

Every window has three little boxes in its upper-right corner. To close a window, click the box farthest to the right—the one with the X in it. You can *minimize* a window by clicking the left box. When you minimize a window, it shrinks to become a small bar near the bottom of the screen, like this:

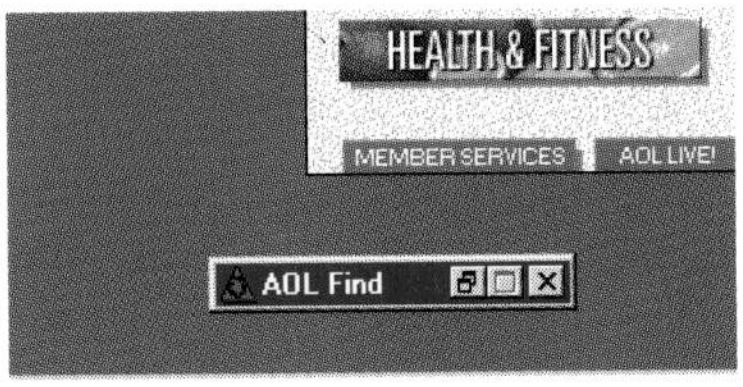

To restore a window to its previous size, click the left box on the minimized bar. (Note: The middle box is for enlarging the window to fill the screen. On AOL, this works only for windows that contain text or windows that you can write in, such as chat room windows and message boards.)

AOL is continually improving its software with new tools and features. But don't worry, you won't have to run out and get the new software. When new technology becomes available, AOL can download it to your computer while you're online.

The Hand That Points the Way

When you really start playing with AOL, you'll find yourself jumping from place to place by clicking links to other areas. In Internet parlance, these links are called *hyperlinks*. When you move the mouse pointer over a hyperlink, the pointer turns into a hand with an extended forefinger, like this:

Hyperlinks can be buttons, images, or even text. On AOL, a single click on a hyperlink will take you to the area associated with the link—either on AOL or out on the Internet. (You'll learn about Internet hyperlinks in the next chapter.)

Online Art—Why the Delays?

As you roam around in AOL, you'll notice that sometimes it takes a minute or so for a window to be completely displayed. That's because the art for the window is being sent to your computer. This delay is especially evident the first time you go to a channel or other graphically rich area. A slight delay also occurs whenever you visit an area to which new art has been added. Art is automatically stored on your hard disk so that you won't have to wait for it the next time you visit the area.

habits & strategies

There's a fair amount of duplication between the menu bar and the toolbar. For instance, five items on the Go To menu have corresponding toolbar buttons. In many cases, AOL provides more alternatives than you really need.

LEARNING YOUR WAY AROUND

AOL provides a menu bar and a toolbar to help you use the service efficiently and access key features quickly. No matter where you go in AOL, they're always perched at the top of the screen, ready to be used. The File, Edit, Window, and Help menus are similar to the menus of the same names on most Windows-based programs. The Go To, Mail, and Members menus are more specific to AOL and provide easy access to some of the most important areas of the service.

A Quick Tour of the Toolbar

There are 18 buttons on the toolbar, each one providing ready access to a feature that the folks at AOL have deemed especially useful.

What if you forget what a tool does? Just place your mouse pointer over the tool. A brief description of the tool will appear in a yellow box.

Personally, I find that some of the tools really are great for a busy person, whereas others seem like a waste. It's great to be able to click one button and begin writing an e-mail message or jump onto the World Wide Web, for instance. But who really needs a button to take you to a channel when you can just use the Channels window? (There are three channel buttons on the toolbar.) It's too bad that you can't customize the toolbar, as you can in many Windows-based applications. Oh well. To use a tool, click it with your mouse. Table 2.1 gives you a rundown of what the various tools do.

Button	Button Name	Function
	Read New Mail	Click here to display a list of your unread mail in the New Mail window.
	Compose Mail	Want to send someone an e-mail message? Click here.
	Channels	Click this button to go directly to the Channels window.
	What's Hot	Click here for the newest features, as well as those that AOL considers to be some of the most exciting.
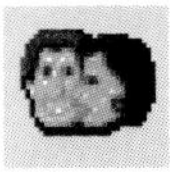	The People Connection	If you want to chat live with other members, this is the place to start.
	File Search	Click here to quickly find and download software for your computer.
	Stocks and Portfolios	How are your stocks doing today? Click here to find out.

Table 2.1 The AOL Toolbar Buttons

Button	Button Name	Function
	Today's News	Click this button for instant access to the latest headlines and stories in news, sports, weather, and entertainment.
	World Wide Web	Click here to quickly get onto the Internet.
	The Marketplace	Shop till you drop without ever leaving your chair—just click this button.
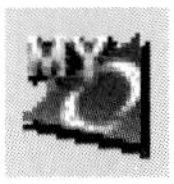	My AOL	Click this button to custom-tailor AOL for your own needs.
	Online Clock	Click here to find out how long you've been online.
	Print	See something you'd like to print out? Clicking this button does it.
	Personal Filing Cabinet	Click here to view saved e-mail and files you've downloaded.
	Favorite Places	Click here to display a list of your favorite places and access those places.
	Member Services	For online help or information about your account, click here.
	Find	Click this to start a handy feature that helps you find people, places, and events.
	Keyword	Click here to instantly jump to almost any area on AOL.

Table 2.1 The AOL Toolbar Buttons *(continued)*

habits & strategies

If an area has a keyword, it will be shown at the bottom of the area's window. During your travels through AOL, be sure to note the keywords for places that you plan to visit again.

KEYWORDS

The fastest way to get around in AOL is to use *keywords*. AOL's Keyword feature is the online version of the transporter in Star Trek, carrying you instantly from place to place. As the name implies, a keyword is a word—sometimes a pair of words, but usually just one—that transports you instantly to a specific area of the service. Often a keyword can save you several steps in the navigational process. As of the summer of 1996, there were more than 5,000 keywords, with new ones being added all the time. To use a keyword, click the Keyword button on the toolbar. You can also choose Keyword from the Go To menu or, if you prefer not to take your hands from the keyboard, press CTRL-K. The Keyword dialog box will be displayed, as shown here:

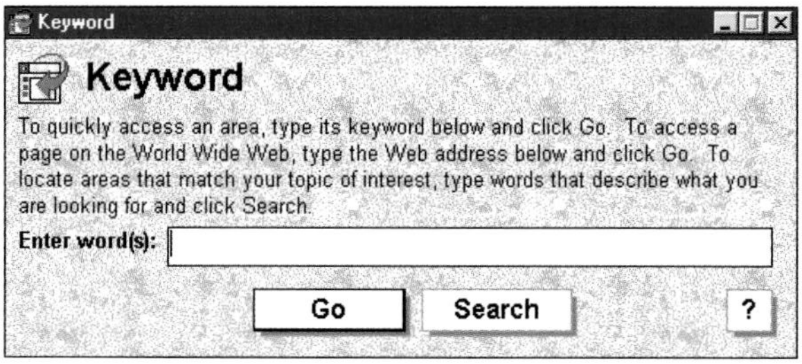

Enter the keyword for the area you want to access and then click Go. Simple, isn't it?

What If You Don't Know the Keyword?

Hey, don't panic. There are several tacks you can take if you don't know the keyword for an area.

- Enter a word that describes the topic you're interested in and click Go. It sounds haphazard, but it isn't—there's a keyword for nearly every major topic you can think of. For example, suppose you're looking for information on mutual funds. It stands to reason that either *mutual* or *funds,* or possibly *mutual funds,* would be a keyword. In fact, *mutual* is not a keyword (or wasn't at this writing). But *funds* is the keyword for Morningstar Mutual Funds, and *mutual funds* takes you to AOL's Mutual Funds Center.

SHORTCUT

You can add frequently used keywords to the Go To menu for easy access. Choose Edit Go To Menu from the Go To menu and enter the name of the area and its keyword. (You can delete the preprogrammed keywords if you need more room.)

- Enter a word or words that describe the topic you want and click Search instead of Go. A list of areas related to the topic will be displayed. You can then view descriptions of the areas and go directly to the areas.
- Use the keyword *keyword* to go directly to AOL's area for keywords, shown here. In this window you'll find up-to-date lists of all keywords, categorized both alphabetically and by channels. You also have the option of downloading the entire list to your computer.

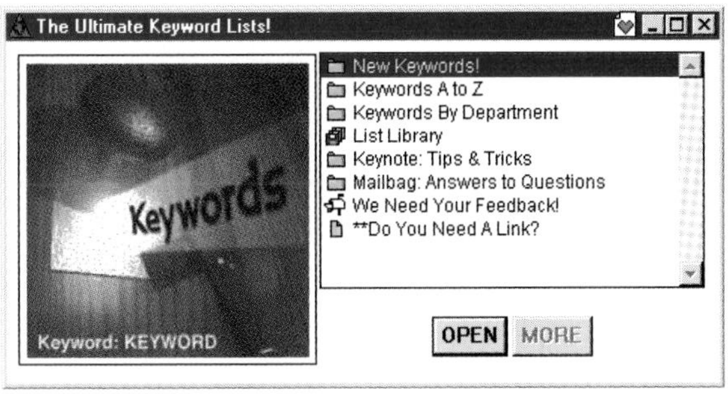

IF YOU'RE LOST, TRY FIND

With version 3.0 for Windows, AOL added a new feature called Find that helps you locate people, places, and events on the service. It includes a good search tool and a point-and-click directory. Use one of the following methods to access the Find feature:

- Click the Find button on the toolbar.
- Choose Find from the Go To menu.
- Click Find in the main Channels window.
- Click Find at the bottom of a channel window.
- Use the keyword *find*.

With that many options, if you can't find Find, you're really lost—maybe you should stop reading right now. Just kidding. Here's what the Find window looks like:

Those who have used AOL in the past may be wondering what happened to the Directory of Services. It's still there, but it has been replaced by Find as the main navigational tool. To access the Directory of Services, now called, simply, Directory, *use the keyword* services.

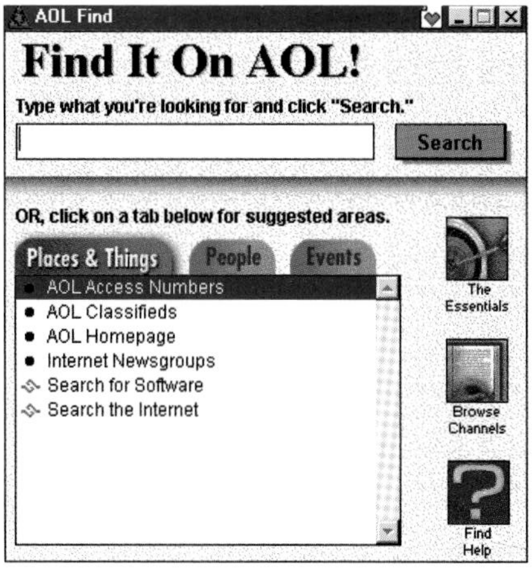

The directory is divided into three tabbed pages: Places & Things, People, and Events. As of this writing, Find was brand new and, from the looks of it, very much a work in progress. As you can see, the Places & Things page contained just six items. We can only hope that AOL will someday enhance Find so that the content is as good as the graphic.

CAUTION

Find's Search function isn't infallible. It looks for words in area descriptions. If the word isn't in the description, Find won't find it. And don't try to use Find to locate information about using AOL—go to Member Services instead.

Search and You Shall Find

The most useful part of Find is its search engine, which lets you hunt for services and features throughout AOL. Just type in the word or words you're seeking and then click Search or press ENTER. A list of items that match your criteria will be displayed. You can double-click an item to view a description of it and then click Go There to access the area.

Browsing the Channels

On the right side of the Find window are buttons labeled The Essentials and Browse Channels. Clicking The Essentials button produces a window with links to the Member Directory, AOL's Software Libraries, and the World Wide Web. It's a convenient window that gathers often-used directories in one place. However, you might find yourself getting more use from the Browse Channels button, which lets you see what's available in all the main channels. Here's how to use it:

1. Click the Browse Channels button to display the Channel Find window.
2. Select the channel you want from the drop-down list at the top.
3. Choose whether to display the channel's resources alphabetically or by topic. The example here shows the By Topic list:

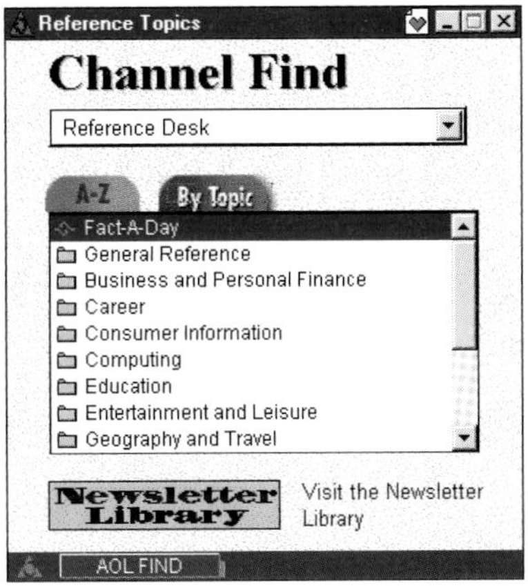

4. The topics are displayed as folders. Double-click any folder to view all the resources available on a particular topic.

The Favorite Places feature can be used for almost any AOL window, all World Wide Web windows, and even Internet newsgroup windows. When you double-click a Favorite Place that's on the Web, AOL's Web browser starts and launches the site.

FAVORITE PLACES

Now that you've found what you want, wouldn't it be great if you could stash it away for quick and easy access in the future? You can, using AOL's Favorite Places feature. Here's how it works: Almost every window in AOL boasts a red heart on its title bar. The heart indicates that the window can be saved as a Favorite Place. This can be done in two ways:

- Double-click the heart icon on the window's title bar. You'll see a message box asking whether you want to add the window to your Favorite Places folder. Click Yes.
- Drag the heart icon from the window to the Favorite Places button on the toolbar.

Managing Your Favorite Places

To view a list of your Favorite Places, click the Favorite Places button on the toolbar. This displays the contents of your Favorite Places folder. Here's what mine looks like:

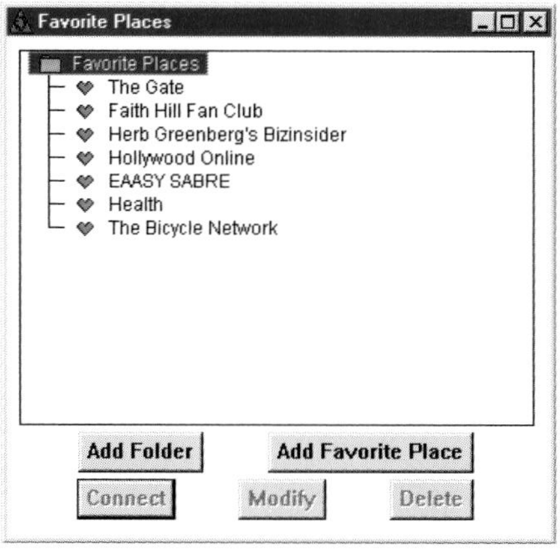

To access a Favorite Place, either double-click it or select it and click Connect. To delete the item from the list, select it and click Delete. To change the description of a selected item, click Modify.

Adding New Folders

Initially, the only folder in Favorite Places is the (aptly named) Favorite Places folder. Every time you drag a heart to the toolbar button, the window you're saving goes into that folder. However, if you're the bureaucratic type, or if you're a stickler for neatness, you can add folders to help you keep track of your Favorite Places. Any folders you add will go inside the Favorite Places folder. You can also add folders inside other folders. To add a folder, open Favorite Places and click the folder within which you want your new folder to go. Then choose Add Folder. Here's an example:

habits & strategies

You say you don't like the way your Favorite Places are arranged? So change them already! You can change the order in which places are listed by dragging them up or down or from one folder to another.

After creating the new Entertainment folder, I dragged the Faith Hill Fan Club and Hollywood Online to it. (Faith Hill, for those who are wondering, is a wonderful country singer.) There, now my favorite entertainment areas are in one place.

YOUR PERSONAL FILING CABINET

Each screen name on an account has its own Favorite Places and Personal Filing Cabinet. However, you can't use your Personal Filing Cabinet or Favorite Places when you sign onto AOL as a guest from someone else's computer.

Speaking of keeping things in one place, as an AOL member you have a Personal Filing Cabinet in which AOL stores stuff that you accumulate during your time online. The cabinet, which you can access by clicking its button on the toolbar, holds and organizes items retrieved during FlashSessions (see Chapters 4 and 5), including e-mail messages and newsgroup articles. It also contains files that you've downloaded. Best of all, it can be used to permanently store copies of all the mail that you send and receive. (Chapter 4 tells you how to do that.) As you can see in the following illustration, the Personal Filing Cabinet has the same basic structure as Favorite Places, though it has a lot more folders:

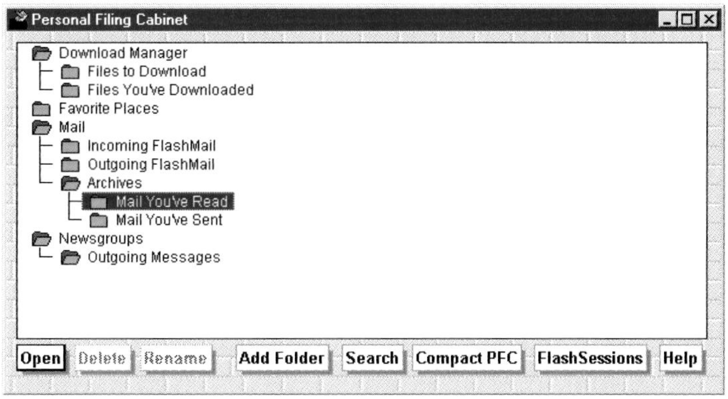

Staying Organized

You can use the buttons at the bottom of the Personal Filing Cabinet window to get rid of items you no longer want to keep or to rename any item. You can also use the Search button to hunt through the entire contents of the cabinet for specific text references, such as names in mail messages. Try THAT with a regular filing cabinet!

HAVE IT YOUR WAY WITH MY AOL

Just because you're now part of a community of 6 million people doesn't mean you forfeit your individuality. AOL allows you to tailor various parts of the service to suit your needs. You already learned in the first chapter how to change and store your password using My AOL. In future chapters, I'll show you how to customize aspects of e-mail, chat rooms, and the World Wide Web. Right now, let's take a look at some of the things you can do to adjust the general way in which AOL works for you.

Shut Up, Already!

If AOL's "Welcome," "Goodbye," and "You've got mail" voice messages start to get to you—or if you work near people who would rather not put up with the noise—you can silence the voice coming out of your computer. Here's how:

1. Click the My AOL button on the toolbar.
2. Click Preferences, then General Preferences, and then Set Up Now to display the following dialog box:

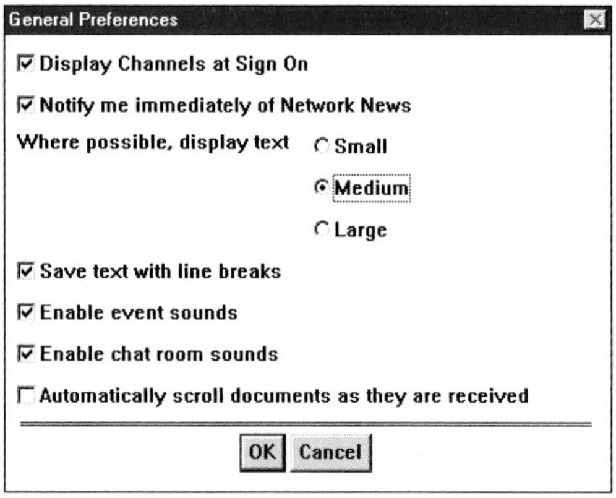

3. Click the box labeled "Enable event sounds" to remove the checkmark from it. Then click OK.

CAUTION

When you turn off "the voice of AOL," you shut down all other sounds as well, including any musical sounds or other sound effects associated with particular areas.

Make It Easier on Your Eyes

If you find the text in your AOL windows hard to read, you can enlarge it. Go to General Preferences the same way you did in the example above. Then, under "Where possible, display text," choose Large instead of Medium. (Medium is the default size for text.) This will increase the size of type in the text windows throughout AOL. It will also give you larger type for e-mail, chat sessions, and message groups. Below are examples of medium and large type:

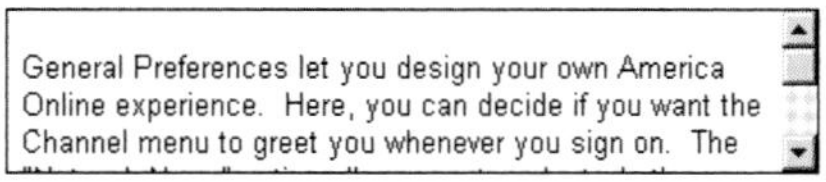
General Preferences let you design your own America
Online experience. Here, you can decide if you want the
Channel menu to greet you whenever you sign on. The

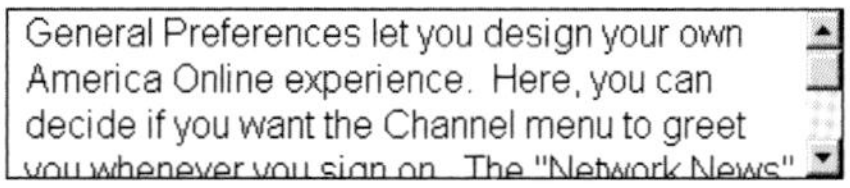
General Preferences let you design your own
America Online experience. Here, you can
decide if you want the Channel menu to greet

Keep Your Address to Yourself

As do many big organizations with lots of members, AOL makes its mailing list available to other companies, which could translate into an increase in the amount of junk mail stuffing your mailbox at home. If you'd rather not have your name and address bandied about, AOL understands and will accommodate you. Just do the following:

1. Choose Marketing Preferences in the Preferences window and then click Set Up Now.
2. In the Marketing Preferences window, double-click Tell Us What Your Mailing Preferences Are to display the Member Mailing Preference dialog box.
3. Place an X in the boxes for the categories that you're interested in. If you don't want to receive any mailings, enter an X in the box in the lower-right corner.
4. Click Send to transmit the form to AOL.

WHAT'S NEXT?

You can't say "online" anymore without also saying "Internet" in the same breath. The folks at AOL have been rushing to incorporate the World Wide Web and other Internet features into their service, so let's rush with them. Next stop: cyberspace and the Web!

Part 2

AOL AND THE INTERNET

CHAPTER 3

Gateway to the World Wide Web

INCLUDES

- Getting to know the America Online (AOL) Web browser
- Using Internet addresses
- Using hyperlinks
- Searching the Web
- Customizing the browser

FAST FORWARD

START THE WEB BROWSER ➤ *pp. 61–62*

Getting onto the Web with AOL is easy. Here are a few ways to launch the Web browser:

- Click the World Wide Web button (the globe) on the toolbar.
- Click Internet Connection in the Channels window, and then choose the World Wide Web icon.
- Click the Keyword button on the toolbar, type **web** or **www**, and then click Go.

USE HYPERLINKS TO EXPLORE THE WEB ➤ *p. 63.*

Moving around on the Web is also easy, especially with hyperlinks. Just click any blue, underlined text or on a linked graphic—you'll be transported elsewhere within a Web site or to another site, perhaps halfway around the world. And don't worry about getting lost. Just click the Back button on the browser's toolbar to return to the previous page or the Home button to go back to the browser's home page.

SEARCH THE WEB ➤ *pp. 65–67*

The Web is a vast, decentralized collection of millions of sites. You can find pages on topics that interest you by using search services that are free to Internet users. Several of the top search services are available via the Search button on the browser's toolbar.

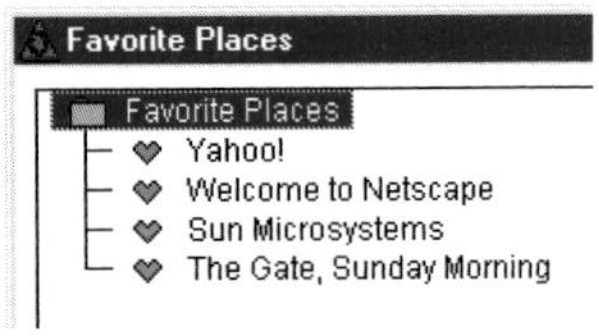

SAVE A FAVORITE PLACE ➤ *p. 68*

If you find a Web page that you really like and plan to visit often, go ahead and save its address using AOL's Favorite Places feature. With the page displayed on your browser, do one of the following:

- Click the heart on the title bar of the browser and then click Yes to save the address to the Favorite Places folder.
- Just drag the heart on the browser to the Favorite Places folder on the AOL toolbar.

CUSTOMIZE THE BROWSER ➤ *pp. 69–71*

You can change some of the features in the browser to suit your own tastes. Two of the most popular modifications are changing the page that the browser displays when it first starts and changing the background from white to gray. Here's how to do both:

1. Click Prefs on the browser toolbar to display the WWW Preferences dialog box.
2. Place a checkmark in the box labeled "Use a gray background in WWW docs."
3. In the space at the bottom, erase the address for AOL's home page on the Web and replace it with another one—for instance, the address of one of the big search services.
4. Click OK.

USE AOL'S LINKS TO THE WEB ➤ *pp. 71–72*

Every channel on AOL includes a button that displays a list of Web pages that complement AOL's own features. Clicking the button displays a list of Web pages. Double-clicking an item in the list starts the browser and loads the page.

When the Internet began to take the world by storm, some commercial online services saw it as a deadly threat. The people at AOL, however, strongly believed that a huge opportunity was at hand. The company launched a drive to integrate its own service with the Internet—and especially with the graphically rich World Wide Web. The campaign has succeeded beyond anyone's expectations. By some estimates, more than 40 percent of all activity on the Web now goes through AOL. And no wonder: AOL has blended its own content so seamlessly with that of the Web that sometimes it's hard to tell where one stops and the other starts. The marriage is a perfect one for busy people who want the best of an online service and the Internet rolled into one.

WHAT IS THE INTERNET, AND WHY IS IT IMPORTANT?

By this time, everybody has heard of the Internet. But it's surprising how many people still don't know exactly what it is. For the record, the Internet is a global network capable of connecting your PC to millions of other computers around the world, including huge mainframes at government agencies and universities, as well as the computer systems of major businesses.

The Internet began a generation ago as a way to maintain crucial communications links within the government in case of a nuclear war. As the Cold War lingered on, the Internet languished in obscurity. With the development of the World Wide Web in the 1990s, however, the Internet was transformed. Today, consumers get a wide range of information and entertainment from the Web, and it promises to become a fast and efficient way for people to buy goods and services electronically.

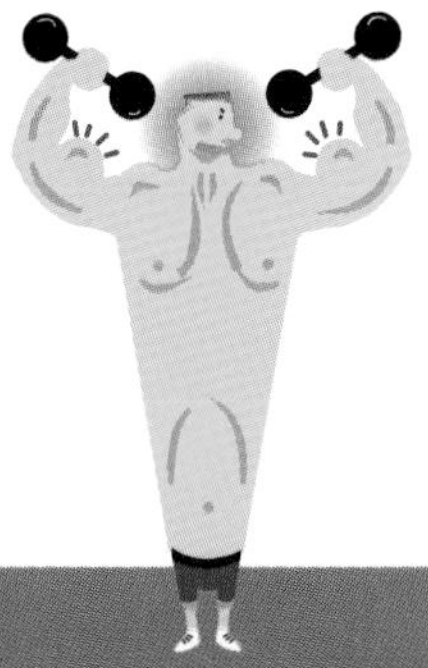

definition

World Wide Web (WWW): *The portion of the Internet that uses graphics, photos, animation, and sound in addition to text. With the Web, you can jump from place to place—even to a computer halfway around the world— with a click of your mouse.*

AOL's INTERNET CONNECTION

There are several ways to use the Internet on AOL, including the following:

- Click the Internet Connection button in the Channels window to go to a window that offers one-click access to all the main features of the Net.
- Click the World Wide Web button on the toolbar to go straight to the Web. (I'll get to that in a minute.)
- Click the big Internet button in the Welcome window to display the following window:

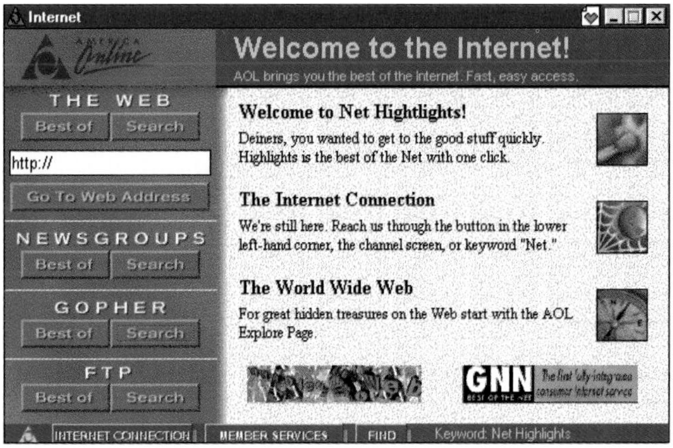

The buttons on the left let you easily search the Net and view what AOL considers to be some of the best sites on it. And at the right are buttons that take you directly to a Net highlights site, the Internet Connection, and the Web.

BROWSING THE WEB

To use the Web, you need a *browser,* a software program that displays Web content on your PC and lets you use your mouse to navigate. There are several first-rate browsers out there, including the Netscape Navigator and the Microsoft Internet Explorer. As of this writing, AOL is using its own browser, which is a pretty good tool. There

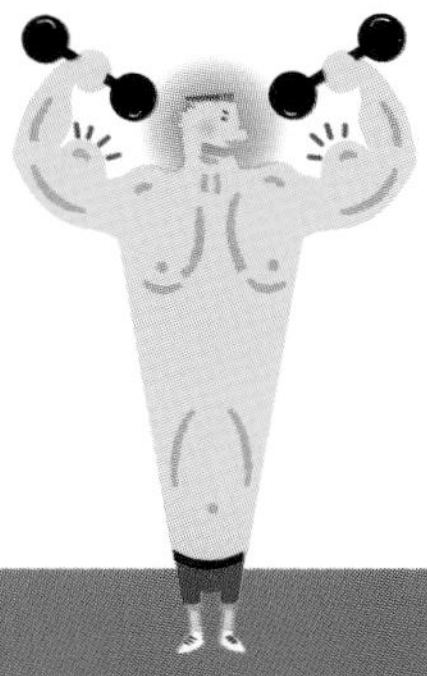

definitions

Web site: *A collection of Web pages. Web pages are viewed one at a time with a browser.*

Home page: *The first page you see when you visit a Web site.*

URL: *Universal (or Uniform) Resource Locator—a fancy way of saying "Internet address."*

HTTP: *Hypertext Transfer Protocol—the standard method of transmitting data on the Web. This is one of those examples of technobabble that has made it into the mainstream.*

are plans, however, to build a version of the Microsoft browser directly into the AOL software.

One Click and You're On

The easiest way to get on the Web is to click the World Wide Web button (the globe) on the toolbar. This will launch the AOL browser and automatically retrieve the home page of AOL's own Web site, shown in Figure 3.1.

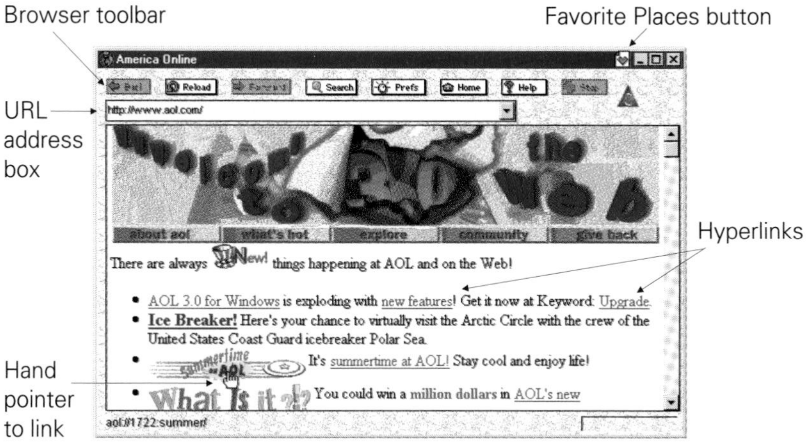

Figure 3.1 America Online's Web browser

This site is not part of AOL's regular online service—anyone with Internet access can view it. It showcases the integration between AOL and the Web and advertises AOL to the Internet community at large. At the same time, however, it provides AOL members with tips on how to get the most out of the AOL browser. For instance, when you click the Help button on the browser toolbar, you're taken to a Help area on the AOL Web site.

IF YOU'RE A NETSCAPE FAN, TAKE HEART

A lot of folks use the Netscape Navigator. By some estimates it dominates nearly three-fourths of the browser market. If you already use Netscape to get on the Internet—perhaps through your corporate network in the office—rest assured that you can keep on using it with AOL; but make sure that you have the version designed for Windows 3.1, because the one for Windows 95 won't work with the new AOL software that came out in June of 1996. To use the Netscape browser, minimize the AOL window while you're signed on, and double-click the Netscape icon on your desktop.

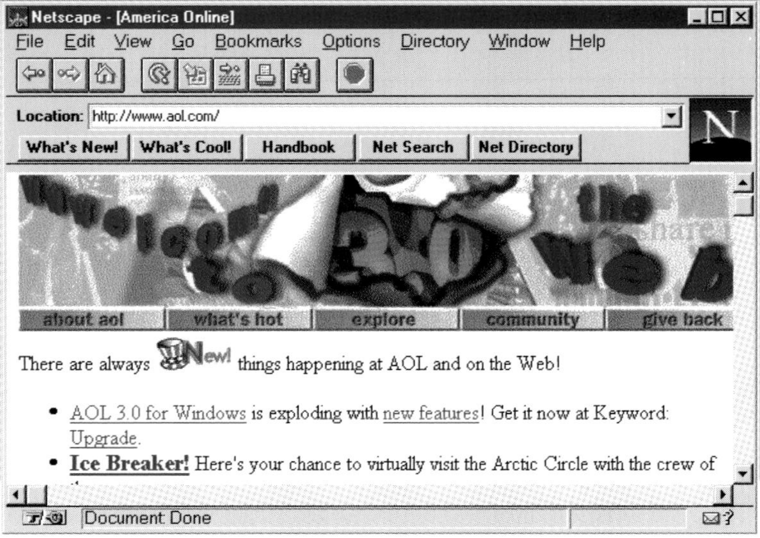

Navigating with Hyperlinks

The best thing about the Web is that it lets you jump around from place to place simply by clicking hyperlinks with your mouse. *Hyperlinks* are text or graphics that have embedded links to other Web addresses. You saw in Chapter 2 that hyperlinks are used within AOL to help you navigate from one area to another. On the Internet, hyperlinks can take you elsewhere within a Web site, or to another site halfway around the world. Any text that's blue and underlined is a hyperlink. And whenever you point to a link—either text or an object—the mouse pointer turns into a hand, as you can see in Figure 3.1.

Internet Addresses

Every Web site has its own unique address, also known as a URL, that lets other computers know where to find it on the Internet. A typical address begins with **http://** and goes from there. With thousands of

SHORTCUT

*You can go directly to a Web site from anywhere on AOL simply by using the Keyword function and typing in the address. (In this case, you must include the **http://**.) This is a great example of the way AOL has integrated itself with the Internet.*

companies now advertising their Web addresses on TV as well as in newspapers and magazines, Web addresses are starting to be commonplace. If you know the address of the site you want to visit, just type it into the box below the toolbar, as shown below. (You don't have to type in http://. The browser knows that that's how Web addresses start and will add it automatically.)

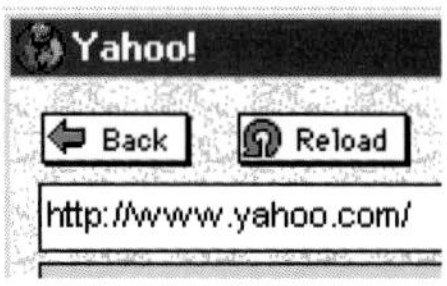

You don't have to worry about capitalizing proper names in an address—use all lowercase if you want to. But you do have to enter addresses exactly right. One missed letter, colon, or slash and you won't be able to access the site. After you type in the address, press the ENTER key. The browser will locate the site and retrieve it. (This is also called *loading* the page.) You can see how the loading process is going in the status bar at the bottom of the browser window.

It Doesn't Always Work

Addresses and hyperlinks aren't foolproof. Sometimes you can't access a page. It could be because the page no longer exists, because its address has been changed, or because there are too many other users trying to access the same page at the same time. You might end up looking at a message like this one:

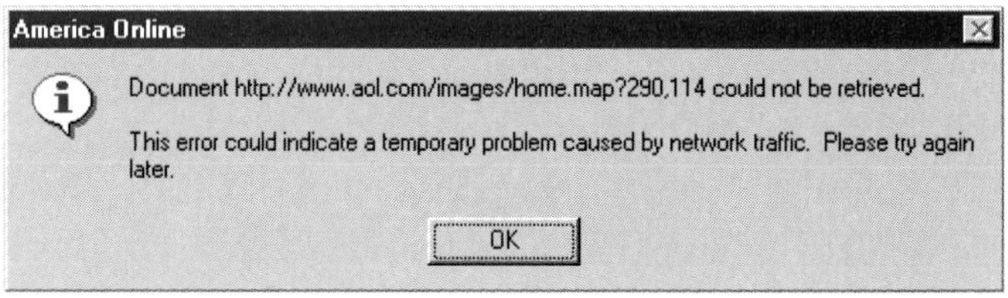

Hey, nobody said the Internet was perfect.

habits & strategies

Even with a fast modem, it can take time for a graphics-intensive page to load. As long as the status box indicates that the page is being loaded, stick with it. If the loading stops for more than a minute or so, give up and try something else.

Going Back and Forth

As you surf the Web, the AOL browser keeps track of the pages you've visited during your current session. This is helpful because it lets you revisit places without having to re-enter their addresses or search for them again. To go back to the last page you viewed, click the Back button on the toolbar. Clicking the Forward button takes you ahead one page on the list of addresses you've been to during your Web session. You can also go directly to any of these pages. Here's how:

1. Click the arrow at the right end of the address box. This displays the list of places you've been, as shown in the illustration below. (The most recent page is at the top.)
2. Click any of the addresses to go directly to that page again.

SEARCHING THE WEB

Even seasoned Web surfers memorize only a small number of addresses, and busy people certainly have better things to do. Fortunately, you don't have to know a site's address to find it. Just use an Internet search service. An easy way to get started is to click Search on the browser toolbar. This takes you to the window shown next:

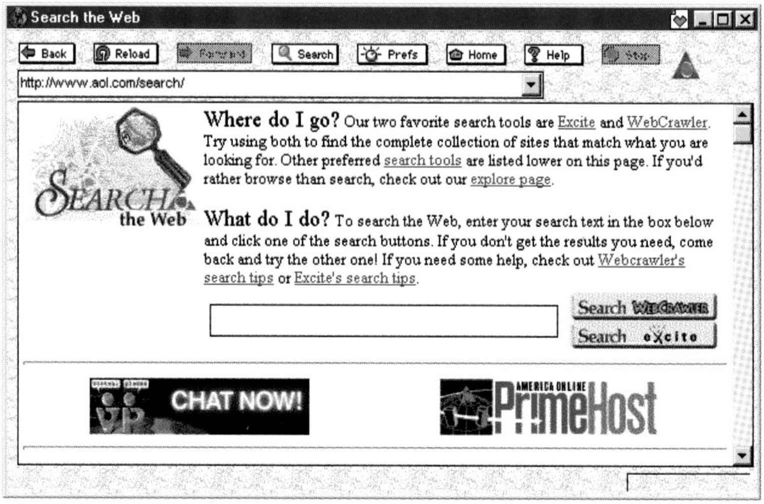

AOL features the Webcrawler and Excite search services, but there are lots of other ones out there that you can also use. Here are a few of the best, along with their Web addresses:

AltaVista	**http://www.altavista.digital.com**
Infoseek	**http://www.infoseek.com**
Lycos	**http://www.lycos.com**
Yahoo	**http://www.yahoo.com**

One of the most popular search services is Yahoo, which was started by two Stanford University students. They took their young company public, and now they're both millionaires. Maybe that helps explain the remark by Microsoft's Bill Gates (one of the richest men in the world), who has referred to the Internet as a "gold rush." Anyway, here's Yahoo's home page:

habits & strategies

Search services all do basically the same thing, but they go about it and display their results in different ways. It's a good idea to give all the big ones a try. You may find that one serves your needs better than the others.

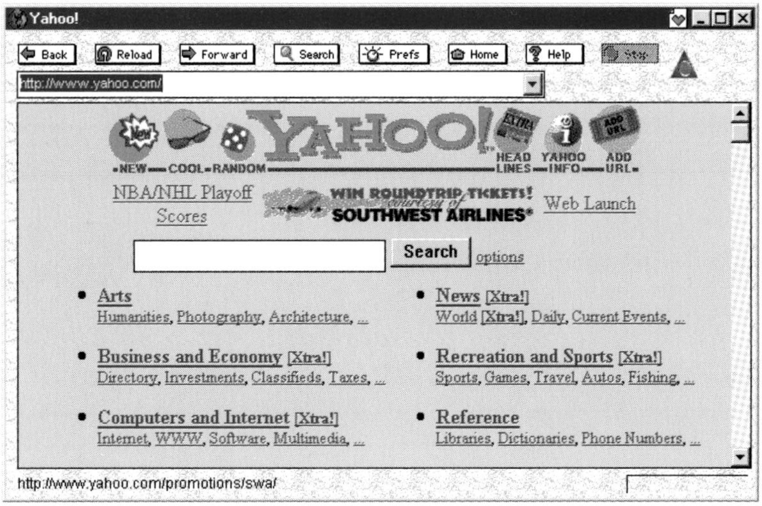

How to Conduct a Search

With most search services, you type in a word or phrase and the service locates pages that match and lists them for you. For instance, if you searched for *Grateful Dead* using Webcrawler, you'd find more than 13,000 pages. Obviously, the death of Jerry Garcia hasn't diminished the popularity of the band. To access any of the pages that are found in a search, just click the hyperlink for the page.

SOME USEFUL TOOLBAR BUTTONS

Here are a few of the browser's toolbar buttons that you might find useful while you're working with Web pages:

- **Stop** Occasionally you'll change your mind after choosing to activate a hyperlink. Or maybe the page you've chosen is taking too much time to load into your PC. No problem. When you click the Stop button, the loading process halts dead in its tracks so you can try something different.

AOL's browser offers some relief while you are waiting for a page to load: You can scroll a page as it's loading, and you can click a hyperlink before a page is completely loaded. The latter aborts the load and takes you to another page.

- **Reload** If you're looking at a Web page that is continually updated (such as a page of news or sports scores), you can click the Reload button to display the page with its latest contents.
- **Home** At any time, clicking the Home button will take you back to the browser's home page. (If you want to return to the home page for the Web site you're in, use the drop-down list of pages you've visited.)

FAVORITE PLACES

Wouldn't it be great if you could save the addresses of pages you really like so that you could access them any time you want? The folks at AOL already thought of that. They've incorporated their Favorite Places feature into the Web browser. To add a Web page to your list of Favorite Places, do one of the following:

- Let's say you want to add the Netscape Communications home page to your list of Favorite Places. With the page showing on the screen, click on the heart near the right end of the browser's title bar. Then click Yes to add the address to Favorite Places.
- Drag the heart from the title bar to the Favorite Places folder on the AOL toolbar.

The Netscape address is now safely tucked away among your Favorite Places, as you can see here:

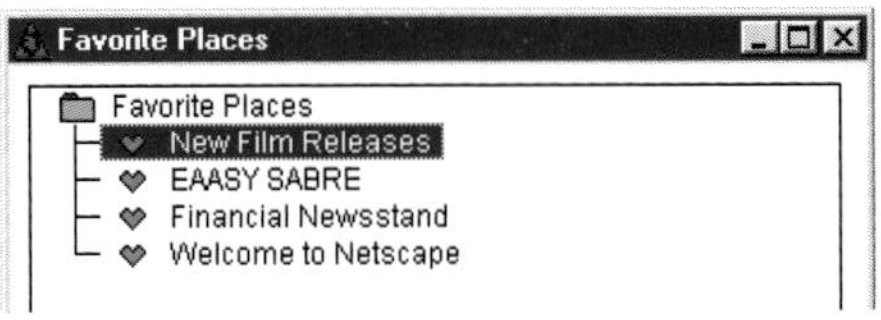

By the way, you don't have to be running the AOL Web browser to go to one of your favorite places on the Web. Wherever you are in AOL, you can open the Favorite Places folder and double-click the name of a Web page, which will automatically start and load the page.

CAUTION

If you use Favorite Places to go to a Web page while you're running the browser, any other pages you've already visited will be erased from your drop-down history list.

CUSTOMIZING THE BROWSER

The Preferences feature allows you to modify the way the AOL browser displays information. Click the Prefs button on the browser toolbar to open the following dialog box:

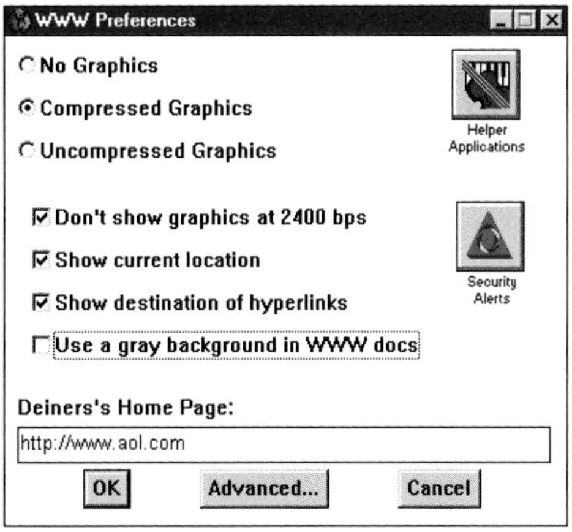

As long as you have at least a 14.4-kbps modem, you probably shouldn't fiddle with the first three options, which deal with graphics. You probably won't want to change the next two check boxes, either. If you deselect the one labeled "Show current location," the address at the top of the browser disappears. Not only will you not see the address of the page you're viewing, but you also won't be able to directly enter an address. This would be a stupid preference to deselect, as would be the next one, "Show destination of hyperlinks." All this option does is display the address of a hyperlink in the status box at the bottom of the browser. What's wrong with that? I ask.

Changing the Browser's Background

As you've seen from some of the illustrations in this chapter, the display area of the AOL browser has a white background by default. This can be hard on the eyes after long periods of uninterrupted browsing. The WWW Preferences feature gives you the option of a gray background. The AOL home page looks like this in gray:

habits & strategies

As a home page for your browser, consider using the page that gives you access to all the big search services plus hundreds of smaller ones on specialized topics. It's called Search.com and its address is ***http://www.search.com.***

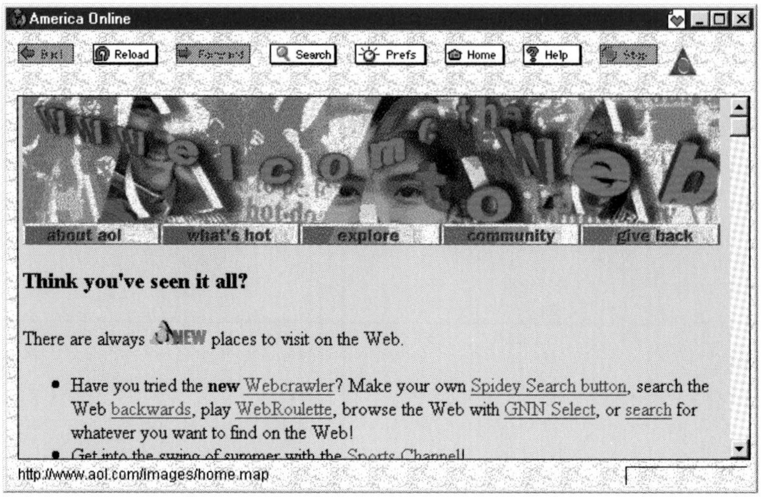

Setting a Different Home Page

If you'd rather not look at AOL's home page every time you go onto the Web, you can change the browser to display a different starting page. At the bottom of the WWW Preferences box, there's a space that allows you to do so. Just erase what's already there and type in a different address. (Remember, you have to enter it exactly as it's written.)

Managing Your Cache

You'll probably notice that once you've loaded a Web page for the first time, it loads more quickly on subsequent visits. This is because the AOL browser stores information about each Web site in a "cache" on the hard disk and uses that information to reload pages. The more you browse the Web, the more items get stored in the cache. This can create problems, stuffing up your disk and slowing down the performance of your PC. You can forestall any difficulties by managing the cache. Start by clicking the Advanced button in the WWW Preferences box to display the following box:

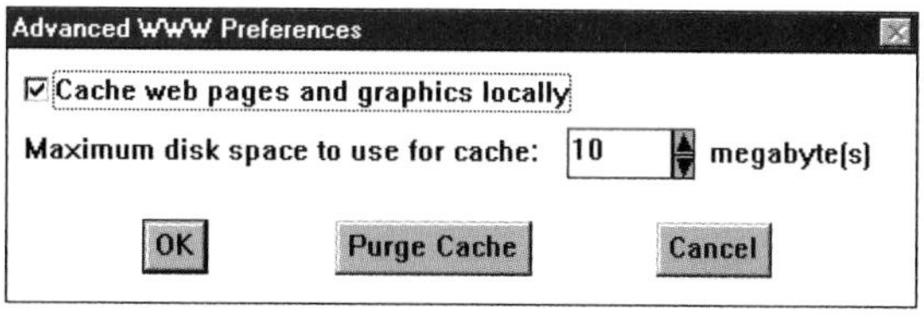

Okay, here are your choices:

- *Disable caching by deselecting the check box.* This is a bad idea, because caching allows the browser to load previously viewed pages faster.
- *Limit the size of the cache.* This is a sensible option if you're really tight on disk space.
- *Purge the cache.* This completely empties the cache—which is both good and bad. It frees up disk space immediately, but it also means that you lose the cached information that lets pages load faster.

That Secure Feeling

The security issue is one of the biggest obstacles preventing people from using the Web to buy stuff. With the regular AOL service, security is not a problem. You deal directly with the AOL computer system, which is as secure as they come.

The WWW Preferences box also includes a Security Alerts button. The AOL browser is set to alert you whenever you enter a Web site that is not secure—that is, one that can't guarantee that any information you send to the computer at the other end will remain confidential. This is only really important if you're buying something over the Web and have to enter your credit card number during the transaction. To view the alert options—and disable them if you want—click the Security Alerts button in the WWW Preferences box.

HOW AOL HAS ADOPTED THE INTERNET

AOL hasn't just accepted the Internet. It has embraced cyberspace wholeheartedly. It's a classic case of "If you can't beat 'em, join 'em." Wherever you go in AOL, you'll find direct links to comparable features on the Web. And, as you'll see in Chapter 4, AOL's electronic mail (e-mail) feature is also Internet e-mail.

AOL and Web Content, Side by Side

Regardless of where you go within AOL, you're never far from the Web. Each channel includes a button that takes you to a list of Web sites that complement AOL's own offerings. Try this as an example:

1. Click Sports in the Channels window.
2. Click the Internet button at the bottom of the window. This will display the following screen, which, as you see, is loaded with links to the Internet.

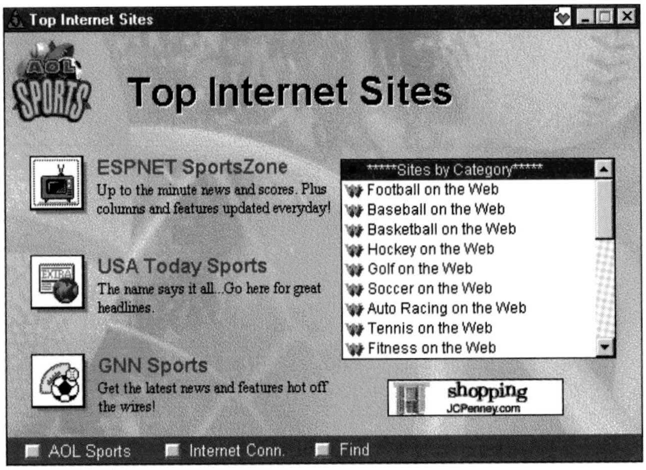

habits & strategies

AOL also offers straightforward help on Internet issues in the One Stop Infoshop section of Member Services. The best part is that this is a free area, in which connect charges don't apply. To go straight to it, use the keyword questions.

HELP FOR WEB USERS

The folks at AOL have provided some of the best help and advice about the Web that you'll find anywhere. Let's go back to the Internet Connection window to demonstrate. (Use the keyword *internet* to go to the Internet Connection window.) The right side of the window features a list of Web resources, one of which is called Help. Double-click it to display the following screen:

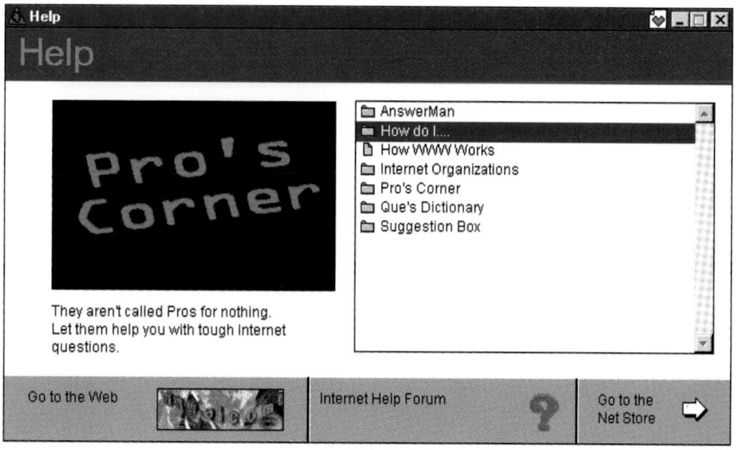

WHAT'S NEXT?

The World Wide Web may be grabbing all the headlines, but there's another Internet-related feature of AOL that you might find at least as useful. It's e-mail, the communications phenomenon of the 1990s, and it's the subject of our next chapter.

CHAPTER
4
CAFE
KING
CAUTION

E-Mail—Corresponding Has Never Been Easier

INCLUDES

- Composing and sending messages
- Using the Address Book
- Attaching files to messages
- Reading new mail
- Sending replies
- Writing offline
- Automating with FlashSessions

FAST FORWARD

WRITE AN ELECTRONIC LETTER ➤ *pp.79–81*

1. Click the Compose Mail (paper-and-pencil) button on the toolbar.
2. Fill in the e-mail address of the recipient.
3. Enter a description of the message in the Subject box.
4. Write your message.
5. Click Send.

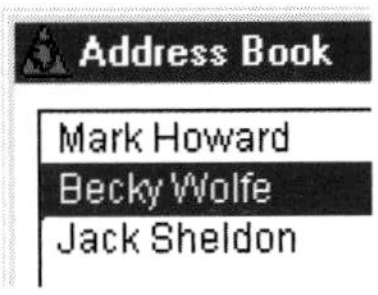

STORE AN ADDRESS IN THE ADDRESS BOOK ➤ *pp. 81–82*

1. Choose Edit Address Book from the Mail menu.
2. Click Create.
3. Enter the person's real name or nickname in the Group Name box.
4. Enter the person's America Online or Internet address in the Screen Names box.
5. Click OK.

ATTACH A FILE TO A MESSAGE ➤ *pp. 82–83*

1. Click the Compose Mail button on the toolbar.
2. Write and address your message and then click the Attach button.
3. Locate the file you want to attach, select it, and click OK.
4. Send the message. A copy of the file will be transferred with it.

CHECK YOUR MAIL ➤ *pp. 84–88*

1. If you have new mail waiting for you, the flag on the mailbox button on the toolbar will be up and the Mail Center button in the Welcome window will say "YOU HAVE MAIL." Click either one.
2. You'll see a list of incoming messages. Select the one you want to read and click the Read button.
3. To read the message again later, choose Check Mail You've Read from the Mail menu.

REPLY TO A MESSAGE ➤ *pp. 88–89*

1. While the message is on the screen, click the Reply button. To include material from the original message, select the text you want before clicking Reply.
2. Write your response and click Send.

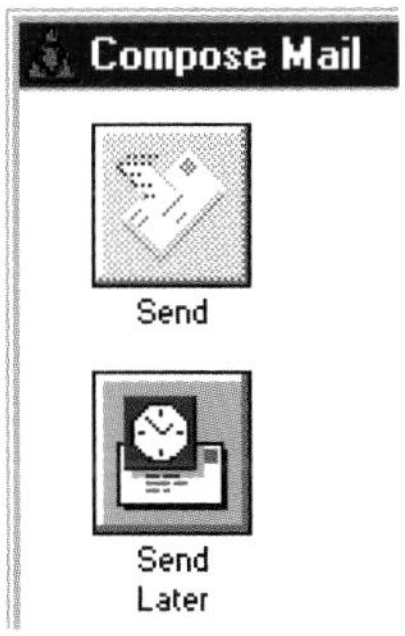

COMPOSE A MESSAGE OFFLINE ➤ *pp. 89–90*

1. Before you sign on, click the Compose Mail button on the toolbar.
2. Write and address your message just as you would if you were online.
3. Instead of clicking Send, click Send Later.
4. Sign on and then choose Read Outgoing FlashMail from the Mail menu.
5. Open the message and click Send.

AUTOMATE WITH FLASHSESSIONS ➤ *pp. 90–92*

1. Choose Set Up FlashSession from the Mail menu. You can do this offline.
2. Click Walk Me Through to choose options and schedule FlashSessions.
3. Once they have been enabled, FlashSessions can periodically sign you on, check and send mail, and then sign you off, thus saving time and money.

Despite the enormous growth of the World Wide Web, it's not the most widely used feature of the Internet. That distinction belongs to electronic mail, or e-mail, as it is popularly known. E-mail is such a widespread phenomenon that it has entered the language as a noun, a verb, and an adjective. It has become an indispensable tool in the workplace, and almost every business card now includes an e-mail address. But it's also great for personal correspondence. Using e-mail is more convenient than writing and mailing a letter, and it even has advantages over the telephone—you needn't worry that the person won't be there, time zones aren't a problem, and you don't have to deal with voicemail. In short, it's ideal for busy people.

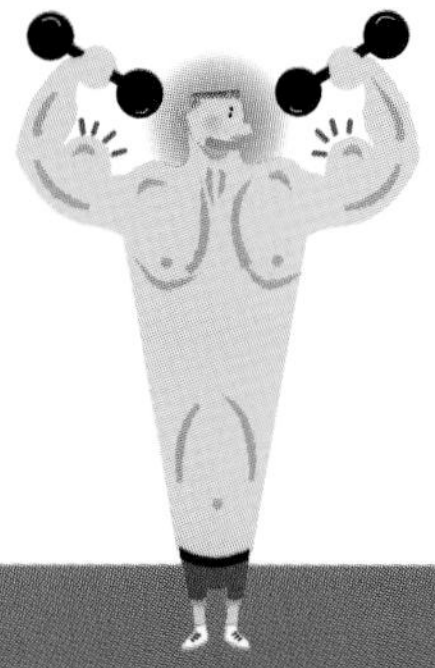

definition

Mail: *A term used by AOL's software to refer to e-mail. It's okay to use mail and e-mail interchangeably. In fact, I think I'll do that.*

ANYONE, ANYWHERE, ANYTIME

You can use America Online's e-mail feature to exchange messages with other AOL members or with anyone in the world who has an e-mail address. You can send and receive messages anytime, day or night. (The only catch is that you must be signed on to send mail.) And there's no extra charge for sending e-mail—it's included in your membership rate. A few special features are available when you're writing to another AOL member, as you'll see later in this chapter. But you use the same basic techniques to communicate via e-mail no matter who's on the other end of your message.

Your E-Mail Address

Everyone who uses e-mail has a unique e-mail address. When you correspond with other AOL members, you can simply use your screen name. But when you go out on the Internet, you need a full-fledged Internet address so that people using other online services or Internet accounts can send stuff to you. Your full Internet address is your screen name followed by **@aol.com**, as in **Deiners@aol.com** (that's me).

SENDING MAIL

There are various ways to access AOL's e-mail functions and, as is the case with other AOL features, there's a good deal of redundancy. Suppose you want to send someone a message, for example. You can start with one of the following steps:

- Choose Compose Mail from the Mail menu at the top of the AOL screen.
- Click the Compose Mail (paper-and-pencil) button on the main toolbar.
- Click Mail Center in the Welcome window and then click the Compose Mail button. (This doesn't work if you have unread mail, in which case the Mail Center button will say "YOU HAVE MAIL." If you click the button, AOL will take you directly to your unread mail.)
- Press the CTRL key as you type the letter M (CTRL-M).

As you can see, this is a lot easier than hunting up a piece of paper, a pen, an envelope, and a stamp. Using any of the methods above will display the following window, which you use to compose and send e-mail:

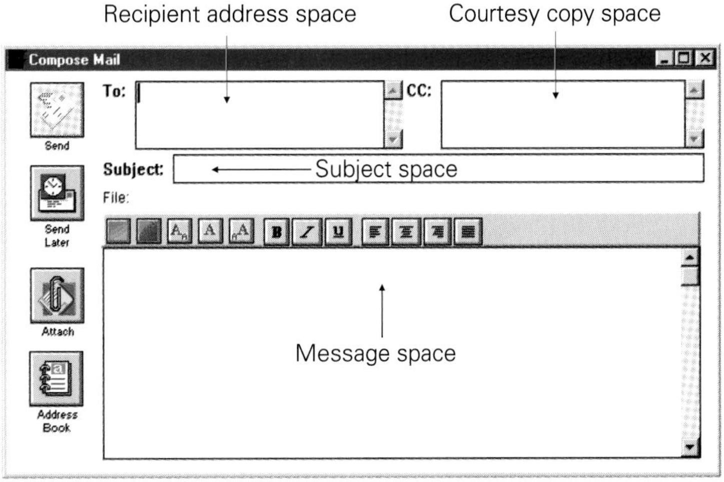

SHORTCUT

You can send the same message to more than one person simultaneously. Just enter addresses one after the other, separating them with commas. This technique works in both the To box and the CC box.

habits & strategies

Write messages to yourself to practice using e-mail. You'll find out how different procedures look to recipients, and you'll always have a pen pal you can rely on.

Composing Your Message

Composing a simple message (or even an extraordinarily erudite one) involves just a few steps and can be done quite quickly. A short message, in fact, can be composed and sent off in a minute or two. Follow these steps to get the job done:

1. In the Compose Mail window, enter the address of the recipient in the To box. If you're sending mail to another AOL member, just use the person's screen name as the address. If the recipient uses another e-mail service, you'll have to include his or her entire Internet address, like this: **president@whitehouse.gov**. (By the way, don't worry about capitalization. E-mail doesn't care, so go ahead and lowercase everything if you want.)
2. To send a courtesy copy of the message to someone else, fill in that person's address in the CC box.
3. In the space labeled *Subject*, type a brief overview of your message. This is the first thing the person at the other end will see before he or she reads your message, so keep it brief and to the point.
4. Write the message in the main blank area of the window. Don't worry if you fill up the space—the window will scroll to accommodate as long a letter as you care to write. When you're done, you'll have a window that looks similar to this:

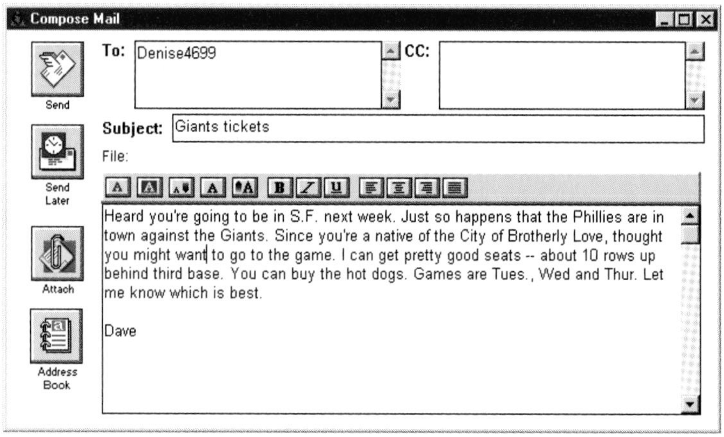

Mail from one AOL member to another is handled by AOL's own computer system and arrives in seconds. Mail sent across the Internet to a nonmember takes a little longer, but not much—usually less than half an hour and often just a few minutes.

Okay, Now Send It

When you've finished writing your missive, send it by clicking the Send button at the left side of the window. If all goes smoothly, you'll see a confirmation box telling you that your mail has been sent.

Check Mail You've Sent

To reread a message, choose Check Mail You've Sent from AOL's Mail menu. In addition to reading sent mail, you can do a couple of other nifty things—but only if the message was sent to another AOL member. The following features don't work on Internet mail:

- Click the Show Status button to check to see if and when your message was read by the recipient.
- Click the Unsend button to retrieve a message after you've sent it. Note that this works only if the message has not yet been read by the recipient.

habits & strategies

You can easily send mail to a group of people. Instead of adding each address in the To box, create a group entry in the Address Book: enter a name for the group in the Group Name box and list the addresses below, separating them with commas.

The Address Book

E-mail addresses can be very difficult to remember. Not to worry, however. AOL has a feature called the Address Book, in which you can keep frequently used addresses and retrieve them with a click of the mouse. To store addresses, open the Address Book window by choosing Edit Address Book from the Mail menu or by clicking on the Address Book button in the Compose Mail window. Then click the Create button to display this window:

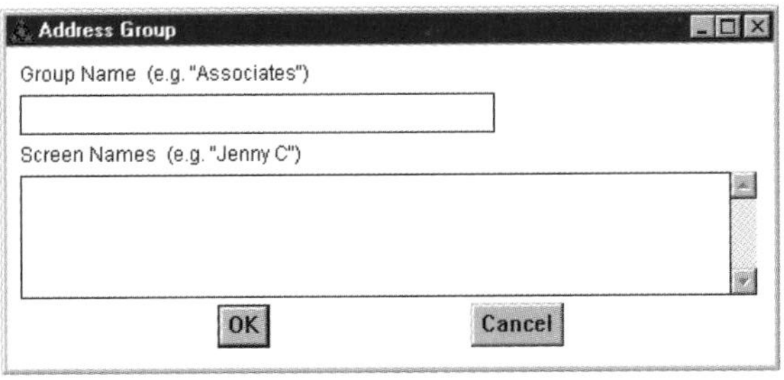

To add an address to your Address Book, enter the person's real name or nickname in the Group Name box and his or her Internet address (or AOL screen name) in the Screen Names box. Then click OK. The next time you want to send that person a message, do the following:

1. Open the Compose Mail dialog box.
2. Click Address Book and select the person's name.
3. Click To. The address will automatically be inserted in the To box in your message.
4. Click OK to close the Address Book.

Attaching Files to Your Mail

Sometimes you might want to send someone a spreadsheet or the draft of a report. No problem. You can send a text document, a graphic, or any other file by attaching it to an e-mail message. The file can be of any size and can go to any Internet address. Here's how to attach a file:

1. Open the Compose Mail window, fill in the address and subject boxes, and write your message.
2. Click the Attach button at the left side of the window. This opens a dialog box that lets you search your hard disk to find the file you want to attach.
3. Once you've located the file, select it and click OK. The name of the file now appears in the Compose Mail dialog box, as you can see here:

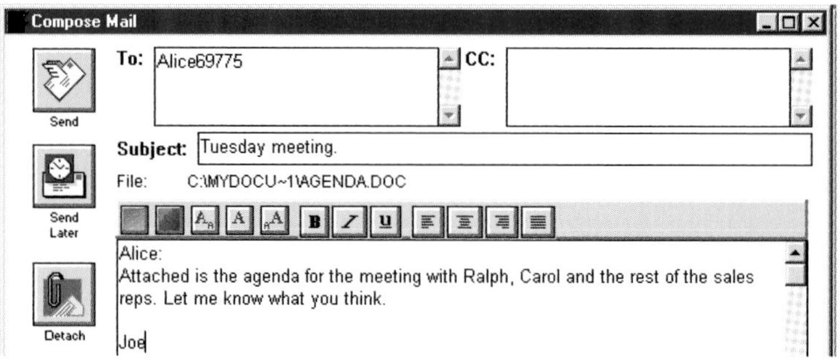

When you send the message, a copy of the attached file will be transmitted along with it. (Don't worry, the original file remains undisturbed on your hard disk.)

CAUTION

In theory, sending attached files is a piece of cake. In reality, it can present problems, especially if complex data and graphics are sent. Before you send a file, make sure the recipient has software capable of viewing and editing it.

habits & strategies

While on the road with your notebook PC, you can back up files you create by sending them to yourself as e-mail attachments. This is also a good way to transfer files between your PC at home and your computer at the office.

How AOL Sends Attachments

AOL's software automatically encodes attachments using the MIME (Multipurpose Internet Mail Extensions) technology. This is a standard technique for sending files via e-mail. Most e-mail programs can decipher MIME attachments. AOL members really get pampered, because the AOL software automatically decodes any MIME messages that they receive.

Dress Up Your Writing

When you're writing to someone out in Internet-land, you're limited to plain text for your message. But if the recipient is an AOL member, you can make your prose a lot more colorful, as in the following example:

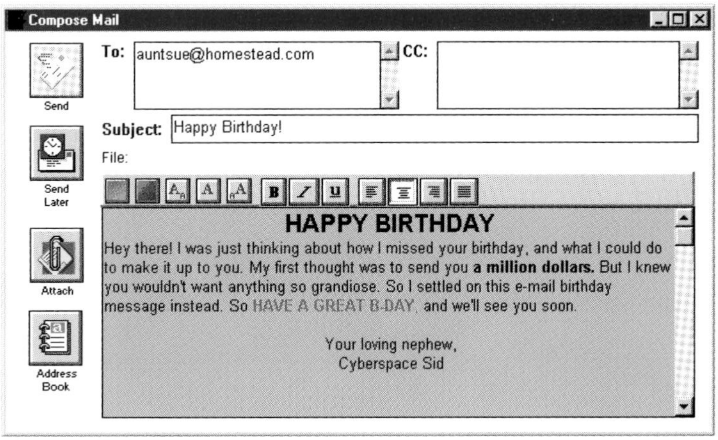

Just why anyone would want to send a green and pink electronic mailgram is beyond me. Most busy people probably have better things to do. But the capability's there if you want it. Hey, I don't invent this stuff, I just write about it! Anyway, to apply attributes to text (boldface, underlining, italics) or to change its alignment or its color, do the following:

1. Select the text you want to change.
2. Click the appropriate button on the formatting toolbar, located just above the writing area in the Compose Mail window.

SHARE YOUR FAVORITE PLACES

Got a favorite place you'd like to share with another AOL member? No problem. Just drag the place-mark from your Favorite Places folder (or drag the heart from the title bar of any window) and drop it into an e-mail message. You'll notice that it turns into a hyperlink. When the other person opens the message, he or she can click it and go right to the favorite place. Cool or what?

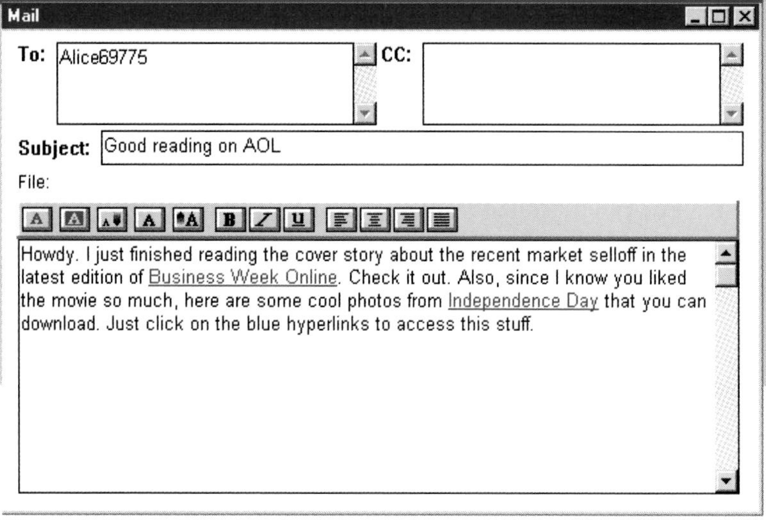

Mail
To: Alice69775
CC:
Subject: Good reading on AOL
File:
Howdy. I just finished reading the cover story about the recent market selloff in the latest edition of Business Week Online. Check it out. Also, since I know you liked the movie so much, here are some cool photos from Independence Day that you can download. Just click on the blue hyperlinks to access this stuff.

YOU'VE GOT MAIL!

Whenever you sign on to AOL, you'll know right away whether there's new e-mail waiting for you. In fact, you won't be settled in your chair before you find out, because an assertive male voice will begin your AOL session with the announcement, "You've got mail!" You'll get the same audio alert if mail arrives while you're online. But even if you're hard of hearing or you've turned off the sound (see Chapter 2), you'll still know as soon as you sign on whether there's anything new in your mailbox. Here's why:

- The big Mail Center button in the Welcome window will read "YOU HAVE MAIL."

- The flag on the mailbox icon at the left end of the AOL toolbar will be up. Clicking this tool is the quickest way to retrieve mail that arrives during an online session. (When the flag is down, there's no new mail, and clicking the mailbox tool does nothing.)

You get the point. Basically, you have no excuse for not reading your mail. You certainly can't say, "Gosh, I didn't realize you'd sent me an e-mail."

Reading New Mail

As with composing mail, there is a surfeit of ways to read mail. Here they are:

- Click the Mail Center button if it says "YOU HAVE MAIL."
- Click the mailbox on the toolbar if the flag's up.
- Choose Read New Mail from the Mail menu on the menu bar at the top of the screen.

Unread e-mail remains in your mailbox for about 35 days, after which it will be expunged. Messages that have been read will be deleted in 3 to 5 days. AOL does this to keep its computer system from becoming stuffed to the gills with e-mail.

In each case, you'll be presented with the New Mail window and a listing of your new messages, as in the example here:

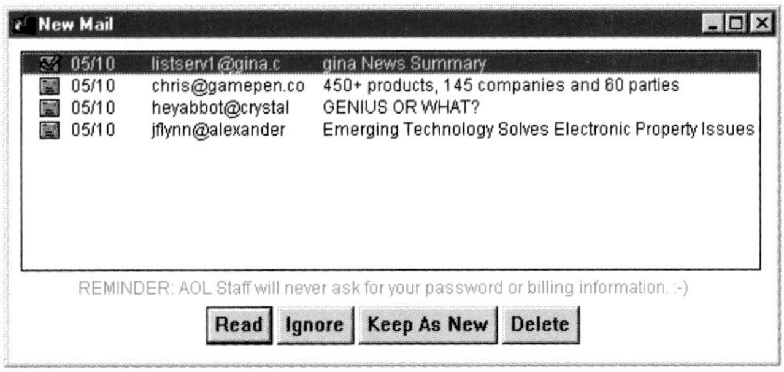

At the bottom of the window are four buttons. Here's what they do:

- **Read** Opens the message so you can read it.
- **Ignore** Moves the message to your Old Mail box. (Be aware that if the message is from another AOL member

SHORTCUT

Whenever you have more than one piece of new mail, you can go from the current one to the next one just by clicking on the Next button in the bottom-right corner of the window. This button appears only when you have multiple messages.

and he or she checks on the status of the message, it will be reported as "ignored.")

- **Keep As New** Keeps the message in the New Mail box.
- **Delete** Gets rid of the message. Think twice before using this one.

If you decide to read the message, it will be displayed as in the example below. This is a message I wrote and sent to my AOL account from an Internet account:

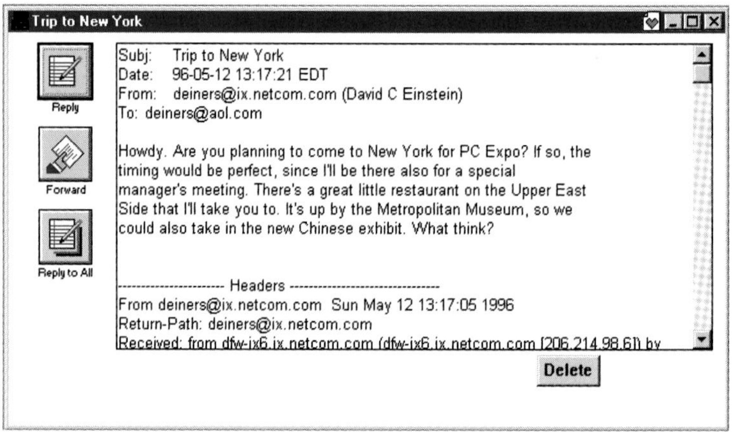

What's All the Garbage at the Bottom?

At the end of the message shown above, you'll notice a pile of gibberish. This is "header" information that shows you how the message was routed over the Internet. Messages from one AOL member to another don't have header material, since they don't go over the Internet.

Reading an Attachment

You'll know that your mail includes an attachment if two buttons—Download File and Download Later—appear beneath the message, as shown here:

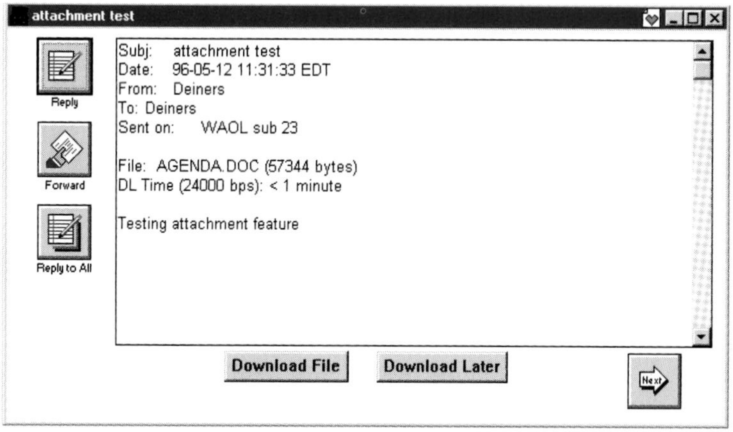

Clicking the Download File button will start AOL's Download Manager. Click OK to automatically decode the file and transfer it to the Download folder inside the main AOL folder on your hard disk. If you'd rather put it somewhere else, choose a new destination folder before clicking OK. (For a full explanation of downloading, see Chapter 7.) Once the file's downloaded, you'll be able to read it using an appropriate program. For instance, if the file was created in Microsoft Word, you must open it in a program that can display Word documents.

habits & strategies

When you get a message that's really important or that contains information you'll need when you're away from your PC, it's a good idea to print it out. To print a message, display it on the screen and then choose Print from the File menu.

Rereading Your Mail

Once you've read a message, it goes into the Old Mail box. To read it again, choose Check Mail You've Read from the Mail menu. This displays the Old Mail window, which lists your previously read messages. Remember, once you have read a message, it will be deleted 3 to 5 days later and will disappear from the Old Mail box.

Keeping Mail Permanently

If you want to keep mail for future reference, you can store it in your Personal Filing Cabinet. Just check the appropriate boxes in Mail Preferences, which you can access by clicking My AOL on the toolbar, then Preferences, and then Mail Preferences. Whenever you want to refer back to old mail, even if you're offline, just click the Personal Filing

Cabinet button on the AOL toolbar. You'll see your mail listed in a folder entitled Mail You've Read, as shown here:

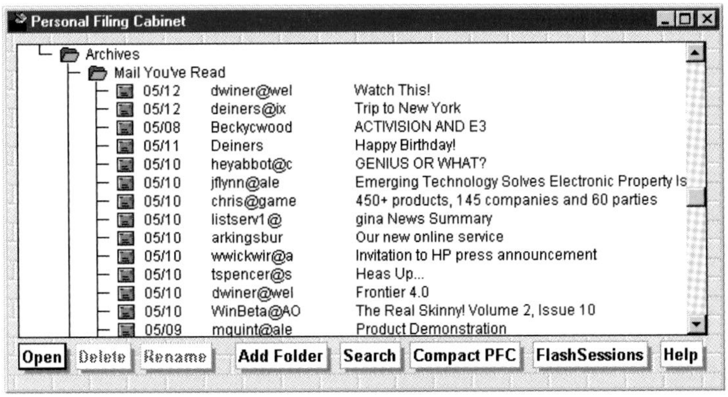

REPLYING TO MESSAGES

One of the best things about e-mail is that it lets you easily respond to mail. And you can even include all or part of the original message in your reply. To reply to a message, display the message and then click on the Reply button. This opens a new message composition window. The address of the person you're responding to is automatically inserted in the To box, and the subject of the original message preceded by Re: appears in the Subject box.

Quoting the Original Message

There will probably be times when you will want to include all or part of the original message in a reply, just to remind the other person what they wrote about in the first place. Use the following steps to do so:

1. With the original message on your screen, use your mouse to select the material you want to quote as part of your response.
2. Click the Reply button. A message composition window that includes the selected text will appear, as in the following example:

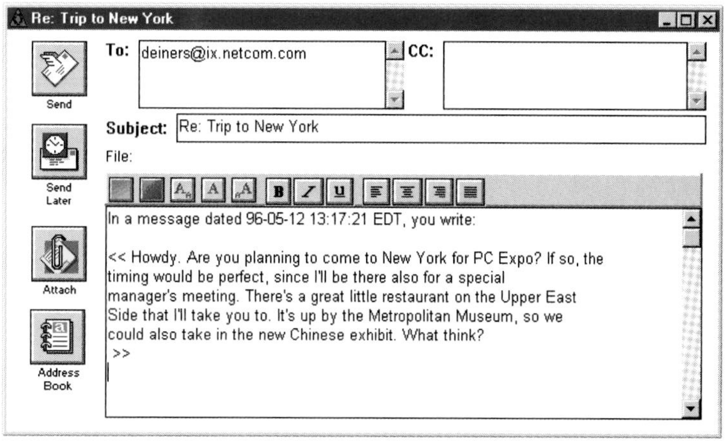

Write your response below the quoted text. You can attach a file, use the Address Book, or do anything else you would do with a regular message. AOL treats the reply exactly as if it were a new message. When you've finished, click the Send button.

Forwarding Messages

Occasionally you might want to send a message you've received to a third person. Maybe somebody has e-mailed you a good joke, and you'd like to pass it on to a friend. It's easy. With the original message on your screen, click the Forward button. A new message composition window will appear. All you have to do is enter your friend's e-mail address and click the Send button. (The message itself will not appear, but it will be forwarded, trust me.)

habits & strategies

Offline mail is probably the biggest money saver offered by AOL. It's especially good for people who do a lot of message writing at one sitting. Just sit down and write all your messages for the day and then go online and send them.

COMPOSING MAIL OFFLINE

Writing messages during an online session can eat up your monthly allotment of connect time faster than you can say, "Wait a minute, Mister Postman." Fortunately, you can compose messages offline. In fact, you compose a message offline the same way you would if you were connected. The Compose Mail button on the toolbar and the Compose Mail option on the Mail menu are both available when you're offline, as is the Address Book.

Sending Mail Composed Offline

When you've finished writing your offline message (or messages), click the Send Later button, which will save the mail for later delivery. If you have FlashSessions scheduled, the mail will go out during the next session. (See the section on FlashSessions that follows.) Or you can sign on and send the mail manually. To do that, follow these steps:

1. Once you're online, choose Read Outgoing FlashMail from the Mail menu. This will present you with a list of messages that were composed offline, as in this example:

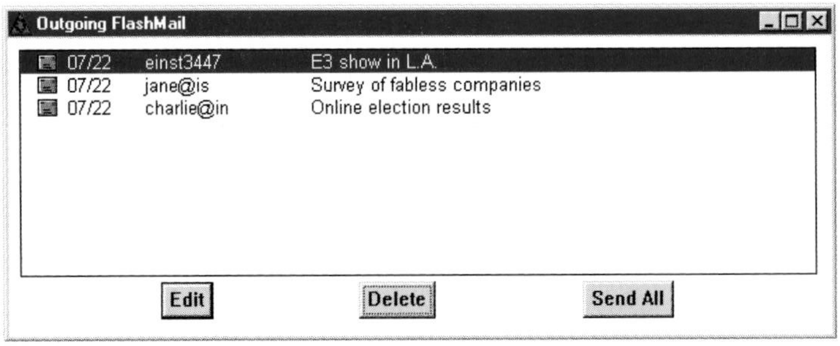

2. Either click Send All to dispatch all the messages in the queue or, if you want to send only one of a group of messages, select the message and click Edit. The message will be displayed in a regular message window, complete with a Send button.

LET YOUR PC PLAY MAILMAN

As I said earlier, you can't check or send mail unless you're connected to AOL. But you can have your computer sign on by itself and do those chores for you if you use AOL's FlashSessions. You can set FlashSessions to operate unattended at regular intervals, from once a week to once every 30 minutes. FlashSessions can also be used to send and retrieve Internet newsgroup postings and download software files. But if you're like most people, you'll probably use them primarily to stay on top of your e-mail.

CAUTION

FlashSessions are great for busy people who use AOL. But if you're going to leave your computer unattended, make sure it's in a secure place. If your password is stored, your AOL account is available to anyone who wants to use it.

A Few Musts for FlashSessions

For FlashSessions to work, all of the following conditions must be met:

- Your computer must be turned on.
- The AOL software must be running. You can either leave the sign-on window visible or minimize it and use other programs.
- The PC's internal clock should be set correctly. This will allow scheduled FlashSessions to work when they're supposed to.

Configuring Your FlashSessions

To set up FlashSessions, choose Set Up FlashSession from the Mail menu. (Is there an echo in here?) You can do this online or offline, but you'll save money if you do it offline. The following window will be displayed:

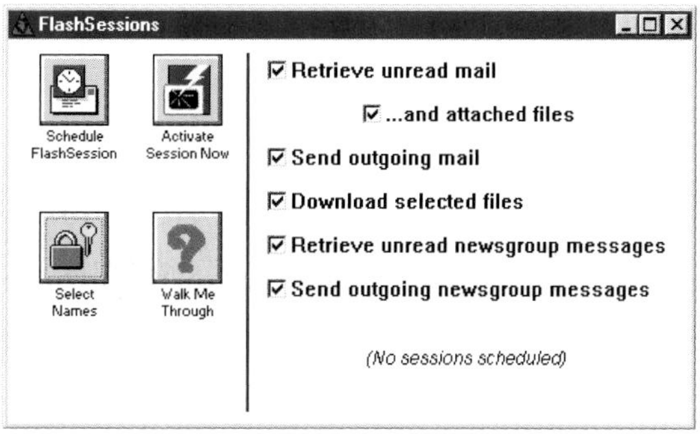

All the options are right there in front of you. If you're a beginner, you might want to click on the Walk Me Through button. This initiates a short step-by-step procedure during which you'll get to choose the features you want to activate. You'll also have the chance to set up the FlashSession schedule. To deactivate FlashSessions (but keep your option settings), do the following:

1. Choose Setup FlashSession from the Mail menu.
2. Click the Schedule FlashSession button.

SHORTCUT

If you don't want to wait for a FlashSession, choose Activate FlashSession Now from the Mail menu. A FlashSession will begin immediately. This is the way to go if you want to send offline mail without waiting for a scheduled FlashSession.

3. Deselect the Enable Scheduler check box, shown here:

What Happens During a FlashSession?

During a FlashSession, the tasks you selected when you set up the session are performed. When the FlashSession begins, a status box like the one shown below appears onscreen.

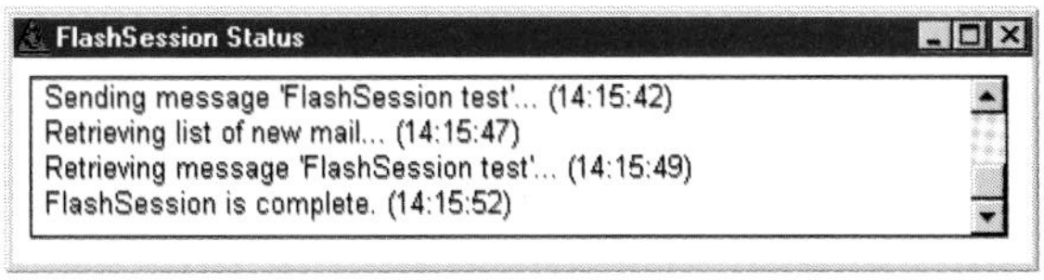

Reading Mail After a FlashSession

Mail retrieved during a FlashSession can be read offline, of course. To read your FlashSession messages, choose Read Incoming FlashMail from the Mail menu. All incoming (and outgoing) FlashMail is stored in folders in your Personal Filing Cabinet. FlashMail messages don't appear in the New Mail or Old Mail boxes, so don't look for them there. And FlashMail messages stay in the Personal Filing Cabinet until you delete them.

You can also use AOL to send a letter by regular mail with the Fax/Paper Mail option. But it's a silly and expensive option—AOL charges $2.50 per letter. Oh, and you can only send a fax or paper mail after you've been an AOL member for 45 days.

SENDING MAIL DIRECTLY TO A FAX MACHINE

What if you want to write to someone who doesn't have e-mail? There still are such people, poor devils. Well, AOL has an answer for that. It's called paper. You can use AOL's Compose Mail window to send a fax from your computer to almost any fax machine. You send a fax either by selecting Fax/Paper Mail from the Mail menu or by using the regular Compose Mail window. (If you are working offline, use the regular Compose Mail form.) All you do is put the recipient's name in the To: box, followed by @ and the phone number of the fax machine, including area code (for instance, **Jessica Rabbit@800-555-1212**). Each fax you send will cost $2.00, which will be added to your AOL bill. You'll get confirmation of the fax transmission by e-mail.

MAILING LISTS

E-mail isn't just for exchanging messages with individuals. It's also used for Internet mailing lists. Don't be put off by the term—these aren't like regular mailing lists, which are used to spread your name around for marketing purposes. Internet mailing lists are global discussion groups that let e-mail users share information. By some estimates, there are more than 20,000 mailing lists floating around in cyberspace. A mailing list can take the form of an electronic newsletter or a forum for public debate, or it can just be a group of people with common interests. Mailing lists are a good way to stay up to date on current issues. And, like most other stuff on the Internet, they're free.

How to Locate Mailing Lists

The place to start if you're interested in mailing lists is the Mailing List Directory window, shown below. To get there, use the keywords *mailing lists.* (Don't use *mailing list,* or you'll be taken to an electronic yellow pages directory, which is something else altogether.)

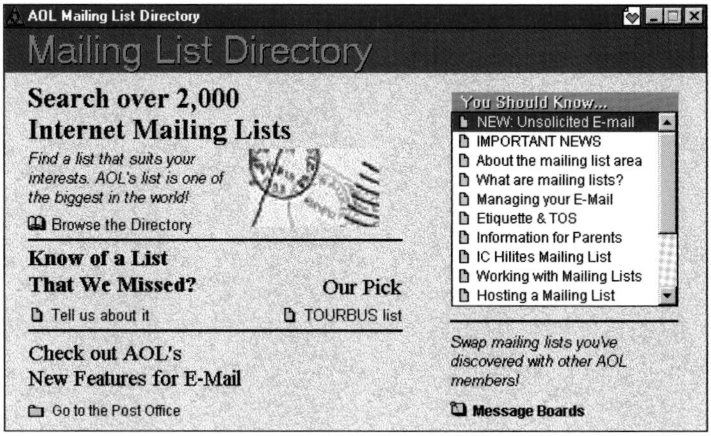

Clicking Browse the Directory will take you to the directory itself, which happens to be located on the World Wide Web. AOL put it there to make it available to anyone with Internet access, not just AOL members. Are these guys thoughtful or what? You can use the directory's index of categories or search by topic to locate names and descriptions of mailing lists.

Many mailing lists are operated by individuals. But large lists are often administered by software programs called Listservers. You'll know you're dealing with a computer if the e-mail address for the list includes the word listserv.

Subscribing and Unsubscribing

Before you can start receiving messages from a mailing list, you must subscribe to it. This is standard operating procedure, and information on how to subscribe (as well as how to unsubscribe) is routinely included in the description of the list. Here, for instance, are the instructions for The NBC Comedy Friends Discussion List:

CAUTION

You can subscribe to as many mailing lists as you like, but be aware that AOL can accommodate only 550 pieces of new mail. When it reaches that limit, it starts killing messages, beginning with the ones that have been waiting longest.

Most lists, like this one, let anyone join. But some can get picky about it, and you might be asked to submit the reasons why you ought to be admitted. (Imagine—snobs on the Internet!) Assuming that your request is approved, you should start receiving messages sent to the list within a day or two.

Sending Messages to a Mailing List

Most mailing lists welcome participation by subscribers. The e-mail address for posting messages is usually included with the description of the list, along with the subscription information. Note that some lists are edited, which means that somebody decides which messages from subscribers will be sent to the entire list.

WHAT'S NEXT?

More Internet stuff, that's what. In addition to e-mail and the World Wide Web, AOL lets you play around with the exciting, informative, and often controversial world of newsgroups. Stay tuned for a look at how to participate in global discussions on everything from science to skiing.

CHAPTER 5

Newsgroups—Your Global Bulletin Boards

INCLUDES

- Subscribing to a newsgroup
- Reading news messages
- Posting messages and replies
- Using proper netiquette
- Limiting your kids' newsgroup access

FAST FORWARD

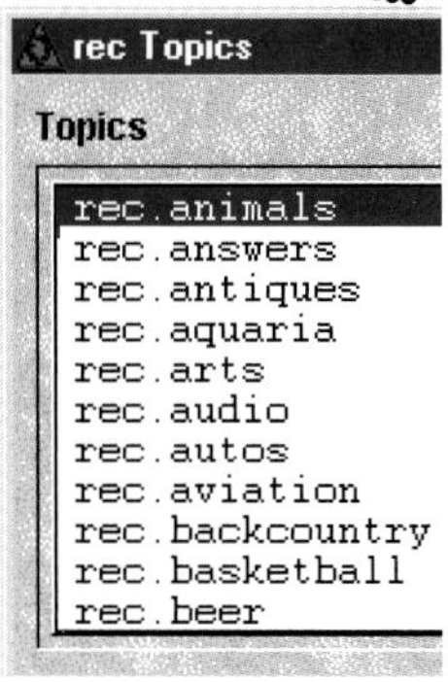

SUBSCRIBE TO A NEWSGROUP ➤ *pp. 100–104*

Start by clicking on the Internet Connection button on the toolbar and then clicking on News Groups to display the main Newsgroups window. Then do one of the following:

- If you know the name of the newsgroup you want to subscribe to, click Expert Add and enter the name. Then click Add.
- To find newsgroups on a specific topic, click Search All Newsgroups, enter a word or phrase, and then click OK. If the search returns a newsgroup you want to subscribe to, select it from the list and click Add.
- If you're a total beginner, try browsing AOL's massive database of newsgroups. Start by clicking Add Newsgroups.

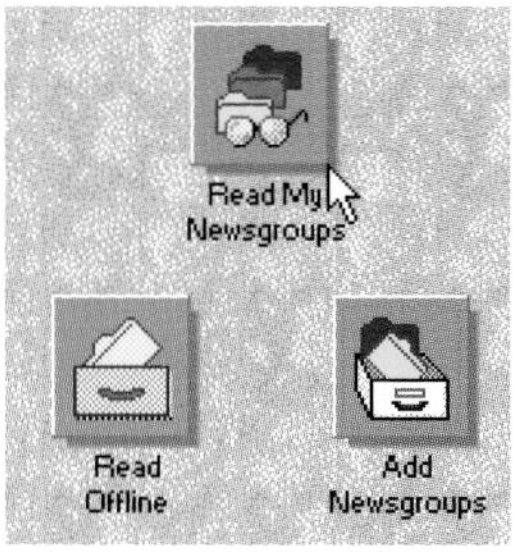

READ A NEWS MESSAGE ➤ *pp. 105–106*

1. Click Read My Newsgroups in the Newsgroups window.
2. In the list of the newsgroups you've subscribed to, highlight the one that contains messages you want to read and click List Unread. You will be presented with a list of all the items you haven't yet seen.
3. To read a message, highlight the subject and click Read.

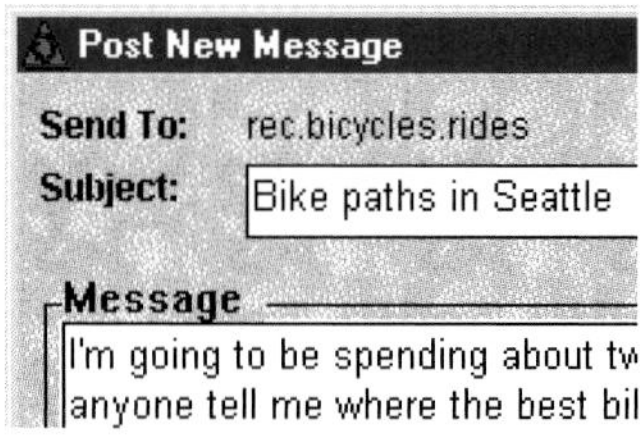

POST A MESSAGE ➤ *pp. 106–108*

1. In the Newsgroups window, click Read My Newsgroups and then double-click a newsgroup to access it.
2. Click Send New Message.
3. Enter a description of your message in the Subject box and write your message in the Message area.
4. Click Send to post the message to the newsgroup.

READ NEWS MESSAGES OFFLINE ➤ *p. 109*

You can use FlashSessions to have your computer automatically sign on to AOL and retrieve unread newsgroup messages, which you can then read offline. Here's how:

1. Click Read Offline in the Newsgroups window.
2. In the dialog box that appears, either click Add All or select the desired newsgroup and click Add. When you've finished adding newsgroups, click OK.
3. Choose Set Up FlashSession from AOL's Mail menu.
4. Select the box labeled "Retrieve unread newsgroup messages."
5. Close the FlashSessions dialog box.

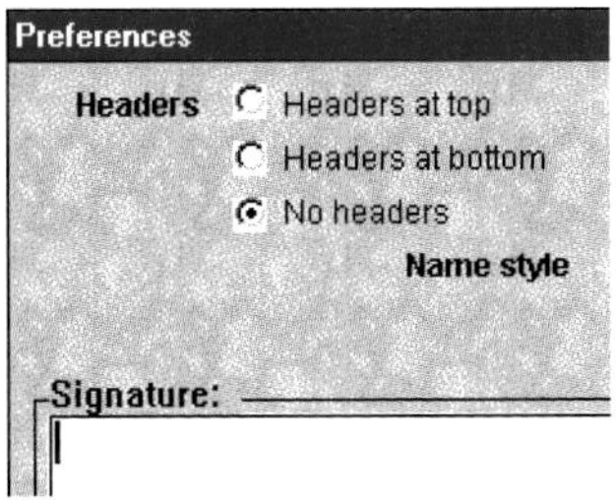

SET PREFERENCES ➤ *pp. 110–111*

Click Set Preferences in the main Newsgroups window to display customization options. You can use the Preferences dialog box to create a personalized "signature" that you can append to messages you send out. You can also change the order in which new incoming messages appear.

BLOCK CHILDREN'S ACCESS TO NEWSGROUPS ➤ *pp. 111–112*

1. In the main Newsgroups window, click Parental Controls.
2. Select the screen name to which you want the restrictions applied.
3. Select the options you want and enter the names of any newsgroups you'd like to keep your child from seeing.
4. Click OK.

E-mail isn't the only method of exchanging information over the Internet. There are also global forums called *newsgroups* that let you post and read messages about particular topics—messages that can be read by millions of computer users. Newsgroups can be an invaluable tool for busy people. A friend of mine whose passion is scuba diving uses newsgroups to scope out great locations for scuba vacations. And people I know in the computer business keep on top of the latest trends through newsgroups, which have given a whole new meaning to the phrase "news travels fast." Newsgroups are similar to America Online's internal Message Boards, but they aren't hampered by AOL's rigid restrictions on language and subject matter. We'll talk about the Message Boards in Chapter 6. Right now, let's take a look at the wild and woolly world of newsgroups.

SOMETHING FOR EVERYONE

Newsgroups, known collectively as Usenet, cover nearly every subject you can imagine, from cats to computers and from politics to poker. New groups are being added on a daily basis, and AOL does its best to keep up with the rush. To get started using newsgroups, follow these steps:

1. Click the Internet Connection button in the main Channels window.
2. Click News Groups, which opens the following main Newsgroups window:

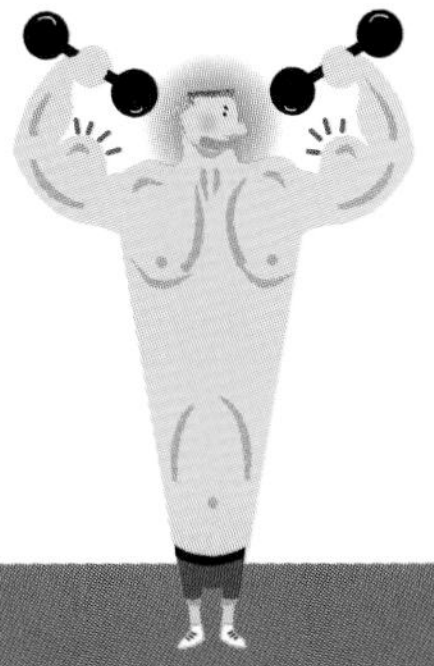

definition

Usenet: *Short for* user network, *an umbrella term for the Internet newsgroups. There is no central governing body for Usenet, and, in fact, it would be extremely difficult to govern because it's so big. As of this writing there are more than 20,000 newsgroups.*

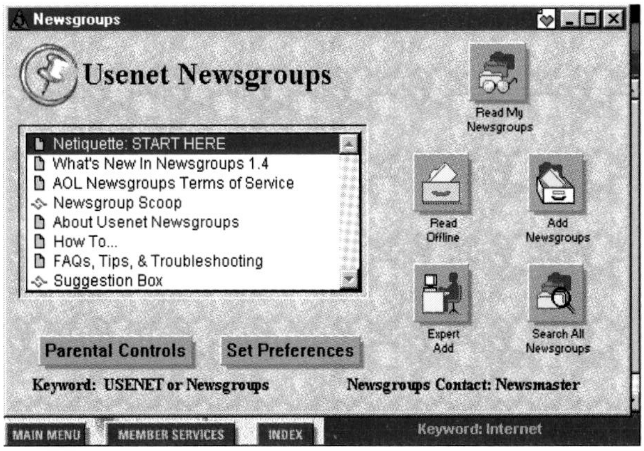

Newsgroup Lingo

Like the World Wide Web, Usenet has its own language. (You didn't know this was a book on linguistics, did you?) Take heart, however: it's a very easy language to learn. Each newsgroup has a name composed of several parts, separated by periods, that together determine the newsgroup's identity within Usenet. Here's a typical newsgroup name:

rec.arts.movies.reviews

The first part of the name is its main category, also known as a *hierarchy*. That's followed by one or more subcategories and finally by a word that denotes the specific subject matter of the group. Here's a rundown of some of the major hierarchies, which contain the most popular newsgroups:

- **rec** Groups involved with recreational interests. This is the most wide-ranging category, encompassing everything from motorcycles to music. If you have a hobby, no matter how obscure, there's probably a newsgroup to accommodate you.
- **comp** Groups that offer computer information. Newsgroups in this category can help you find answers to questions about your hardware and software.

- **alt** "Alternative" groups. The alt category is an immense grab bag of interesting, dull, and even lurid subjects. This is the category that contains the sexually explicit groups.
- **soc** Groups that deal with social issues such as religion, history, and politics.

For a comprehensive discussion of newsgroups and their terminology, click on FAQ (frequently asked questions) in the Internet Connection window and then on Newsgroups to display the following window:

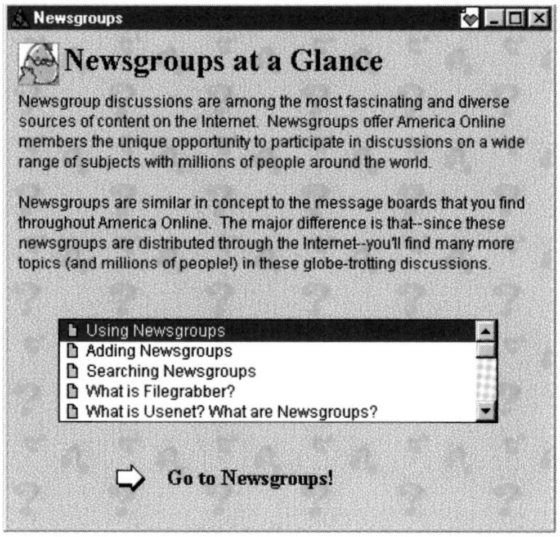

YOU HAVE TO SUBSCRIBE—BUT IT'S FREE

To participate in a newsgroup, you must first subscribe to it. (AOL uses the term *adding,* which means that you add a newsgroup to the list of the groups you subscribe to.) This is a lot easier than subscribing to a newspaper or a magazine. There are no forms to fill out and mail, no telephone calls to make, and—best of all—no payments. You can subscribe to as many newsgroups as you want—it's absolutely free.

Adding Newsgroups

There are several ways to subscribe to a newsgroup. (There are several ways to do everything on AOL, so why should this be any

habits & strategies

You can't send a message to a newsgroup until you've subscribed to it, but you can read messages in newsgroups that you view via Add Newsgroups. This is a useful way to get a feel for a newsgroup before you decide whether to add it to your list.

different?) If you have no idea what you're looking for, try clicking Add Newsgroups in the main Newsgroups window. You will be presented with AOL's database of newsgroups. Bear in mind, though, that the selection is enormous. Here, for example, is the first part of a list of 145 newsgroups dealing with world cultures:

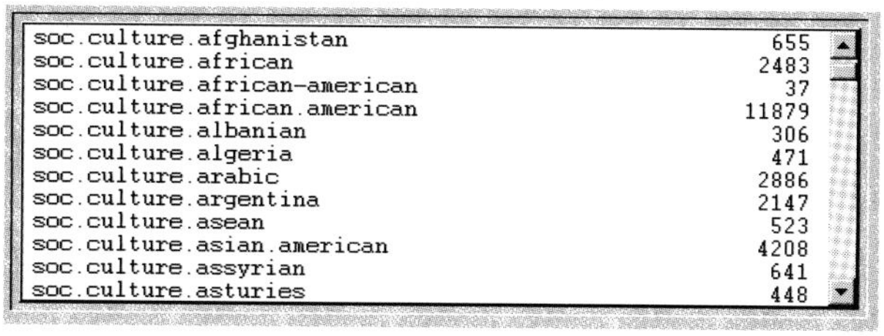

Searching for Newsgroups

A second option is to use the Search All Newsgroups feature. This presents you with a dialog box in which you enter words or phrases that describe a topic that interests you. Although this feature can be a helpful tool, it has its limits because it finds only those newsgroups that have the words or designations in their names. That's great in some cases—you'll find more than 150 groups devoted to IBM, for instance. But try searching for *science fiction* and you'll come up empty. That's because science fiction newsgroups are denoted by *sf*. And if you try searching for *sf* you'll get this mishmash, which includes stuff on the San Francisco 49ers and on Bakersfield, California:

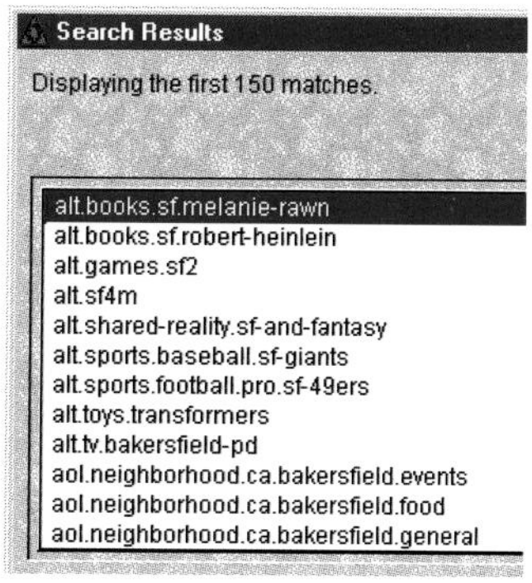

habits & strategies

AOL has deliberately omitted sexually explicit and other controversial newsgroups from the database that's connected to Add Newsgroups and Search All Newsgroups. But with Expert Add, you can add any group that's out there.

The names of newsgroups can be cryptic, but AOL can help: click the Internet Names button in the Read My Newsgroups window for descriptions in plain English. (Note: Not all groups have descriptions.)

The Expert Approach

If you know the name of the newsgroup you want to subscribe to, you can use the Expert Add feature:

1. Click Expert Add in the Newsgroups window.
2. Enter the name of the newsgroup. Be absolutely precise, because one misplaced period or misspelled word will prevent the Expert Add feature from locating the newsgroup and adding it to your list. (It may be expert, but it's not very smart.)
3. Click Add.

YOUR NEWSGROUP LIST

Once you've subscribed to a newsgroup, you can read messages that other people have written and you can post your own. (By the way, newsgroup messages are also called *articles* and *posts*.) Clicking Read My Newsgroups in the Newsgroups window displays a list of your groups, like the one shown here:

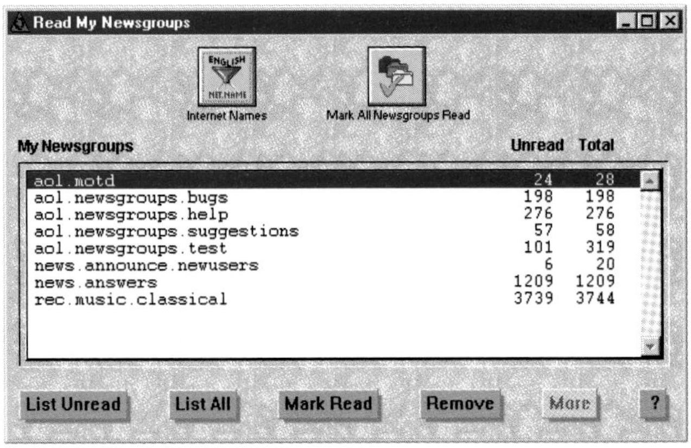

You'll notice that the list includes several newsgroups that you didn't subscribe to. AOL took the liberty of adding them for you. They include groups that pertain to AOL itself, along with groups that deal with Usenet issues.

If You Don't Like It, Dump It

It's even easier to unsubscribe to a newsgroup than it is to subscribe to one. Any time you get tired of a group, highlight it in your newsgroup list and click on Remove. You can subscribe and unsubscribe to newsgroups as often as you like.

Messages often prompt responses from other users. AOL combines these responses with the original message. This is called threading, *and it's a good way to keep track of a discussion in which messages may be posted hours or days apart.*

PERUSING A NEWSGROUP

Messages in newsgroups are listed by subject. To display a list of subjects in a newsgroup, click List Unread or List All in the Read My Newsgroups window, and you'll see a window like the one below. (Choosing List Unread will show you only the items that you haven't already looked at.)

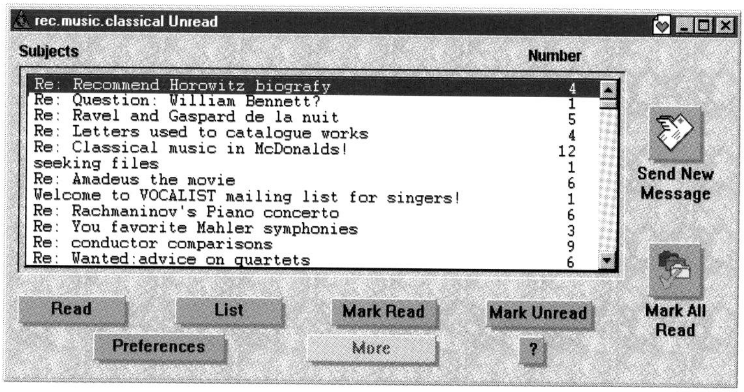

SHORTCUT

Use the cursor keys on your keyboard to move quickly through long lists of subjects. The PAGE UP *and* PAGE DOWN *keys move you a screenful of items at a time, and* HOME *and* END *take you directly to the first and final entries, respectively.*

Reading a Message

Select the subject you want to explore and click Read. If the subject contains more than one message, you'll see the message that began the thread. (Use the Next button to move through the messages in the subject and then on to the next subject.) A newsgroup message looks a lot like an e-mail message. It shows you who wrote it and when it was sent. It also might include text quoted from another message to which the author is responding. Here's a typical newsgroup message—in this case, one from AOL itself:

habits & strategies

Once you mark an entire newsgroup as read, you can't undo the procedure. But it is possible to reverse the damage. Simply remove the newsgroup from your list and then resubscribe to it. All the items in the group will reappear, just like that!

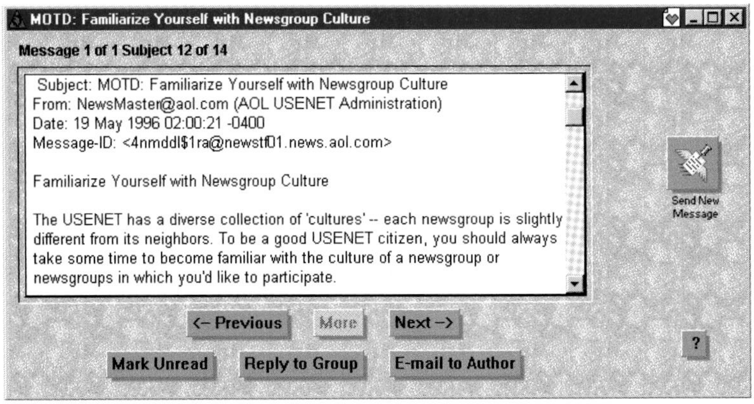

Marking Stuff as Already Read

Suppose you don't want to sift through dozens, hundreds, or even thousands of messages in a newsgroup, you just want to read messages that have been posted since you last checked out the group. No problem. Highlight the newsgroup in the Read My Newsgroups window and click Mark Read. All of the messages currently in the group will be given the bum's rush so that the next time you go to read your newsgroup they won't be there. You can even mark all your newsgroups as read (with the Mark All Newsgroups Read button), which will let you start fresh with all your newsgroups the next time you sign on.

OKAY, NOW IT'S YOUR TURN

Once you get comfortable reading newsgroup messages, you probably will want to join the millions of users who post messages every day. You can use newsgroups to request information or opinions from other users, or you can put in your own two cents' worth in response to other messages.

But First, a Few Words About Netiquette

Despite the decentralized nature of the Internet, certain standards have arisen that govern what people should and should not put into newsgroup messages. This loose, self-imposed code of behavior is

CAUTION

Another reason you should watch what you say is that your e-mail address is right at the top of every message you post, so anybody knows where to find you—at least in cyberspace.

referred to as *netiquette*. Basically, if you respect the following guidelines, you'll be a model newsgroup citizen:

- Don't try to sell anything. Newsgroups are supposed to be commercial-free zones.
- Don't use foul language. As a rule of thumb, don't write anything you wouldn't say in person to a group of people.
- Don't flame anyone. *Flaming* is the public, and often profane, criticism of another individual on the Internet.
- Don't propagate chain letters.
- Avoid spamming. Spam in this case is not a lunch meat. *Spamming* means posting a lot of messages to a newsgroup on an irrelevant topic.
- It's possible to send messages to many newsgroups simultaneously. Don't cross-post messages to large numbers of newsgroups for which the messages aren't appropriate.

Posting a Message

Newsgroup messages take two forms: original messages with new subjects and responses (also called *follow-ups*) to messages already posted. To send a new message, click Send New Message, which is available when you're viewing a newsgroup or an individual message. The Post New Message window looks like this:

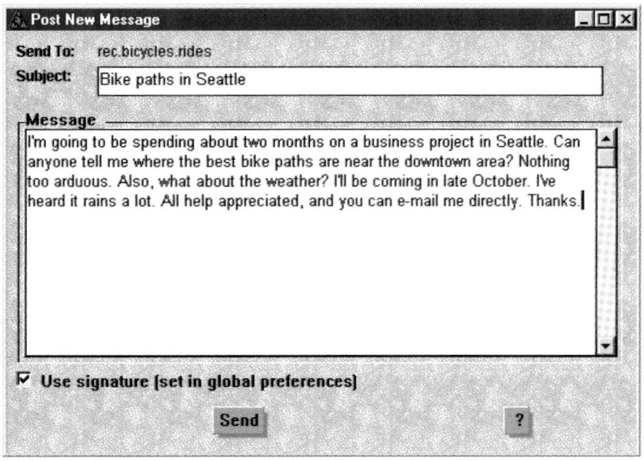

habits & strategies

If you want to send out some test messages, don't post them to bona fide newsgroups. AOL has a newsgroup called **aol.newsgroups**.test *specifically for that purpose. It's one of those groups that AOL automatically adds to your list.*

You see that I've already filled out this form, entering a subject and the text of the message. I've also set my newsgroup preferences to add a personalized signature. (See the section "Preferences" later in this chapter.) Now the only thing left to do is click Send.

Sending a Response

To post a follow-up message on a particular subject, click Reply to Group in the window that displays the message to which you're responding. The window that appears next will be nearly identical to the one for sending new messages, the difference being that the subject box will already be filled in. The subject will be preceded by Re:, which lets people know that the message is a response. If you'd rather not share your reply with the world, you can e-mail the author of a message directly instead of sending a reply to the newsgroup. Just click E-mail to Author rather than Reply to Group.

Quoting from a Previous Message

When you send a response, it's a good idea to quote some of the message you're responding to. That way, anyone reading your message will understand what you're talking about. To include text from a previous message in your response:

1. Highlight the text you want to include.
2. Copy it by choosing Copy from the Edit menu or by pressing CTRL-C.
3. Insert it at the top of your reply by choosing Paste from the Edit menu or by pressing CTRL-V.
4. Indicate that the text is from a previous message, and give the identity of the author.

Wait a Minute, Cancel That!

Let's say you've fired off a newsgroup message and then immediately regret it. Believe it or not, it's possible to cancel the message. To do so, you'll need the Message ID number, which appears beneath the date at the top of the message. If you don't have that number, use the screen name you used to post the message, the date it was posted, and the name of the newsgroup to which it was sent. E-mail the information to the AOL screen name *Newsmaster.* AOL can cancel messages up to four days after they were posted.

READING NEWSGROUP MESSAGES OFFLINE

The same FlashSessions that you use to automatically retrieve e-mail (see Chapter 4) can also be used to fetch new newsgroup items so that you can read them when you're not connected to AOL. To use this feature, follow these steps:

1. Click Read Offline in the main Newsgroups window. You will see the following dialog box:

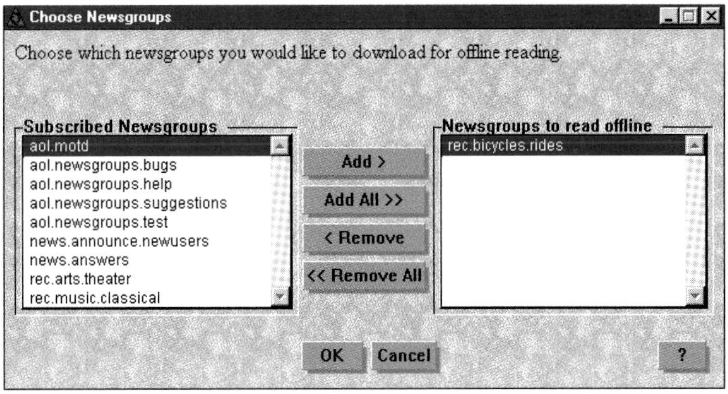

2. Select each newsgroup you want to read offline and click Add to place it in the box at the right. Click Add All if you want to include all your groups. When you've finished, click OK.
3. Choose Set Up FlashSession from the Mail menu.
4. Select the box labeled "Retrieve unread newsgroup messages."
5. Close the FlashSessions dialog box.

The next time a FlashSession is activated, all unread messages in the groups you've chosen will be placed into your Personal Filing Cabinet. To read them, click the Personal Filing Cabinet button on the toolbar and then double-click each message listed in the Newsgroups folder. (You can also compose replies to messages offline and send them via FlashSessions.)

CAUTION

During a FlashSession, ALL unread messages in the selected groups will be downloaded to your PC. Before the first FlashSession, mark those groups as having been read. If you don't, you may end up with thousands of messages on your hard disk.

PREFERENCES

A few newsgroup features can be customized. Choose Set Preferences from the main Newsgroups window to display the following dialog box, which contains your options:

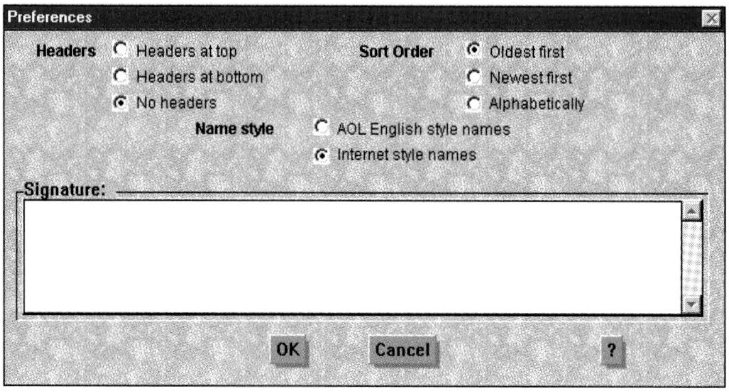

- **Headers** If you want to see headers—the routing information that shows how a message traversed its way over the Internet—you can have them appear at the top or bottom of the message. But headers are essentially worthless. Do yourself a favor and stick with the default choice, which is to hide them.
- **Sort Order** You can change the order in which messages are displayed in your newsgroups' windows. Normally, the most recent messages are at the bottom of the list. If you'd rather have them at the top, choose "Newest first."
- **Name Style** If you'd like to have newsgroup names displayed in plain English rather than in their rec-comp-alt form, choose "AOL English style names" instead of "Internet style names." For example, if you choose this option, the newsgroup **rec.music.classical** will be renamed to *Discussion about classical music.* The only downside to this is that there are many newsgroups for which AOL doesn't provide common names. It's a hit-or-miss affair.

SHORTCUT

You can save newsgroups to your Favorite Places folder, thereby giving yourself ready access to them. Just drag the heart from the title bar of the newsgroup window to the Favorite Places folder on the AOL toolbar.

Signing with a Flourish

The space at the bottom of the Preferences box is for a "signature" that you can automatically append to any newsgroup message you send. It's not your real signature—AOL isn't equipped to duplicate your handwriting. But it is a time-saving way for you to include information about yourself—your name, your nickname, or your company's or organization's name. But remember, newsgroup messages can be read by millions of people, so be frugal with sensitive personal information.

Limiting the Number of Messages

By default, AOL displays unread newsgroup messages for two weeks after they've been posted. If you discover that there are too many messages piling up, you can shorten this time limit for any newsgroup. This option is selected in a different Preferences dialog box. To invoke it, click Preferences in the window that displays the newsgroup you want to limit. At the bottom of the dialog box there's a section, shown below, for setting the number of days after which newsgroup items will be bounced.

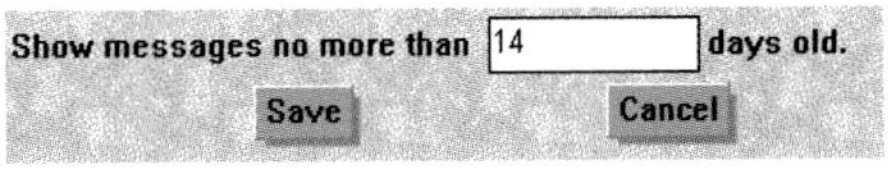

PARENTAL CONTROLS

Because newsgroups reside on the Internet, they aren't subject to AOL's rules about language and behavior. So if you let your kids read any newsgroup they want, they're apt to run into subject matter that would make the devil himself blush. For example, it's possible to download sexually explicit photos from some newsgroups. The proliferation of controversial newsgroups has raised hackles in Congress, but so far the government hasn't figured out a way to clamp down on them without also clamping down on the First Amendment.

AOL, however, lets you block access to newsgroups that you think are too risqué for the younger set. You do so by using the Parental

Controls option, which just happens to be available right in the main Newsgroups window. Click Parental Controls, select the screen name of the child to whom the restrictions will apply, and then click Edit. This will display the following dialog box:

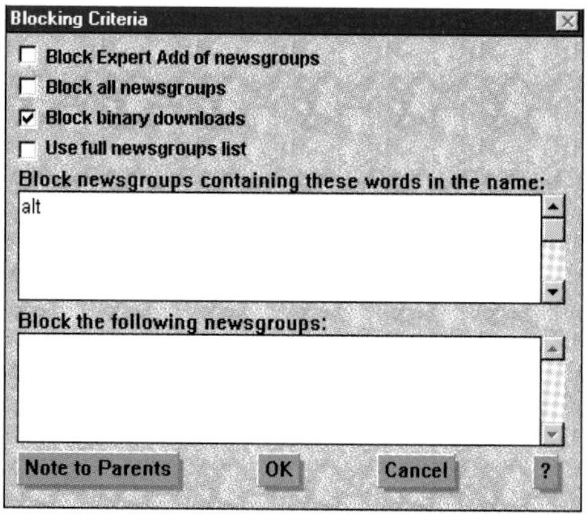

As you can see, the options are impressive. You can block only those groups with specific words in their titles, or you can shut off the entire Usenet. You can even prevent your child from using Expert Add—an option that any smart ten-year-old would use in a New York minute. And the best part is that Parental Controls are impossible to disable unless your kid knows your password and can sign on as you. (Only the person with the primary screen name can set Parental Controls.)

habits & strategies

Unless you block all newsgroups, it's impossible to guarantee a safe experience on the Internet. But you can eliminate more than 90 percent of the trouble spots by typing the letters alt in the top space of the Parental Controls dialog box.

OTHER INTERNET STUFF ON AOL

In addition to the World Wide Web and newsgroups, AOL's Internet Connection gives you access to two other Internet features: FTP and Gopher. Neither one of these is of much use to busy people, so for all practical purposes you can ignore them. However, for the record, this is what they do:

- *FTP*, which stands for *file transfer protocol*, is a technology that allows you to download files to your computer from vast libraries of files maintained by big institutions,

As of this writing, the AOL button for Gopher was labeled Gopher & WAIS. But WAIS (Wide Area Information Server), which searched the Internet with keywords, is gone, and I wouldn't be surprised to see FTP and Gopher disappear as well.

especially universities. But using FTP to find files can be treacherous—and besides, most major FTP sites are now linked to the World Wide Web, which is a whole lot easier to use.

- *Gopher* is a system that uses menus to help you find stuff on the Internet. It was developed at the University of Minnesota and named after the school's mascot. But, like FTP, it's a leftover from the days before the emergence of the Web.

WHAT'S NEXT?

The rest of this book is devoted to helping you get the most out of AOL. In the next chapter, I'll start by showing you how to use Message Boards—the AOL equivalent to Internet newsgroups—and Chat Rooms, where you can hold live electronic conversations with other members on just about any topic that strikes your fancy.

Part 3

MAKING THE MOST OF YOUR TIME ONLINE

CHAPTER 6

Message Boards and Chat Rooms—That's the Community Spirit

INCLUDES

- Finding and using forums
- Using message boards
- Making the People Connection
- Finding your way around chat rooms
- Sending Instant Messages
- Attending big-time events on AOL Live

FAST FORWARD

POST A MESSAGE TO A MESSAGE BOARD ➤ *pp. 123–124*

Many areas of AOL have Message Boards that let you share thoughts and opinions on specific topics with other members. To post a message for others to read, use these steps:

1. In the window for the Message Board, click List Messages.
2. Click Post Another Message.
3. Type in a subject line for your message, making it catchy but to the point.
4. Type your message in the space provided. You can write as much as you want, but be aware that concise, short messages are most likely to draw responses.
5. Click Post to send the message to the board.

FIND A CHAT ROOM TO VISIT ➤ *pp. 125–129*

Most forums on AOL have chat rooms. If you're not sure where a room is, check out the forum for the subject in which you're interested. Or use the following procedure:

1. Click the People Connection button on the toolbar to enter a chat lobby.
2. Click List Rooms to display the Public Rooms window. To see a list of rooms created by members, click Member Rooms in this window.
3. To go to a room on a list, select it and click Go.

SAFEGUARD YOUR CHILDREN ➤ *pp. 129–130*

Some chat rooms deal with sensitive topics, and their language can get bawdy. To prevent youngsters from seeing what they shouldn't:

1. Either choose Parental Control from the Members menu or click the Help button in any chat room window and then click Parental Controls.
2. Choose Custom Controls. If your child doesn't have a screen name, you must create one at this point. You can't impose restrictions without it.
3. Click Chat and then Chat Controls.
4. Check the options you want and then click OK.

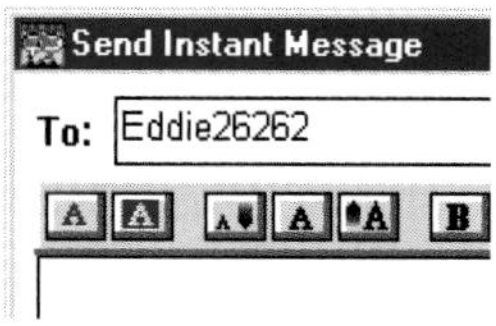

HAVE A PRIVATE CHAT ➤ *pp. 130–131*

➤ *pp. 130–131*

You can have a private conversation with another member in a chat room. Just follow these steps:

1. Double-click the person's name in the list at the right that shows who's in the room.
2. In the dialog box that appears, click Message.
3. Enter your message and click Send. If the other person is up for it, you can have a running private conversation.

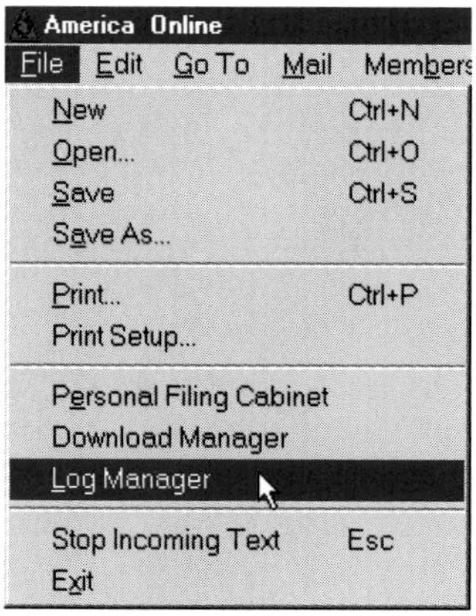

LOG A CHAT SESSION ➤ *pp. 134–136*

To record a major AOL online event or even a small chat room session for posterity, do the following:

1. Choose Log Manager from the File menu.
2. In the Chat Log section of the Log Manager, click Open Log.
3. Enter the name and location of the file in which the transcript will be saved.
4. Click OK. From that point on, all text that appears in a chat window will be saved. You can stop logging any time by going back to the Log Manager and clicking Close Log.

America Online is often called a virtual community, and with good reason. Each day, thousands of its members exchange ideas, questions, answers, and opinions among themselves online. In fact, AOL may be the most vibrant community on the planet. It sure beats the town I live in, where the city council meets once a month and very few people even care. Anyway, this chapter is about the tools that let you get in on the action—AOL's message boards and chat rooms. If there's a hot topic—or even one that's not so hot—there's probably a message group or chat room devoted to it.

FORUMS

Message boards and chat rooms can usually be found in forums, which are areas that bring together resources on specific topics. There's no central listing for forums—and sometimes areas that have all the characteristics of forums aren't even called forums. (Don't ask.)

How Do You Find a Forum?

So where are these forums? Well, they're sprinkled throughout AOL, so you'll probably stumble upon many of them during your online explorations. You'll know you've found a forum when you come across a screen that has buttons for messages and chatting, as in the example shown on the next page.

To view a list of forums, click the Find button on the toolbar, enter the word **forum** into the search box and click Search. You can get a description of any forum on the list by double-clicking it, and then you can access the forum by clicking Go There.

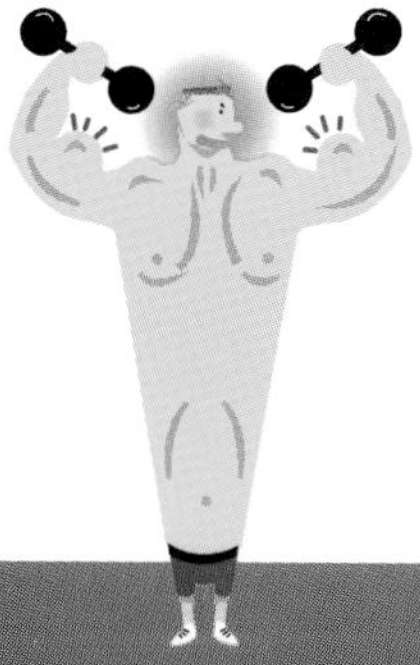

definitions

Posting: *An item sent to a message board.*

Message: *An item sent to a message board.*

Confusion: *The result of having to deal with more than one word that means the same thing.*

MESSAGE BOARDS

AOL's message boards are similar to Internet newsgroups. The difference is that participation in them is limited to AOL members. There are many more Internet newsgroups than message boards, but AOL message boards offer advantages that newsgroups do not: each of AOL's boards is associated with other resources on the same topic, including chat rooms, news and information, and even free and inexpensive software. (We'll get to that in Chapter 7.)

Bringing Order to Chaos

Many AOL message boards contain thousands of postings on dozens of topics. To keep things organized, message boards place messages into topic folders. If there is an unusually large number of topics in a particular message board, the topics in turn can be placed into category folders. But most message boards don't merit categories.

At the top of each message board window is a brief description of what you'll find inside. These descriptions can help you decide whether the board has what you're after.

Navigating Through a Message Board

To use a message board, you'll have to work your way through at least a couple of screens—including a list of topics, as shown here:

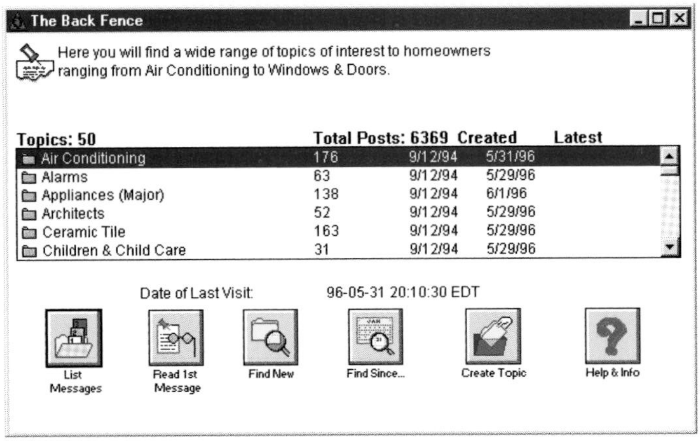

The central space of this window lists the topic folders that contain messages. To the right you'll see the number of messages in each folder, along with the date the folder was created and the most recent date that something was added to it. Below the central list you'll see the date you last visited the board. Along the bottom is a row of buttons. Here's what the most important ones do:

- **List Messages** takes you to the next level down in the message board. Select a topic and then click the List Messages button to display a box like the one shown in Figure 6.1.
- **Find New** displays topics and messages that have been posted since you last visited the board. (This is similar to the option for viewing only unread messages in an Internet newsgroup.) The date of your most recent visit is shown just above the buttons.
- **Find Since** lets you view stuff that's been posted within a certain number of days. You set the number of days in the dialog box that appears when you click the button.
- **Create Topic** lets you make a new folder if none of the topics applies to what you've got to say.

If a message board has more messages than you can view by scrolling the window, use the More Messages button to access the additional items.

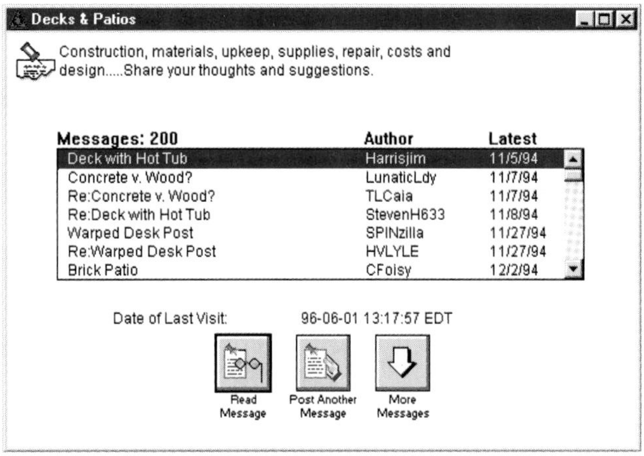

Figure 6.1 A message board topic window showing a list of messages

Posting a Message of Your Own

As you can see in Figure 6.1, there are 200 messages in the topic on decks and patios. If you came to the board seeking information, answers, or opinions—which many busy people do—first scroll through the messages already there to see if perchance your issue has been addressed. If it hasn't, it's time to brush off your writing skills. Start by clicking the Post Another Message button, which brings up the following window:

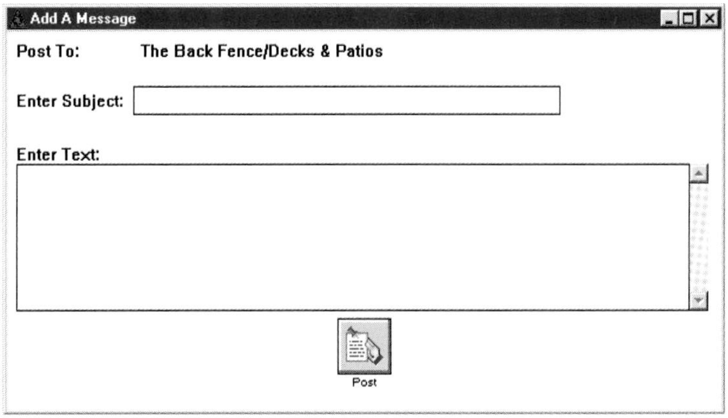

This is just about the simplest form one could imagine. Come up with a subject line that gets straight to the point, enter a brief message, and click Post. Your message will appear on the board shortly.

Message Board Posting Guidelines

Rules for message boards are roughly the same as those for Internet newsgroups:

- No chain letters
- No pyramid schemes
- No commercial offers
- No harassment or foul language

Reading and Responding

To read a message, select it and click the Read Message button shown in Figure 6.1. Here's a typical posting—simple, concise, and sure to draw responses:

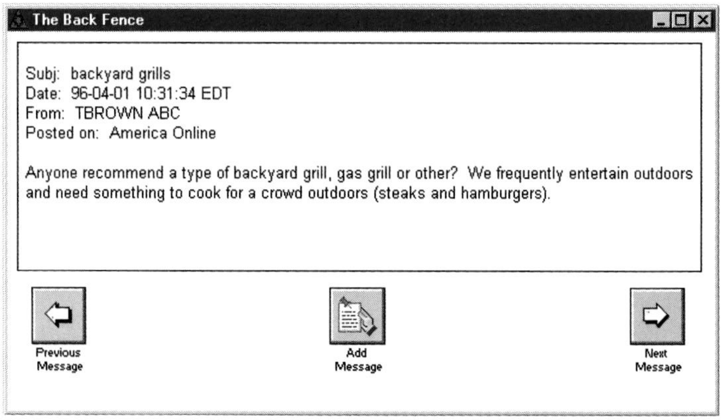

To respond to the message, click the Add Message button. This will bring up a form that is almost identical to the one for adding a new message. The one difference is that the Subject box will automatically be filled in with "Re:" followed by the subject of the message to which you're responding. If you were answering the plea shown above, for example, your Subject box would read "Re: backyard grills."

habits & strategies

Individual message boards don't have keywords, and you can't add them to your Favorite Places folder. If you find a board you really like, add the forum that contains it to your Favorite Places folder.

Keeping Track of Responses

If there is a drawback to AOL's message boards, it is that most of them do not support threading. Threading is a system that places responses to a message together with the original message so that you can follow the dialogue on a particular subject. Without threading, each response is posted to the board as a regular message. If there are many responses to a message, it can be really hard to keep track of them. Internet newsgroups routinely use threading, and some AOL message boards do also. Here's a threaded board in the forum for bird watchers:

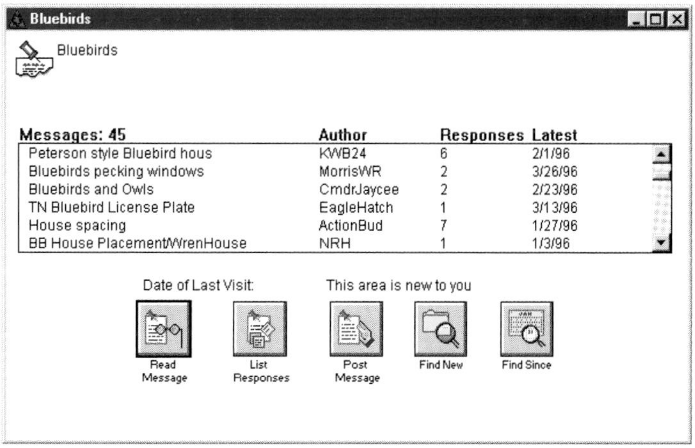

Notice that there's a column listing the number of responses to each message. When you open a threaded message, you'll find buttons at the bottom of the window that let you read the responses. This is definitely a superior way of doing things, and it is hoped that more message boards will adopt threading.

THE PEOPLE CONNECTION —AOL'S CHAT ROOMS

The best way to introduce yourself to AOL's chat rooms is to click People Connection in the main Channels window or the People Connection button on the toolbar. Either one will transport you like greased lightning into a "lobby" in which you will find yourself milling about aimlessly with other members. Like other regular chat rooms, a lobby can hold only 23 members, so when one fills up, another one is automatically created. There can be dozens of lobbies open at any given time, so don't be surprised to find yourself in Lobby 23 one time and Lobby 49 the next. Here I've landed in Lobby 56:

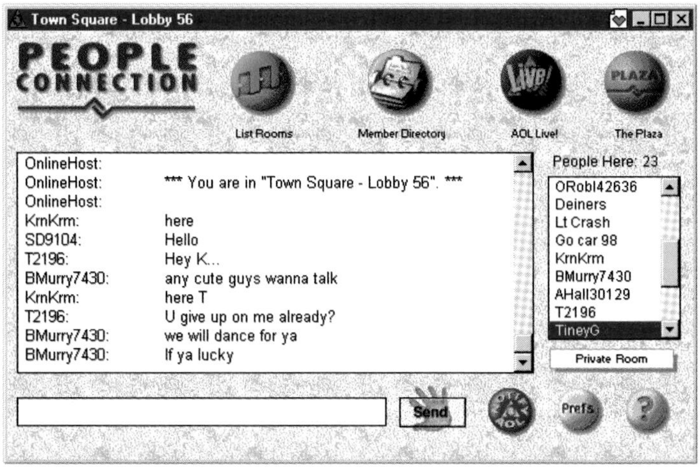

As you can see, lobbies are a little unfocused. As a matter of fact, it's not really clear to me why they even exist. If you're smart, you'll find a room on a topic that interests you by going to the AOL forum devoted to the subject. For instance, suppose you're a Civil War buff. Use the keyword *Civil War* to go to the Civil War forum, in which you'll find the Mason-Dixon Line chat room, which on some evenings resembles an electronic version of the Battle of Gettysburg.

Different Kinds of Rooms

Anyway, once you're in a lobby, the first thing you're probably going to want to do is get out. See that List Rooms button at the top? Click it to display the following view:

SHORTCUT

At the bottom of the Public Rooms window is a button labeled Find by Name. *You can use it to quickly locate a room instead of scrolling through lists of rooms. Just click the button, type in the name of the room, and click Find.*

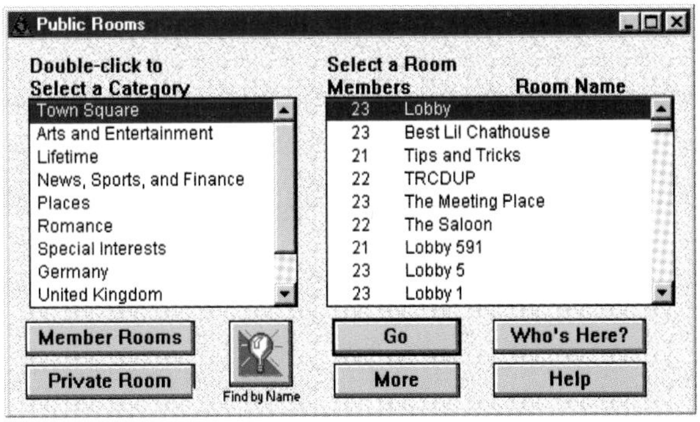

The list on the left shows the categories of *public rooms*—that is, rooms that are available to anyone who wants to come in. The list on the right shows the rooms in the selected category, along with the number of members in each room. By default, you start out in the Town Square category, which includes the lobbies. You can go to any public room that isn't full by double-clicking on it or selecting it and clicking on Go. If the room is full, you'll be given the option of going to another room on the same subject.

Member Rooms and Private Rooms

In the bottom-left corner of the Public Rooms window are buttons labeled Member Rooms and Private Room. Here's a description of these types of rooms:

Member Rooms These rooms are named by members. Like public rooms, they are open to anyone, but the subjects they cover are usually more specific and can get quite bawdy. Clicking on Member Rooms displays a list of these rooms (which you can enter by selecting one and clicking on Go). You can even create a member room of your own.

Private Rooms These also are created by members. They are considered private because their names don't appear on any list. Private rooms can be great for conducting long-distance conferences without relying on telephones. Just create the private room, give the name of the room to everyone involved in the conference, and then have them all enter the room at the same time. To go to the room, click Private Room, enter the room's name, and click Go.

Taking Roll in a Chat Room

If you're thinking about entering a public room or a member room, you can first take a look at who all is there. In the window listing the rooms, select the room you want to check out and click on the Who's Here? button. You will see a list of participants, as in the example below, which shows a list of members in the Chat About the Web room:

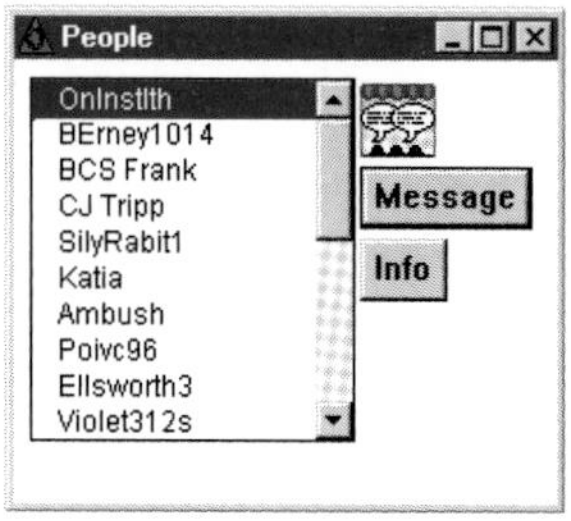

By selecting a name and clicking on Info, you can see that person's Member Profile—assuming that he or she has created one. In addition, you can send the person an Instant Message. I'll get to that in a minute.

Chat Room Basics

All AOL chat room windows are identical and look just like the Lobby window with which I began this section. As people in the room contribute comments, their remarks appear on the screen, which scrolls automatically when it gets full. If you want to put in your own two cents, type your remarks in the space at the bottom of the window and then click Send. Your comments will appear just like everyone else's. Comments appear onscreen in no particular order, so if there are a lot of people in the room, the conversation could look quite disjointed. That's the way it is. Get used to it.

Online Shorthand

Experienced chatters often use a computer-age version of shorthand to convey thoughts and emotions with a minimum amount of typing. You may not ever want to do this yourself—it is pretty nerdy—but it can save you time, and to a busy person that's always appealing. Here's a list of some of the most common examples of online shorthand:

Want to see something cute? Turn this page 90 degrees clockwise and look at the shorthand symbols. Many of them actually look like what they represent. The smile symbol, for instance, looks like a person smiling.

:) = smile
:D = smile/laugh/big grin
:* = kiss
;) = wink
:X = "my lips are sealed"
:P = sticking out tongue
{} = hug
:(= frown
:'(= crying
O:) = angel
}:> = devil
LOL = Laughing Out Loud
ROTF = Rolling On The Floor (laughing)
AFK = Away From Keyboard
BAK = Back At Keyboard
BRB = Be Right Back
TTFN = Ta-Ta For Now!
WB = Welcome Back
GMTA = Great Minds Think Alike
BTW = By The Way
IMHO = In My Humble Opinion
WTG = Way To Go!

Safeguarding the Kids

Chat rooms can be like the Wild West. A lot of raucous and sometimes foul language gets tossed around, despite AOL's strict guidelines. If you have a young child who goes online without supervision, you might consider letting AOL act as a nanny by blocking access to some kinds of chat rooms. Here's how:

1. Either choose Parental Control from Members menu or click the Help button in any chat room and then click Parental Controls.
2. Choose Custom Controls. If your child doesn't have his or her own screen name, click Create a Screen Name. (Controls must be applied to individual screen names.)
3. Click Chat and then Chat Controls.

SHORTCUT

If you can't find someone, choose Locate a Member from the Members menu, enter the person's screen name, and click OK. If your friend is online and in a chat room, this will track 'em down. Then you can send an Instant Message and touch base.

4. Select the options you want in the screen shown here. When you are done, click OK.

Screen Name	Block Instant Messages	--- People Connection --- Block All Rooms	Block Member Rooms	Block Conference Rooms
Deiners	☐	☐	☐	☐
Aaron39587	☐	☐	☑	☐
Dan66666	☐	☑	☐	☐

Chatting One-on-One

In addition to chatting in public, as it were, you can have private conversations with other members in a chat room by using AOL's Instant Message feature. To do so, use the following steps:

1. In the list of participants on the right side of a chat window, double-click the name of the person for whom your message is intended.
2. In the dialog box that appears, click Message to display the Send Instant Message window.
3. The screen name of the recipient is automatically entered, so just type your message in the space provided for it, as shown in the example here. Then click Send.

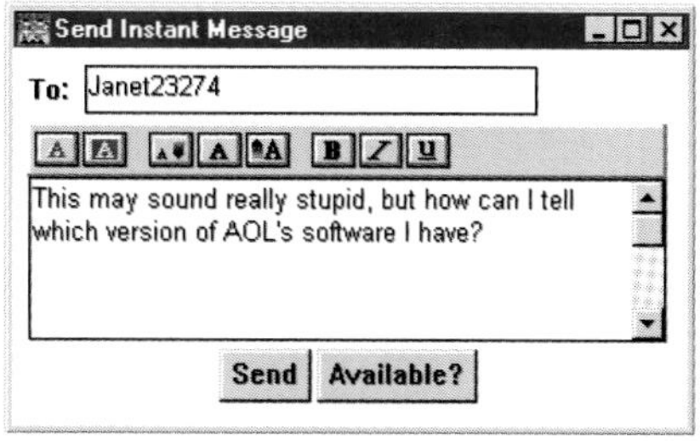

You don't have to be in a chat room to send an Instant Message, as long as both you and the recipient are online. Just choose Send an Instant Message from the Members menu. To make sure your recipient is online, click the Available? button.

The message will appear instantaneously (that's why they call them Instant Messages) on the screen of the person at the other end. If that person replies to your message, the response will appear on your screen. As you continue to exchange messages, the text of the online conversation is recorded at the top of the screen, and you write new messages below it, like this:

Instant messages are a good way to talk to someone far away without paying long-distance charges. Just exchange e-mail and agree on a time when you'll both be online, then conduct your phone-like conversation via Instant Messages.

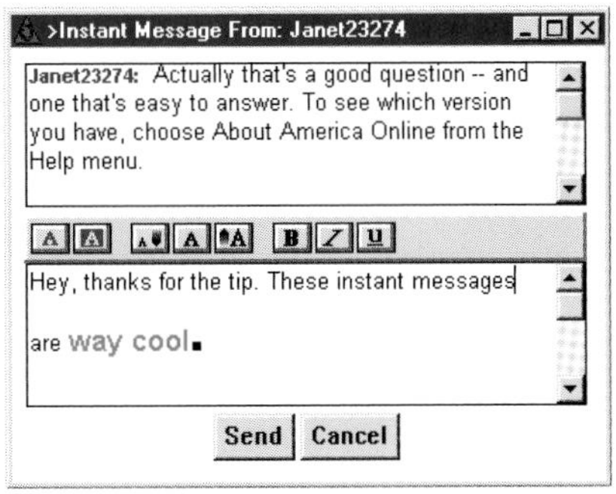

Notice that you can alter the appearance of text in Instant Messages. Just highlight the words you want to change, and use the formatting buttons above the writing area. It's the same procedure you use to dress up e-mail (see Chapter 4). Oh, yeah, you can also drag and drop favorite places into Instant Messages, the same way you do with e-mail.

Getting Rid of a Distracting Chatter

Occasionally you'll encounter someone in a chat room who insists on ruining the experience for everyone else, whether with four-letter words, insults, or perhaps distracting sounds. No problem. Just double-click on the person's name in the list of chat room participants and then check the Ignore box. That person's comments will no longer show up on your screen. Boy, don't you wish you could do that during some corporate meetings?

Setting Chat Preferences

There isn't a whole lot you can do to customize your chat room experience. To see your options, click on the Prefs button in any chat window. You'll see the following dialog box:

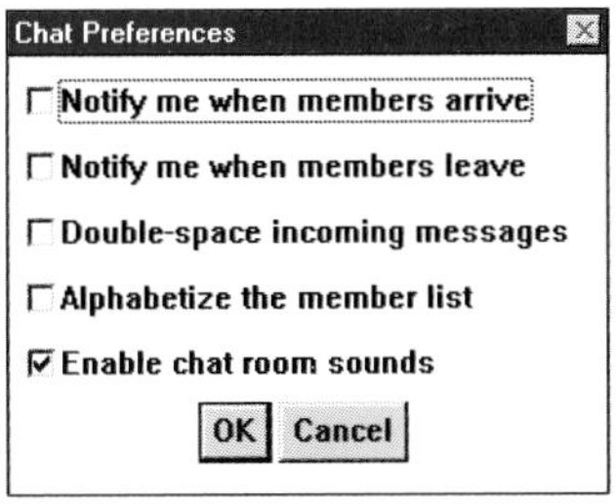

The only option checked by default is the one that lets you hear sounds that are sent by other members in a chat room. (To hear the sounds, you must have a PC with a sound card. Some PCs also require speakers.) You, too, can send sounds if you want to. They have to be in .wav files stored in the AOL folder on your computer. The sounds you send will be heard only by other members who have sound-capable computers and who have the same files. (The actual sounds aren't transmitted, just commands to play the sounds.) AOL comes with a bunch of .wav files that play sounds you hear all the time, such as "Welcome." All that having been said, this is a silly thing to even bring up in a book for busy people. Forgive me. The point is, you can turn off chat sounds if you want to.

habits & strategies

If you don't want to see your buddy lists when you sign on, or be notified when buddies sign on and off, click Preferences in the Buddy Lists dialog box and disable those options.

Keeping Track of Your Friends

There are probably times when one or more of your friends are online at the same time you are. Why not set it up so that AOL automatically notifies you with a beep each time one of your buddies signs on? That way you can exchange Instant Messages and maybe get together in a chat room. All you have to do to set this up is create a Buddy List, which you can do with the following steps:

1. Choose Buddy Lists from the Members menu to open the dialog box shown here:

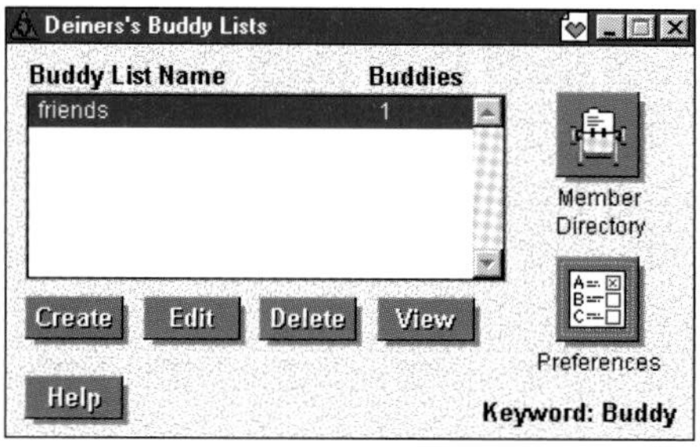

2. Click Create and follow the instructions, entering a name for your list and adding your buddies' screen names to it.
3. When you're done, click Save.

You can have up to ten Buddy Lists per screen name, and each list can have as many entries as you want—with a maximum total of 50 names for all your lists. But that should be enough. I don't know anyone with 50 close buddies.

Once you've created a Buddy List, a beep will alert you whenever one of your buddies signs on or off during your AOL session (assuming you have a multimedia PC capable of sound). Also, your buddy list (or lists) will be displayed every time you sign on, so you can see who's already online. And any time you want to see your buddy list, just choose Buddy Lists from the Members menu, select the list you want (if there's more than one), and click View.

AOL LIVE

Virtual events offer advantages over the real-life kind. You don't have to drive to get there, you don't have to pay to park, they're never sold out, and you can see perfectly from anywhere. Also, you never have to hunt for a restroom.

Regular chat rooms are great for small gatherings, but they're woefully inadequate for staging large events, such as question-and-answer sessions with movie stars, professional athletes, famous business people, and national politicians. For that, the place to turn to is AOL Live, which features auditoriums capable of holding thousands of people. Click AOL LIVE at the bottom of the Channels window to go to the AOL Live window, shown here, in which you will find schedules of events and from which you can enter auditoriums:

Taking in a Live Event

Auditoriums differ from regular chat rooms in several ways. In the first place, you're in a virtual row with as many as 16 other members. And there's a virtual stage for the featured speaker or speakers along with a master of ceremonies.

You can participate in a live event in two ways:

- Send comments to other people in your row. Just type your remark in the space at the bottom and click Send, as you would in any chat room.
- Submit questions or comments for the speaker. To do this, click the Interact button at the top of the window.

By the way, the only text that will appear on your screen in an auditorium will be the dialogue coming from the stage and the comments from people in your row. (The latter will be preceded by the row number in parentheses.)

If You Don't Like Your Seat, Move

To find out who else is in your row, click the People button. Or click the Chat Rows Button to open the Chat Rows dialog box, which lets you see who's in any row. Just select the row you want and click List People. If you don't like the company you're in, you can move to a different row (as long as it's not full) or even create a new row for yourself and any friends who are also in the auditorium. And if you don't want to see comments from other row-mates, there's a button in the Chat Rows dialog box labeled Turn Off Chat that will silence the online chatter so you can concentrate on what's happening on stage.

RECORDING LIVE EVENTS AND CHATS FOR LATER VIEWING

Chat sessions can progress quickly, with text scrolling on your screen at a rate that can make the online conversation hard to follow. If you're really looking forward to a big event on AOL Live, why not tape the whole thing so you can view it again at your leisure after you've signed off? It's easy to do. Just use AOL's logging feature, which lets you capture incoming text to a file on your hard disk. Click Log Manager in the File menu to bring up the Logging dialog box, shown on the next page.

CAUTION

The Chat Log works only for chats and won't record other kinds of text. Similarly, the Session Log won't record a chat session. Make sure you pick the right option for what you want to do.

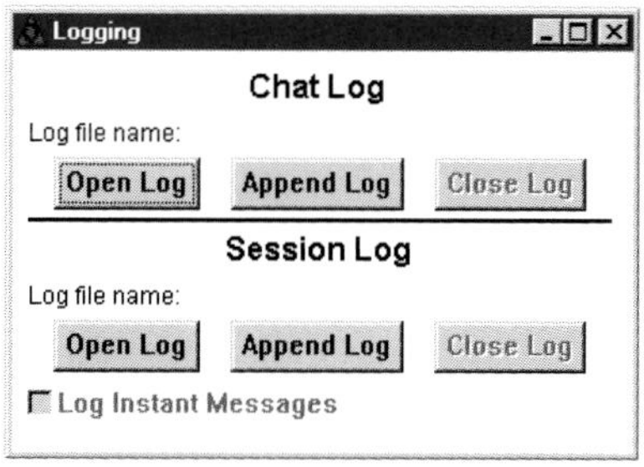

As you can see, there are two options: Chat Log and Session Log. The Chat Log is for recording chat transcripts and can be used in conjunction with any chat room or auditorium. The Session Log is for recording incoming text that you access while online, such as magazine articles and excerpts from reference materials. Both the Chat Log and the Session Log work the same way.

Ready, Set, Log!

You can start logging before you sign on or at any point when you're online. Here's how:

1. Choose Log Manager from the File menu.
2. To record the transcript of a chat, click Open Log in the Chat Log section.
3. In the dialog box that appears, enter the name and location of the file in which the transcript will be saved and click OK.
4. Close the Logging dialog box.

Logging automatically begins as soon as you enter a chat room. Whenever you want to stop logging, go back to the Log Manager and click Close Log. To resume logging to the same file, click Append Log. This lets you pause the logging during periods when the conversation gets too dull or starts to ramble.

The AOL software can handle only files up to 30 kilobytes in size. For anything longer, you'll have to use a word processor.

Viewing a Logged File

Logged chat transcripts are stored in plain text format. You can view the text either with any Windows-based word processor or with AOL itself. To use AOL, choose Open from the File menu. (You don't have to be signed on.) Locate the file in the Open a File dialog box that appears and click OK to view the file.

WHAT'S NEXT?

As a service that you access on a computer, AOL could be expected to have a lot of resources for computer users. And boy, does it. In the next chapter, we'll take a look at the Computers and Software channel and how to get free and inexpensive software right over the telephone line.

MOM

CHAPTER 7

Looking for Software? You've Come to the Right Place

INCLUDES

- Accessing software libraries
- Searching for files
- Downloading software
- Using the Download Manager
- Finding software on the Internet
- Connecting with companies

FAST FORWARD

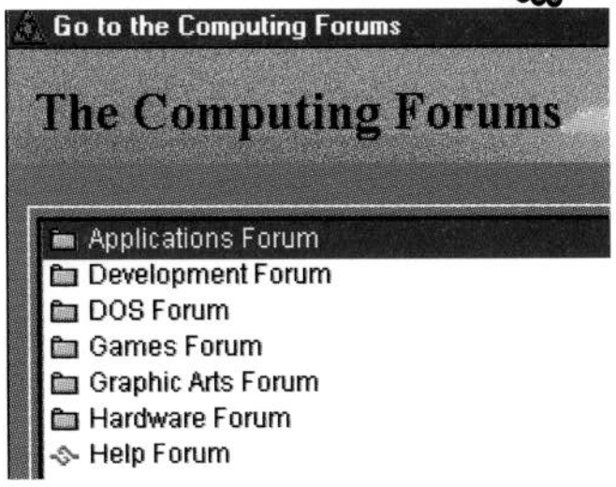

CHECK OUT THE FORUMS ➤ *pp. 143–144*

Almost every forum on AOL includes a link to a library of software files that you can download. For example, check out the finance forums on the Personal Finance channel for software that can help you do your taxes. Or go to the computing forums on the Computers & Software channel for files that can make your PC easier to use.

SEARCH FOR A FILE ➤ *pp. 144–147*

A surefire way to find a file is to use the File Search feature:

1. Click the File Search button on the AOL toolbar.
2. Select the categories you want to search, such as Windows.
3. Type in a word or phrase that describes the file you're seeking.
4. Press ENTER or click on List Matching Files to see a list of files that meet your criteria.

DOWNLOAD A FILE ➤ *pp. 147–149*

When you find a file you want, you can transfer it from AOL's computer system to the hard drive on your PC by following these steps:

1. Click Read Description to see how large the file is and how long it will take to download.
2. Click Download Now to start the process.
3. You will see a dialog box that tells you the name of the file and the folder to which it will be downloaded. (By default it goes to the Download folder in the AOL folder.) You might want to make a note of the filename and location.
4. Click OK to download the file.

VIEW A GRAPHIC ➤ *pp. 149–150*

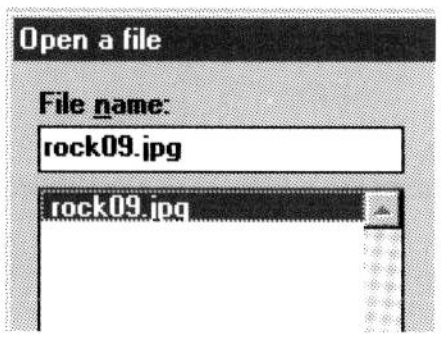

If you have downloaded a graphical image, you can probably use AOL's own software to view it. Here's how:

1. Choose Open from the File menu. (You don't have to be signed on to do this. Just have the AOL software running.)
2. Use the dialog box to locate the file.
3. Click OK to open and view the file.

DOWNLOAD MORE THAN ONE FILE AT A TIME ➤ *pp. 150–153*

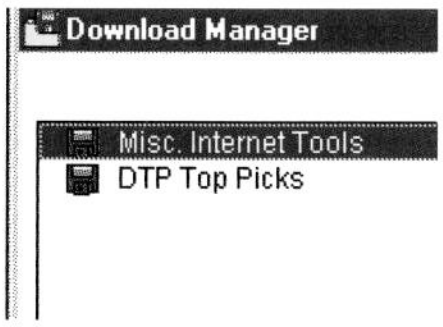

1. During an online session, select files to download, but click Download Later rather than Download Now. This will send the filenames to the Download Manager.
2. Before signing off, choose Download Manager from the File menu.
3. Click Start Download.
4. When the File Transfer dialog box appears, check the box labeled Sign Off After Transfer. When the last file has been transferred, you'll be automatically signed off.

SEARCH THE INTERNET FOR SOFTWARE ➤ *pp. 153–155*

The World Wide Web is a great place to find software. Just follow these steps to get started:

1. Choose The Software Center from the Computers & Software channel.
2. Click the Web button and then double-click the folder labeled Web: Shareware Distribution Sites.
3. Double-click one of the search sites, such as C|Net Shareware at shareware.com, which lets you search through a database containing some 200,000 files.

America Online is a service that is targeted at the personal computer, so it makes sense that it would cater to PC users—and that it does. On the Computers & Software channel, you can find news about personal computer companies, products, and trends. But AOL gives you more than just information. It gives you software. That's right, actual software that you can install on your PC and run, without ever having to go to a store or load up a disk. Stashed in AOL's software libraries are more than 100,000 files, ranging from complete programs and games to graphical images. And that's not all—you also have access to hundreds of thousands of software files that reside on the Internet. Is that cool or what?

WHAT CAN YOU GET, AND WHAT DOES IT COST?

There are three general categories of software that you can download from AOL or the Internet:

- **Shareware** These are programs that you can try out for free. If you like a piece of shareware, you're expected to pay for it. In almost every case, shareware is significantly less expensive than comparable programs in software stores. And just because it's less expensive doesn't mean it's inferior. Some of the best programs you can find are shareware.
- **Freeware** As the name implies, this is stuff that is available at no charge. Freeware generally consists of knickknacks such as clip art and simple file management utilities, but some excellent programs also fall into this gratis category.

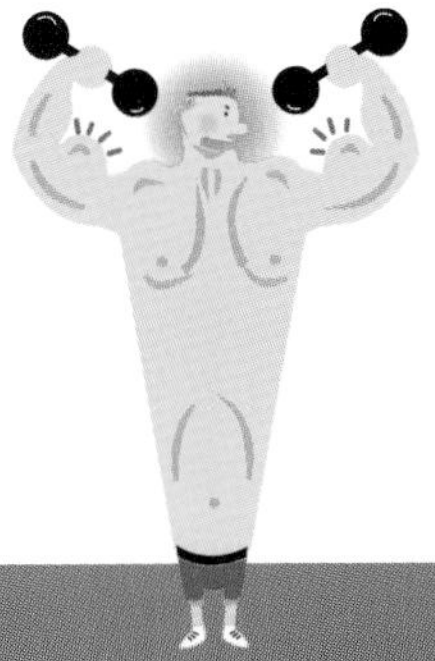

definitions

Download: *To transfer data directly to your computer from another computer. You can download anything, from simple text to complex graphics, using a telephone line and a modem.*

Upload: *To transmit information from your computer to another computer (the opposite of download). You can even upload files to AOL for other members to use, although if you're a busy person, this thought probably will not occur to you.*

- **Demoware** To entice customers, many software companies make "demonstration" versions of their programs available online so that you can try them at no charge and decide whether they're worth buying. Basically, demoware is software from which some key features have been excluded, rendering the program less than fully functional. For instance, you might not be able to save files that you create using the demoware program.

THE SOFTWARE CENTER

AOL organizes its vast storehouse of software into virtual "libraries," each containing files related to a particular topic. There are libraries specifically for clip art, for instance, and others for such things as Windows utilities and desktop publishing tools. Libraries can be found in forums throughout AOL—almost every forum has a Software Libraries button in its main window. But you don't have to go out and find a forum to locate software. Instead, go to the Software Center, shown here. To get there, click The Software Center in the Computers & Software channel window.

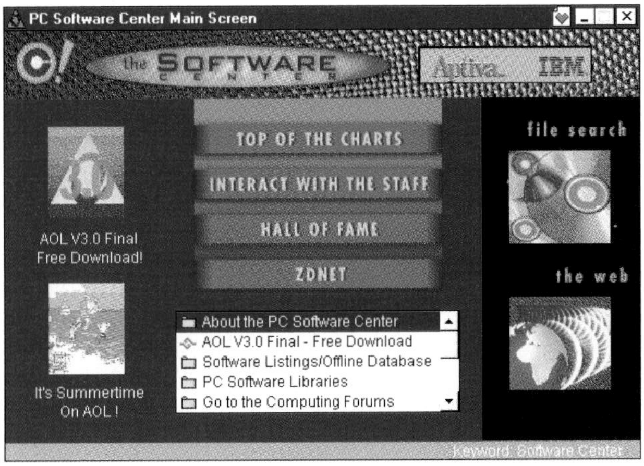

For easy access to computer software libraries, double-click the PC Software Libraries folder. You'll be presented with a list of category folders. Double-click a category folder to view a list of libraries and then double-click a library to see a list of available files.

Let AOL Be Your Guide

Downloading software is like shopping for new clothes—you don't know whether something will fit until you try it on. There's no way to tell whether a file will be useful until you use it. Fortunately, AOL offers some expert recommendations. Just click The Software Center in the Computers & Software channel window, and then click TOP OF THE CHARTS to display the following window:

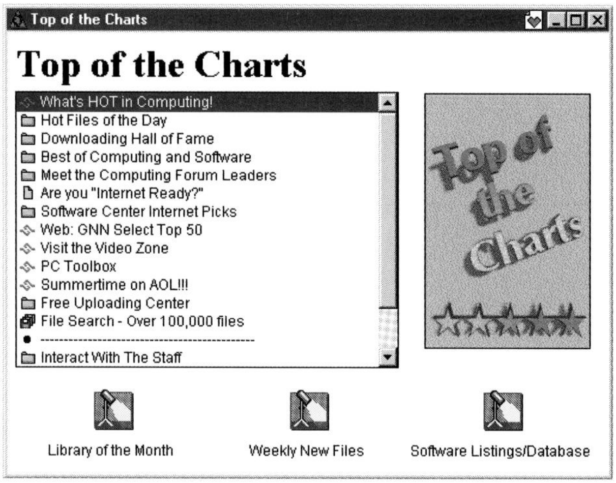

Many popular files are contained in more than one library. For example, some programs in the Personal Finance forum's taxes library can also be found in the PC Applications forum's library.

Here you'll find the hottest new downloadable software, plus collections of some of the best and most popular files in AOL's database. In particular, check out the two folders called Downloading Hall of Fame and Best of Computing and Software. They contain some of the coolest shareware programs available anywhere.

SEARCHING FOR FILES

The options discussed so far are great for browsing through lists of files apropos to a specific topic. But what if you want to search the entire system? Hey, that's what AOL's File Search feature is for. It's a powerful tool that lets you explore the entire database using words and phrases. To start the search process, click File Search in the Software Center window. Or, from anywhere in AOL, just click the File Search button on the toolbar. Either way, the Software Search window is displayed, as shown here:

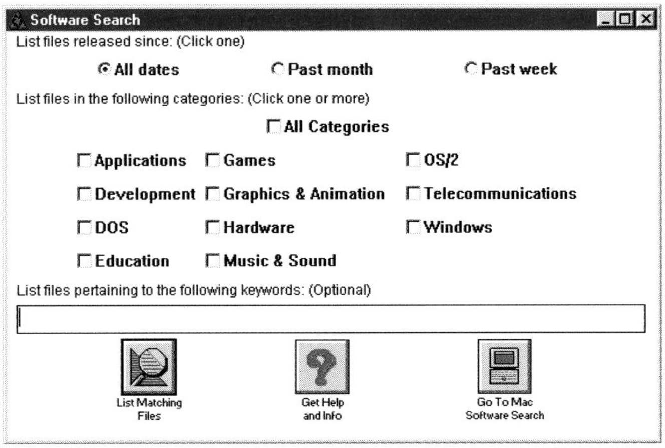

Type in what you're looking for—*pictures of birds* for instance, *or tax preparation software*—and click List Matching Files to view a list of files that meet your criteria. Remember, however, that there are more than 100,000 files in AOL's database. So it usually helps to narrow your search by checking in the Software Search window. To illustrate the point, I searched for *screen saver* without checking any categories, and came up with 1,071 files. When I checked the Windows category box, the number dropped to 708.

Narrowing the Hunt

Still, who wants to plow through 708 files—especially considering that the File Search window can display only ten items at a time? To really track down the software you want, use the right words to focus your search. Suppose, for example, that you're looking for pictures of animals to add to a newsletter. Searching for the word *animals* produces 6,062 possibilities, which is far more than you, as a busy person, have time to sort through. So try narrowing the hunt. Searching for the phrase *animal art* produces 594 files. Putting the name of the animal in the search really cuts it down. I tried searching just for *warthog* and was rewarded with 14 matches, including one that looked like this after I downloaded it. It's amazing what you can find on AOL.

habits & strategies

To locate free files, include distribute freely *in your search phrase. This will find files that you can use without incurring a fee. Similarly, if you're looking just for shareware files, include* shareware *in your search phrase.*

Boy, This Thing Works Fast

When you conduct a search, AOL's heavy-duty database search engine proceeds to ferret out the files that match your search criteria. The process takes just a few seconds, after which the files are listed in the File Search Results window, as shown below:

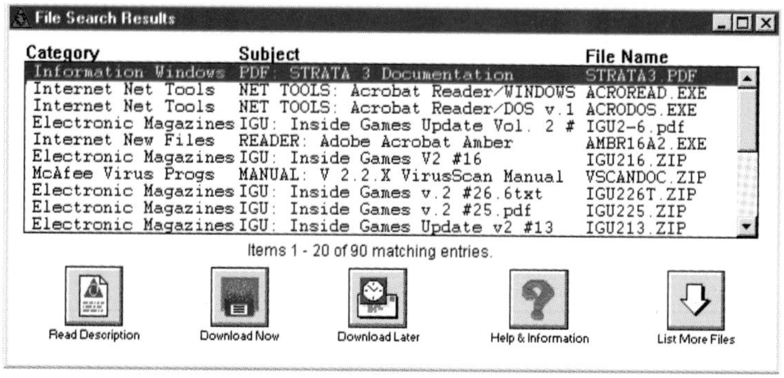

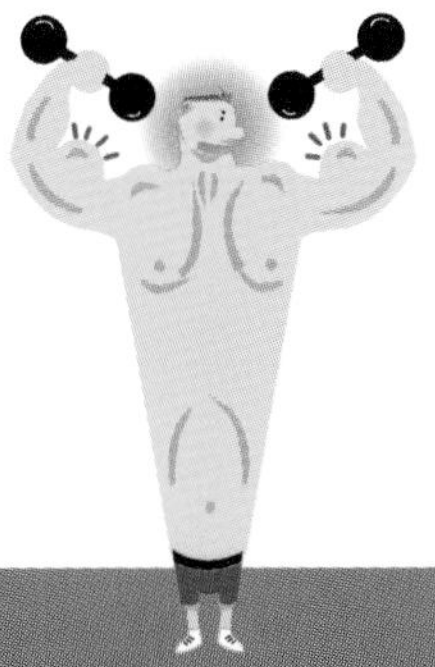

.exe: *The file extension of an executable file. A compressed file ending in .exe is a self-extracting file. Running the file automatically extracts any files within it and restores them to normal size.*

.zip: *The file extension of a file compressed with a zip utility. Files with this extension must be decompressed with an unzip utility. AOL automatically unzips zipped files when you sign off after downloading.*

In this search, I was looking for Acrobat Reader, a program that lets you view files that have been formatted with Adobe's Acrobat technology. Acrobat enables a document to appear on your computer exactly as it does in print. Many companies and government agencies now use Acrobat to publish such documents as annual reports and tax forms on the Internet. You yourself may well have occasion to need the Acrobat Reader (which is freeware). My search for the word *Acrobat* produced the results shown in the illustration. A quick look tells me that the second item is the one I am seeking: Acrobat Reader for Windows.

Checking Out the Particulars

When you select a file and click Read Description at the bottom of the window, you'll be able to view some germane facts about the file before you commit to downloading it. For example, you can see how large the file is (for Acrobat Reader, a hefty 1,528,560 bytes) as well as the approximate time it will take to download (13 minutes with a 28.8kbps modem). You'll also get a brief description the file, including instructions on how to install and use it once it's been downloaded.

Thank Goodness for File Compression

Large programs involve several files, which would take forever to download separately. But it's possible to pack many files into one file and shrink the file down to a manageable size. This is called *file compression*. Most compressed files that can be downloaded end in either .exe or .zip.

DOWNLOADING

If you decide to download a file, you can do so either from the file's description window or from the File Search Results window. In either case, clicking Download Now will begin the downloading process. If you'd rather download the file later—in a FlashSession, for

CAUTION

If you change the name of a file to be downloaded, don't mess with the last three letters that follow the period. If you alter the extension of a program file, a compressed file, or a graphics file, the file won't work.

instance—click Download Later, which I'll discuss in a minute. If you choose Download Now, the following dialog box will appear:

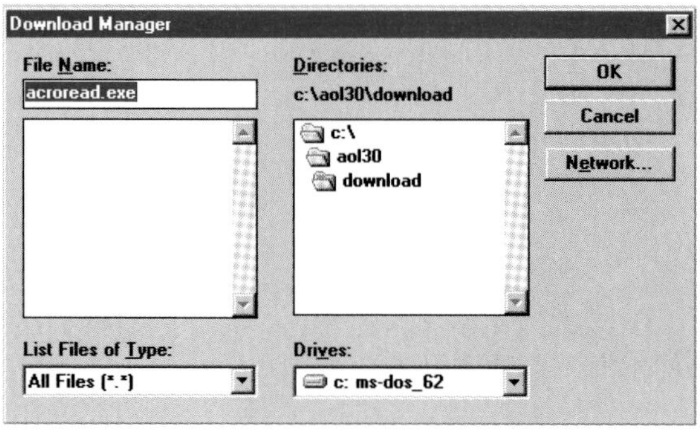

A name is automatically assigned to the file—in this case, acroread.exe. Likewise, files are automatically downloaded to the Download folder in the AOL folder on your hard drive. You can change the filename or the destination if you want, but in most cases there's no reason to.

Ready, Set, Transfer!

When you're satisfied with the information in the dialog box, click OK to start the download. You'll be presented with a File Transfer dialog box that shows you the progress of the download, lets you know approximately how much more time the transfer will take, and gives you the option of canceling the operation or pausing and finishing it later. Here's a File Transfer box in action:

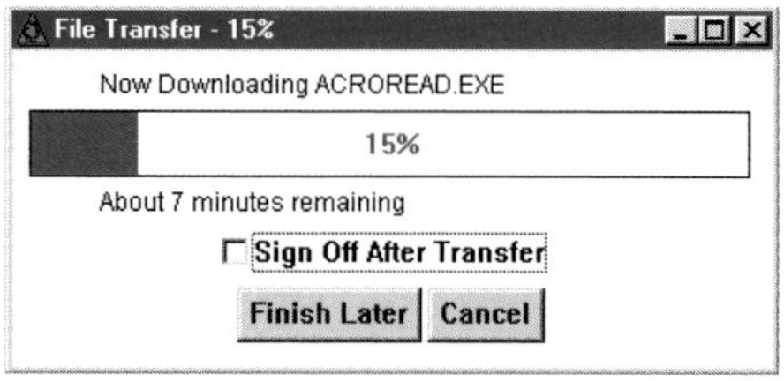

Okay, It's Been Downloaded—Now What?

Installing and using programs that you have downloaded is fairly simple. Here's how to go about it:

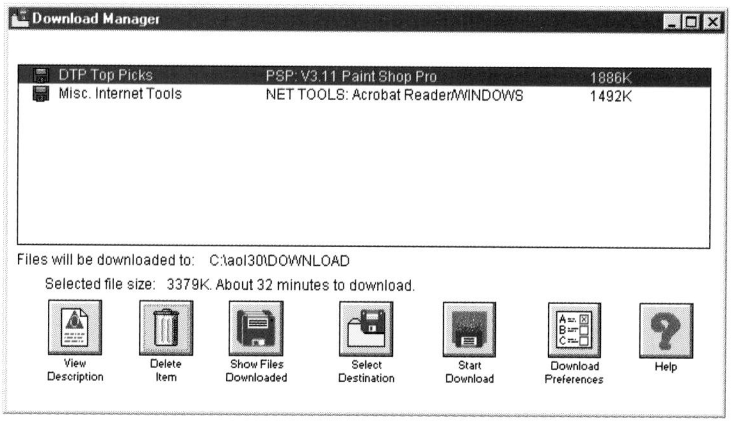

habits & strategies

You can use a FlashSession to download files listed in the Download Manager during off-peak hours. Just set a FlashSession for the time you want and make sure you've checked the Download Selected Files box in the FlashSession preferences.

Okay, now click the Start Download button. When the File Transfer dialog box appears, select Sign Off After Transfer. From that point on, AOL takes over. The files you've listed will be downloaded, and when the last one has been transferred, AOL will sign you off. How's that for convenience?

Keeping Track of Files You've Downloaded

AOL keeps track of your downloads. To see a list of the files you have downloaded, click Show Files Downloaded in the Download Manager. This will display the Files You've Downloaded window, which looks like the Download Manager window but has some different buttons at the bottom. One of them, Show Status, displays the name of a selected file as well as the directory (folder) to which it was downloaded. The information window looks like this:

Downloadus Interruptus, or Finishing Later

At any time while you're performing a download, you can pause the process without losing the time you've already invested. Say, for example, that you're halfway through a 30-minute download and you remember that you're supposed to pick up your son after soccer practice. Like right now. Don't panic. Just click Finish Later in the File Transfer dialog box. The portion of the file that has already been transferred will be stored on your hard drive, and the file will be listed in the Download Manager. You can resume the download at any time by selecting the file in the Download Manager and clicking Start Download.

Downloading Preferences

The Files You've Downloaded window also includes a button that lets you set download preferences. Click it to display the following dialog box:

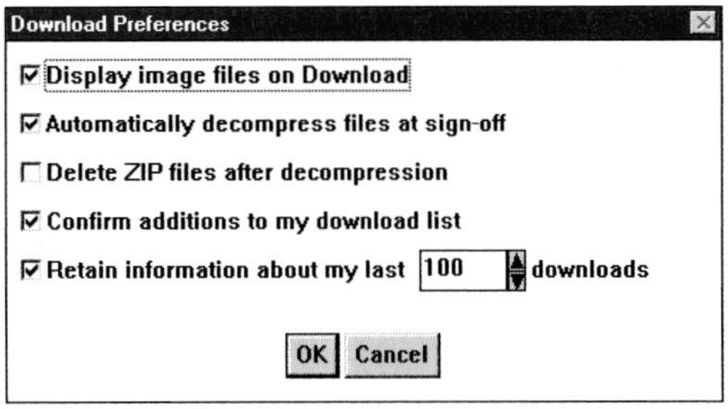

This box offers you several options. Here are descriptions of the most useful ones:

- **Display image files on Download** AOL can display images onscreen while they're being downloaded. This is useful because it lets you evaluate an image as it's coming in. You can then decide to cancel the download if the picture is a dog (unless, of course, you're downloading a picture of a dog).

- **Automatically decompress files at sign-off** When you sign off, AOL will automatically decompress zipped files if you have selected this option. The other way to do this is to select the file in the Files You've Downloaded window and click the Decompress button.
- **Delete ZIP files after decompression** You can have AOL delete zipped files after it decompresses them. This is safe to do because after the files have been extracted you'll no longer need the zipped file itself. However, it's not a bad idea to keep the zipped file at least long enough to save it on a floppy disk (if it will fit). That way you'll have it if you ever need it again.

CAUTION

AOL checks its files for viruses, but there is no such check for Web files. Get a program such as McAfee's WebScan, which you can download from AOL. The keyword McAfee *will get you to the company's area.*

THE INTERNET—A SOFTWARE TREASURE TROVE

AOL's enormous repository of files is impressive, but it's nothing compared to the wealth of software that resides on the Internet. Major universities, corporations, and other large organizations maintain huge libraries of freeware, shareware, and demoware. Much of it duplicates the software found on AOL, but there's also a lot of esoteric, rare stuff on the Web that you can't find anywhere else.

Searching the Web for Software

To access a list of resources that can help you find software on the World Wide Web, do the following:

1. Select the Computers & Software channel from the main Channels window.
2. Click yourself into the Software Center.
3. Click the button for the Web.
4. Double-click the folder labeled Web: Shareware Distribution Sites, which will display this window:

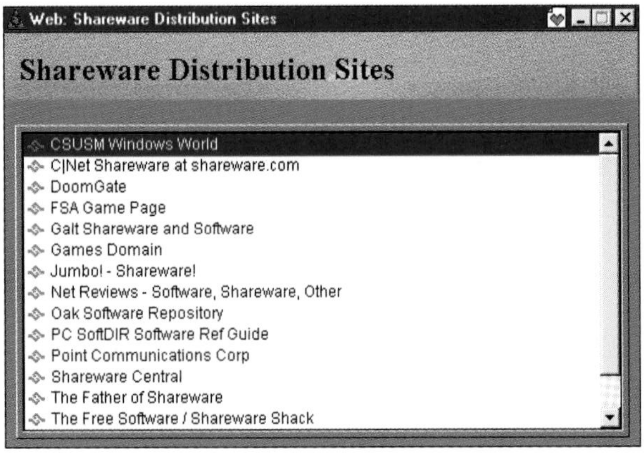

If you can't find what you're looking for with one of these powerful search sites, it probably doesn't exist. One site in particular, C|Net Shareware at shareware.com, has become one of the most popular destinations on the Internet, boasting access to some 200,000 files in various locations around the world. You use these sites much as you do AOL's own File Search feature: enter a word or phrase describing the file you'd like to find and then let the search engine do its stuff.

Downloading from the Web

You download files from the Internet in basically the same way that you download files from AOL. When you have found a file you want to download, you click the hypertext link to start the downloading process. A Save As dialog box appears, with the name of the file already entered and the AOL Download folder designated as the default destination. Click OK to start the download.

Now for the Bad News

Although the Web offers a wealth of software, there are some distinct advantages to using AOL's libraries whenever possible. These include

- **Manageability** You can't use the Download Manager for Internet files.
- **Reliability** You can almost always get software from AOL without a hitch, whereas many Internet software libraries suffer from traffic jams that can keep you from even accessing sites.

- **Speed** Depending on the amount of traffic on the Web, downloads can take an excruciatingly long time. AOL, by comparison, is much more consistent.

And You Might Need a Zip Program

In addition, AOL does not automatically unzip zipped files that you download from the Internet. For that, you'll need a special program. But don't fret—one is right around the corner. Just click the File Search button on the toolbar and search for *PKZIP*. This is an inexpensive piece of shareware that has become something of an industry standard. It's easy to use and can both zip and unzip files—which gives it an advantage over AOL, which can only unzip.

THE COMPANY CONNECTION

One of the big advantages you'll get from using AOL is the ability to access technical support and advice from hundreds of computer and software companies. Anyone who has ever tried to use a big software company's telephone support line knows what a nightmare it can be. It's great to know that you can find answers right there on AOL. To find a particular company, choose Company Connection in the Computers & Software window and then click Company Search. You'll be able to search for a company by name or check out an alphabetical listing of companies with a presence on AOL. The company areas are really forums, such as this one for AST, a personal computer maker:

SHORTCUT

You can reach most of the companies that have areas on AOL by using the Keyword feature. Just type in the name of the company as the keyword.

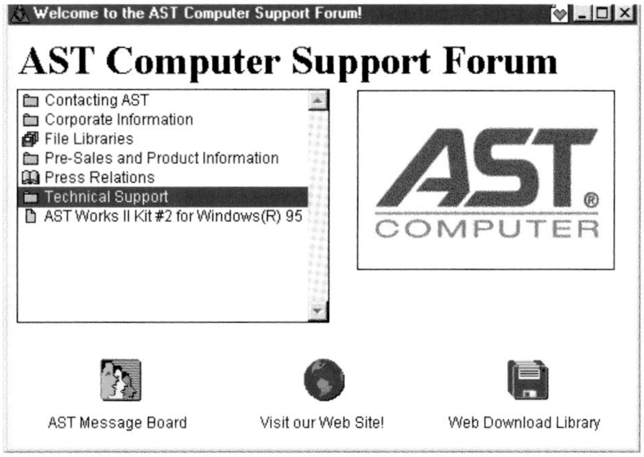

habits & strategies

The Company Connection is the place to go for demoware. In fact, there's a button labeled Demo Library in the Company Connection window that will take you to the best AOL has to offer in demonstration software for business applications, utilities, games, and multimedia.

The forum includes message boards that you can use to pepper the company with technical questions. (They're very good about responding.) Like many companies, AST also provides a direct link from its AOL area to its extensive site on the World Wide Web.

ZDNET—YET ANOTHER OPTION

As if AOL and the Internet didn't give you enough options for finding and downloading software, there's another one in the Computers & Software window. It's ZDNet, an elaborate area operated by Ziff-Davis, the computer-magazine publishing giant. The main ZDNet window includes a big old button labeled Download, which takes you to a window whose title is "Get top-rated software from people you can trust." Well, who knows whether you can trust anyone these days. But I must admit, the ZDNet Download area is impressive. When you find a file that interests you, you can view a colorful description window that even includes a rating. Here's the ZDNet description of PKZIP (the utility I mentioned earlier):

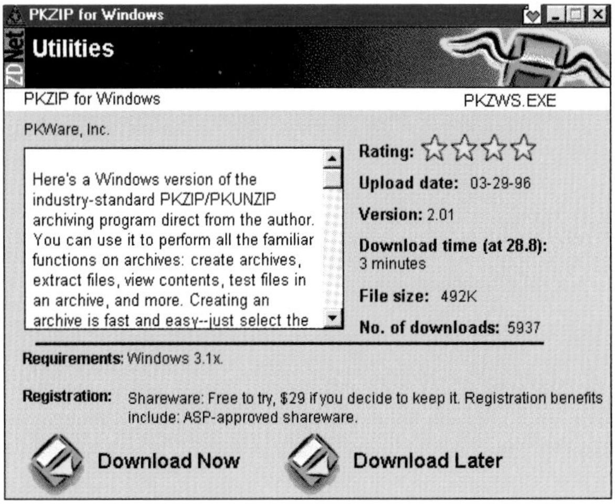

WHAT'S NEXT?

Just about the only thing I didn't cover in this chapter was the computer industry news that abounds on AOL. That's because the next chapter is all about news, from *The New York Times* to *Wired* magazine. Take out your reading glasses—here we go!

CHAPTER 8

Online News You Can Use

INCLUDES

- Today's News
- Conducting a search
- Saving and printing
- News Profiles
- The Newsstand

FAST FORWARD

CHECK OUT THE TOP NEWS ➤ *pp. 162–165*

1. Click the Today's News channel in the main channel window, or the Today's News button on the toolbar.
2. Click Highlights in the section you want (for example, US & World or Business).
3. To view an article from the list of top stories, double-click it.

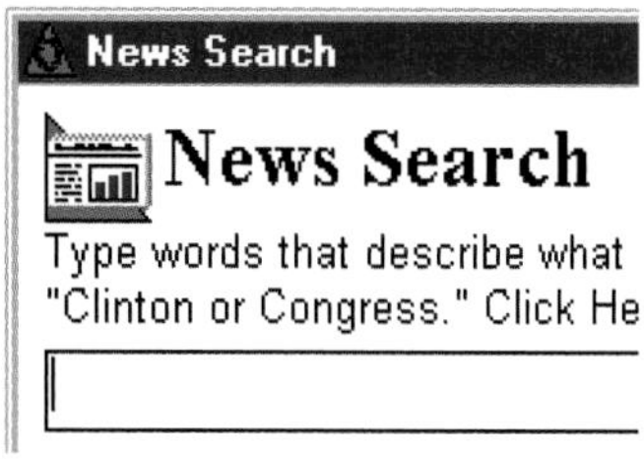

SEARCH FOR ARTICLES ➤ *pp. 165–167*

Using simple but powerful search techniques, you can search for stories on specific topics in AOL's news database:

1. Click News Search at the bottom of the Today's News window, or any other news window.
2. Enter words or phrases to search for. Use "and" to connect terms and narrow the scope of the search, "or" to expand your search with alternatives, and "not" to narrow the search by eliminating topics.
3. Press ENTER or Click List Articles to begin the search.

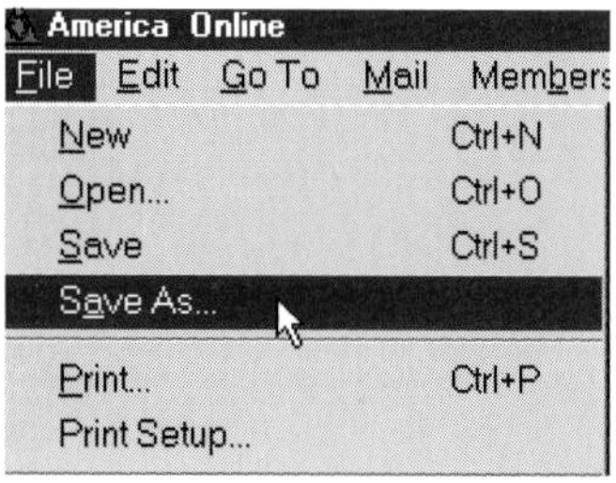

SAVE A STORY ➤ *p. 167*

There are several ways to keep articles so you can refer to them later. Here's one:

1. With the article onscreen, choose Save As from the File menu.
2. Enter a name for the article—and a destination folder if the default folder isn't acceptable.
3. Click OK, which will save the article to your hard disk in text format.

CREATE A NEWS PROFILE ➤ *pp. 168–171*

Have AOL deliver customized news to you every day via e-mail. To set up a News Profile:

1. Click the My AOL button on the toolbar, then click the button labeled "Customized news to your mailbox."
2. Click Enter News Profiles, click Create Your Profile, then click Continue.
3. Fill out the three boxes with words and phrases to customize your search, then click Continue.
4. Give the profile a name, choose news sources that will be used in searching, and set a maximum number of articles that the profile should generate each day.
5. Click Create to activate the profile.

READ A MAGAZINE ONLINE ➤ *pp. 172–175*

The Newsstand channel features more than 100 magazines and newspapers. To peruse one, just double-click its name in the list of publications. That will take you to the main window for the publication. From there you'll be able to read the current issue, search back issues, and take advantage of any special features exclusive to AOL.

One of the first kinds of information offered by online services was news. Today, news is still one of the most popular features on AOL, and boy, has this area grown! More than 100 newspapers and magazines now adorn the service, including some of the most prestigious and informative publications in the country, such as the *New York Times* and *Atlantic Monthly*. You can also stay right on top of news as it happens with wire service reports. And, as you will see, you can even customize AOL to get news about your favorite subjects delivered directly to you via e-mail. In other words, you'll never again have to stay up till 11 o'clock to stay on top of the news.

TODAY'S NEWS

Two of AOL's channels are dedicated to news—Today's News and Newsstand. As the name implies, Today's News is where you'll find the latest headlines, so let's go there first. Just click Today's News in the Channels window or the Today's News button on the toolbar to open the channel, which is shown here:

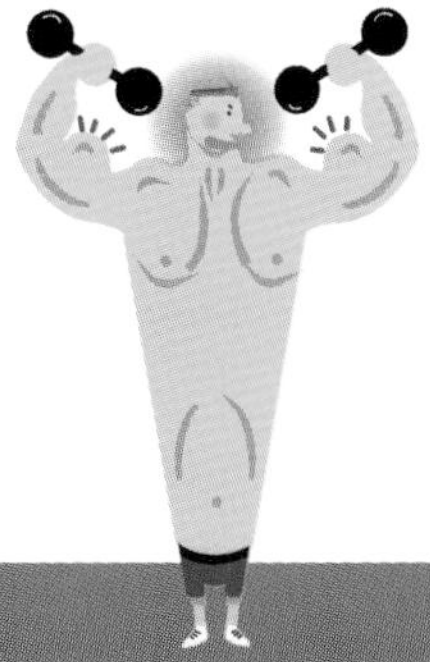

definitions

AOL draws breaking news from several major sources. These include

Reuters: *An international wire service with a large presence in the United States.*

Associated Press: *The largest news gathering organization in the world.*

Knight-Ridder/Tribune Business News: *News from more than 60 newspapers around the country.*

PR Newswire and Business Wire: *Services that electronically publish press releases from corporations and organizations.*

SportsTicker: *Up-to-the-minute news on sports.*

The Today's News channel window is divided into six sections, corresponding to the sections you might find in a daily newspaper. The center of the window is occupied by two panes. In the upper one you'll find a quick summary of top world and national news from Reuters, updated each hour. Below that is a list of important daily news stories. To view an item on the list, double-click it. Most items include not only a breaking news story, but also photos and links to related articles. Here, for example, is a roundup of news on the Middle East peace process.

Flipping Through the Headlines

By default, the Today's News window displays summaries and lists of stories about U.S. and World News. But you can change the contents of the center panes to display news about sports, business, or any of the other sections. Just click the Highlights button in the section you want. (Not all of the summaries are updated every hour. Go to the end of the summary to see the time it was posted on AOL.)

So How's the Weather Out There?

There's one section you definitely ought to know about—the weather. Whether you're traveling to the coast on business, or you just want to see how deep the snow is back in Vermont where your brother-in-law lives (ha-ha), AOL can give you the scoop. Here, for instance, is a map showing the national forecast, which I got by clicking Highlights in the Weather section of Today's News, then double-clicking U.S. Weather Forecast for Today:

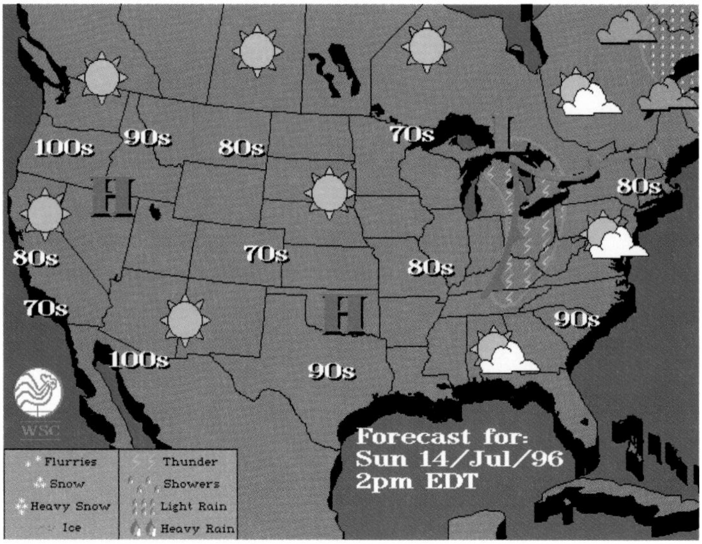

Dig Deeper If You Want To

Some people reach for the sports section before anything else. Others have to know what's going on in Hollywood, while still others are business news junkies. AOL lets you go directly to any section of Today's News simply by clicking the In Depth button for the section. You'll be presented with a news window like the one shown here for Enterterntainment News:

As you can see, there's a list of categories down the left side. Clicking the arrow for a category displays a list of news items. To read any item, double-click it.

But Wait, There's More!

Each news window also gives you links to other resources. In Business, for instance, you can get a stock quote by clicking the Quotes & Portfolios button. All of these resources are also available elsewhere in AOL. (You can also get stock quotes, for instance, by clicking the Stocks & Portfolios button on the toolbar.) It's just a nice convenience to have them in the news windows as well.

The AOL news database contains up-to-date articles on news, business, and sports. Most articles remain accessible for several days after they're published, and some items, especially sports and entertainment, stick around a lot longer.

SEARCHING FOR NEWS

If you want news on a particular topic, there's no need to wade through headlines to find it. Click News Search at the bottom of any of the news windows. This will display the News Search dialog box shown here:

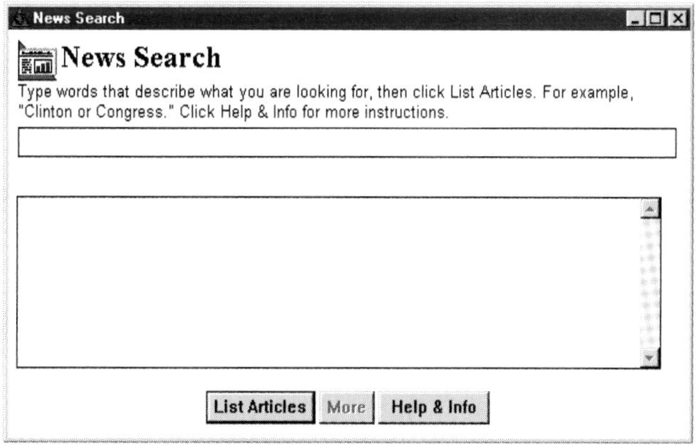

News Search is a great tool for sifting through the mounds of information in AOL's news database. To conduct a search, type in the subject you're looking for and press ENTER or click List Articles.

Some Useful Search Techniques

To use News Search effectively, you need to become familiar with some basic search terms known as *Boolean operators*. The main ones are AND, OR, and NOT. (They needn't be capitalized. In fact, you don't

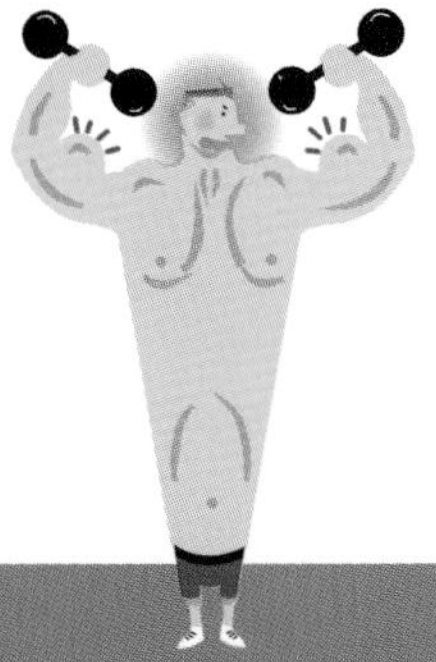

definition

Boolean search: *A search for specific information, using the operators AND, OR, and NOT. Named after George Boole, a nineteenth-century English mathematician who specialized in logical functions. One can imagine him telling his wife "I want beef OR mutton AND potatoes but NOT rice."*

have to capitalize anything in a search. America, america, and AMERICA all work the same.) Here's how to use them:

- Use AND to connect words and phrases and narrow your search. For example, if you're eager for election campaign news, search for *Clinton AND Dole* to find only stories mentioning both of them.
- Use OR to expand your search by providing alternatives. For instance, searching for *car OR automobile* will locate articles containing either one.
- Use NOT to narrow a search by eliminating items you don't want. If you enter *Clinton NOT Dole*, you'll get articles that mention the president but not his GOP rival.

You can use Boolean operators more than once in a query to really get specific. For instance, to get the latest dirt on the world's most famous royal divorce, you could search for *Charles AND Diana AND Camilla*! In fact, I did just that and came up with five juicy stories, as you can see here:

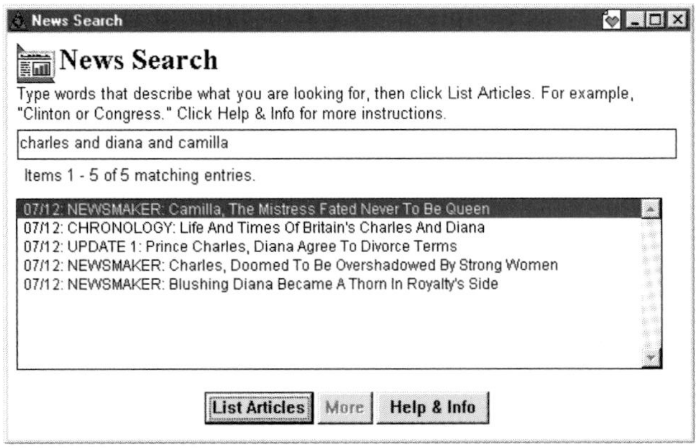

Searching with Names and Phrases

In addition to searching for individual words, you can use phrases or combinations of words, such as first and last names. Each phrase or word combination should be enclosed in single quotation marks. If you don't use the quotes, AOL will look for the words separately, as if they

CAUTION

Every scrap of news on AOL—from wire service reports to newspaper and magazine articles—is covered by a copyright. That means you can't reprint it for commercial purposes without first getting permission. It's OK to use it for schoolwork or as a reference for a business report, but even then it's a good idea to attribute it to its original source.

were connected by AND. For example, a search for *America Online* fetched 453 results—every article in the database containing the words *America* and *Online*. But when I searched for '*America Online*,' it turned up 344 items, all of them having to do with AOL.

Reading, Saving, and Printing Articles

When you conduct a search, the list of articles complying with the search criteria appears in the lower box of the News Search dialog box. To read an article, double-click it. The article appears, as shown in this example, headline and all:

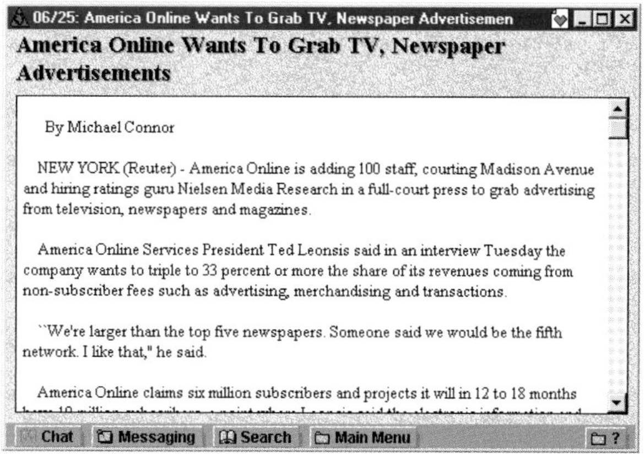
06/25: America Online Wants To Grab TV, Newspaper Advertisemen

America Online Wants To Grab TV, Newspaper Advertisements

By Michael Connor

NEW YORK (Reuter) - America Online is adding 100 staff, courting Madison Avenue and hiring ratings guru Nielsen Media Research in a full-court press to grab advertising from television, newspapers and magazines.

America Online Services President Ted Leonsis said in an interview Tuesday the company wants to triple to 33 percent or more the share of its revenues coming from non-subscriber fees such as advertising, merchandising and transactions.

``We're larger than the top five newspapers. Someone said we would be the fifth network. I like that," he said.

America Online claims six million subscribers and projects it will in 12 to 18 months

Chat | Messaging | Search | Main Menu | ?

Suppose you want to keep the article so you can refer to it later. No problem. AOL gives you several options, the easiest of which is simply to print it out. With the article onscreen, just choose Print from the File menu. This function acts like Print in any word processor. You don't have to worry about type fonts or anything else.

Saving an Article to Disk

To Save the article to your hard disk drive, use the following steps:

1. With the article onscreen, choose Save As from the File menu.
2. Enter a name for the article and select a destination folder for it.
3. Press ENTER or click OK.

Copying to Another Program

You can also copy all or part of the story to another program, such as a word processor. Here's how:

1. Select the portion you want to copy, or choose Select All from the Edit menu, as shown here:

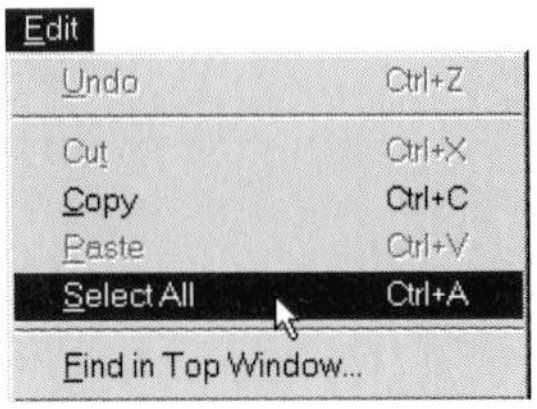

2. Choose Copy from the Edit menu. This places the text on the Windows Clipboard.

Open the second program, place the insertion point where you want the text to go, and choose Paste from that program's Edit menu.

Finding Something in an Article

With long articles, it's nice to be able to quickly locate a word or phrase without having to read the whole thing. And this, too, can be easily accomplished. With the article onscreen, choose Find in Top Window from the Edit menu, which displays the following dialog box:

Enter the word or phrase you're looking for and click Find Next.

NEWS PROFILES

Sure, it's great to be able to scan headlines and search for the latest news. But wouldn't it be great if you could get stories about your favorite topics delivered directly to you every day? Say no more. AOL has created just such a service, called News Profiles. It's a powerful tool, letting you draw from the entire range of AOL's daily news sources.

SHORTCUT

There's a quick way to save part of an article to your hard disk. Select the text and choose Copy from the Edit menu. Then choose New from the File menu. Paste the text in the Untitled window that appears, then choose Save As from the File menu and save the file. To view the text later, choose Open from the File menu, locate the file, and click OK.

Stories come to you as e-mail, an extraordinarily convenient way to get your daily dose of news. The best part is there's no newspaper to toss at the end of the day. Just delete the stories you don't want and keep the ones you do.

You can have up to five news profiles for every screen name on your account. That means you can customize one profile to get stories about your favorite baseball team, another to follow the presidential election, a third to grab news on companies whose stock you own. There are all kinds of possibilities.

Creating a News Profile

To take advantage of this nifty feature, you must set up one or more News Profiles for yourself. Each profile generates specific kinds of news based on criteria that you set. To create a profile, do the following:

1. Click the My AOL button on the toolbar, then click the icon labeled "Customized news to your mailbox." Or go to the Newsstand channel and double-click AOL News Profiles from the list of publications.
2. Click Enter News Profiles to display the News Profiles window.
3. Click Create Your Profile, then click Continue to display the following dialog box:

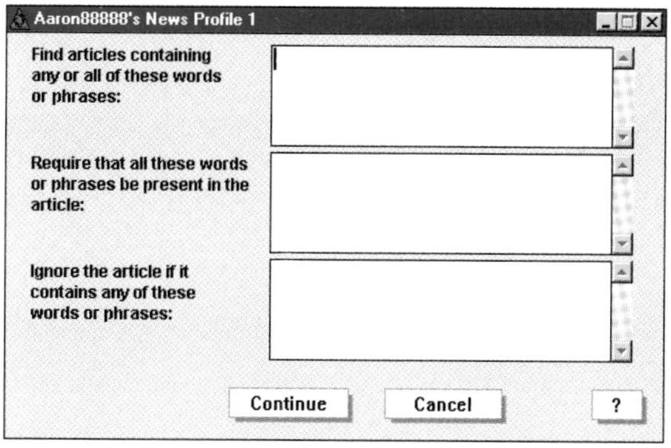

As you can see, there are three boxes for search criteria. You can use single words or combinations of words. Separate terms with commas, and enclose phrases with single quotation marks. (Capitalizing isn't necessary, but you can if you want.) OK, now let's set up a profile to find stories about the Cleveland Indians, who, as I write this, are striving for a second straight division title.

- In the top box, enter words or phrases that describe what you're looking for. For our sample profile, you might fill out the box like this: **Cleveland, Indians, baseball, 'American League'**.
- The center box is for terms that must appear in any story that the profile generates. In this case, good words would be Indians and Cleveland.
- In the bottom box, enter words that you want the profile to ignore. You might type the word **India** here, so that you don't get stories about real Indians (however, you might get a few politically incorrect stories referring to Native Americans as Indians).

habits & strategies

If you've chosen your search criteria wisely, there's really no reason to limit the news sources contributing to your profile. I'd go ahead and use them all. If you find some funny stuff sneaking into your mailbox, you can always eliminate one or more sources.

Choosing News Sources

Once you've filled in the boxes, click Continue to display a dialog box in which you can give your profile a name and choose news sources for it. You can also set a limit for the number of stories that the profile will dump into your e-mail each day (the default is 10). Here's how I set up the sample profile:

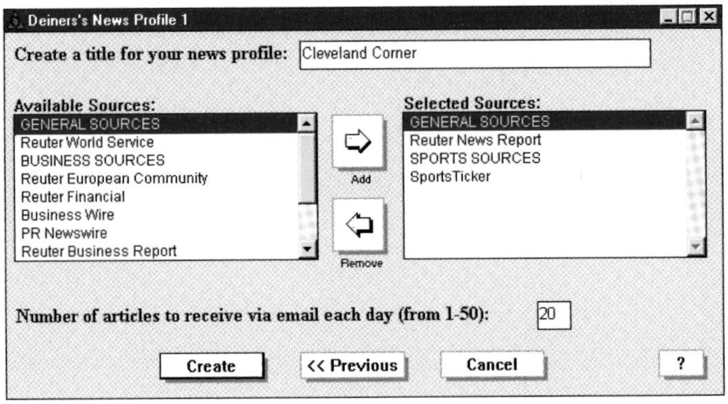

When you finish filling out the dialog box, click Create to close the box and then OK to create the profile.

Viewing News Profile Articles

Reading news profile articles is just like reading e-mail. In fact, it *is* e-mail. The only difference is that all news articles have the return address of **AOLNewsProfiles@aol.net**. (Don't try replying to this address. It doesn't belong to anyone.)

How to Avoid a Jammed Mailbox Your AOL mailbox can only hold 550 pieces of mail—and that includes mail you've already read. If you have several news profiles active, and they're each delivering up to 50 items each day, your mailbox could fill up fast. Once it's full, your news profiles are automatically turned off, and as regular e-mail comes in, old items are deleted to make room. The best way to avoid such a catastrophe is to monitor your news profiles closely for the first few days. If the situation starts to get out of hand, reduce the limit on the number of articles that you get, or try more selective search terms.

Managing News Profiles

AOL lets you easily manage news profiles. You can change the maximum number of articles generated, apply new search terms, or even delete the profile entirely. Here's how:

1. Repeat the first two steps listed earlier in the section "Creating a News Profile."
2. Click Manage Your Profile in the News Profiles dialog box. This will display the following dialog box:

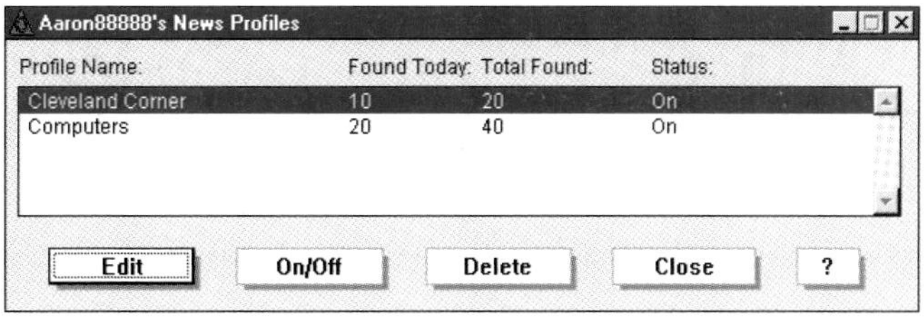

As you see, I've got two news profiles at work: the one on the Cleveland Indians, and another, much bigger one following the personal computer industry for me. To change any of the settings you made when a profile was created, select the profile and click Edit. To stop the profile from working—or to turn it back on—click On/Off. Why would you want to turn a profile off? Well, you might be going out of town and don't want dozens of articles to pile up in your mail. (Also, if your mailbox reaches its 550-piece capacity and your news profiles are turned off, you'll have to turn them back on manually.)

SHORTCUT

To view news articles generated by a news profile without wasting online time, have your computer download them automatically via FlashSessions. Since they're technically e-mail, you can download them with the rest of your incoming messages. See Chapter 4 for directions on setting up a FlashSession.

Some publications in the Newsstand are also available on the World Wide Web. In general, however, the AOL versions are easier to use and offer more features, such as the ability to search for articles in previous issues.

THE NEWSSTAND

The Newsstand may be the most aptly named of all AOL channels. It is, in fact, an electronic newsstand, featuring more than 100 magazines and newspapers covering an impressive range of topics. As of this writing there are seven publications devoted to business and finance, eight on computers, and six on science, as well as others on sports, religion, music, and even the military. In many cases, you get photos and graphics along with text, and most major publications even let you search through back issues—at no charge, of course. But the best part about this newsstand is that you can browse to your heart's content.

All The News That's Fit to Print—Online

For all you newshounds, the first place to stop in the Newsstand is the online version of the *New York Times,* America's newspaper of record. The paper was at one time so influential that each evening radio stations would read a list of what it was planning for the front page the next day. With AOL, you can go that one better by reading the stories themselves when you get up in the morning. Here, for example, is the top story for the day I'm writing this:

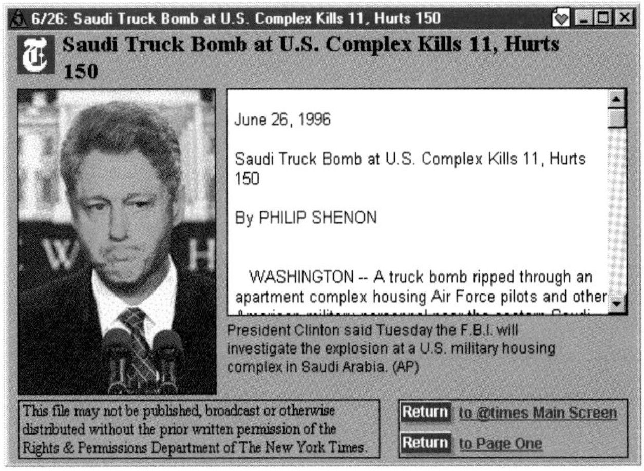

SHORTCUT

A really fast way to save an article for later viewing is to put a copy of it in your Favorite Places folder. Just drag the heart on the title bar of the article to the Favorite Places button on the toolbar.

Any article from a Newsstand publication can be printed, copied, or saved using the same procedures you used for Today's News earlier in this chapter. And, like all proprietary material on AOL, magazine and newspaper articles are protected by copyright law. The *Times* makes sure you know that—see the note in the lower-left corner of the preceding illustration.

Getting Down to Business

One of the most comprehensive of all Newsstand destinations is *BusinessWeek Online*. Here you'll find the complete text of the weekly magazine, along with photos, charts, and other graphics. The main window for *BusinessWeek Online* is shown here:

In addition to the regular magazine, *BusinessWeek Online* offers a special service, BW Plus, which is chock-full of information aimed straight at busy people. There's a list of the top business schools, information on mutual funds, even a Small Business Center.

A Cornucopia for Consumers

One example of a magazine that really benefits from being online is *Consumer Reports*. You can find reviews about products that have appeared in the magazine faster online than you can with the printed issues. I know this because for years I saved *Consumer Reports* so I could look stuff up. On AOL, you can search back issues by subject, or quickly find reviews, test results, and ratings under topics such as Automobiles, Electronics, and Food & Health. Shown below is the Automobile section, a very cool and easy way to learn what the folks at *Consumer Reports* think of your car.

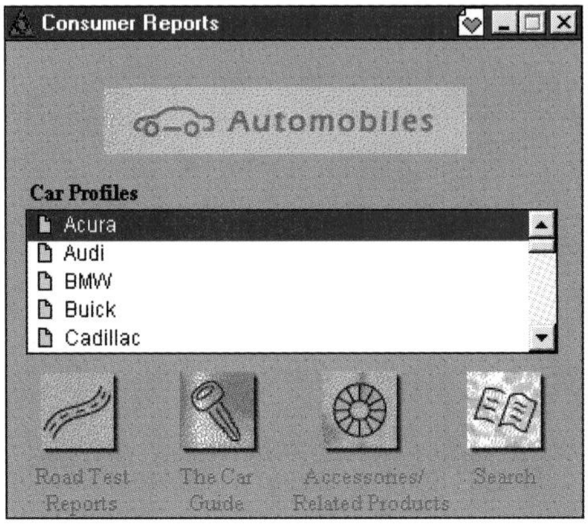

The marvelous convenience of having Consumer Reports on AOL is best evidenced by the speed with which you can search for stuff in past issues. Want to know whether that lawn mower you've been thinking of buying cuts the mustard? Find out by using the following steps:

1. In the main Consumer Reports window, click Search to display a search window.
2. Type in words or phrases that describe what you're looking for. You can use broad categories, types of products, even brand names. Press ENTER or click List Articles to begin the search.
3. The search results will be listed in the lower box of the window, as shown here. Double-click an item to view it.

Many publications offer files for downloading. They consist of photos, charts, even movies. For example, Business Week *lets you download a video clip of Reebok's computer-generated 3-D ad featuring basketball star Shaquille O'Neal. And from* Elle *magazine's area, you can download videos of the latest swimsuit fashions.*

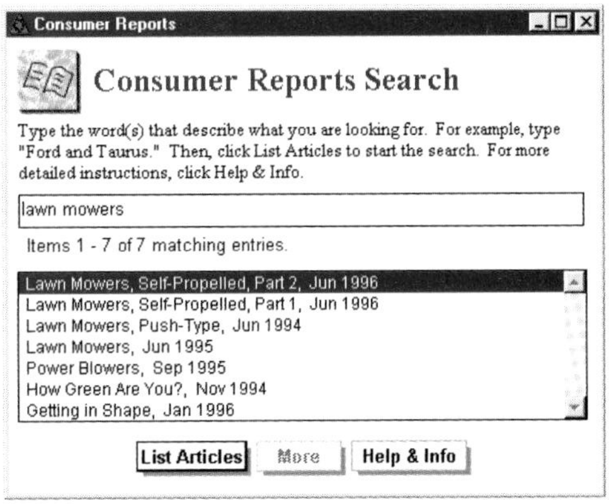

The Computer Magazine Stand

It stands to reason that AOL's Newsstand would include a lot of computer-oriented magazines, and that is indeed the case. In fact, there's an entire section of the Newsstand set aside for them. It's called Computing's Magazine Rack, and you can access it from either the Newsstand or the Computing Channel. The Rack features AOL versions of *PC World, Home PC, Game Pro,* and other top magazines, as well as World Wide Web links to additional publications such as *PC Week* and *PC Computing.* There's even an AOL area for *Wired,* the irreverent canon for the Internet generation.

In Case You Think This Chapter Is Too Serious

Let's end with something on a lighter note. When you get tired of all the crime and sex and violence of regular news, try turning to *Weekly World News,* the supermarket tabloid that happens to be available in the Newsstand. Here you'll find, well, you'll find crime and sex and violence, but there's also a lot of other stuff that never seems to make it into the mainstream press. You'd never see the *New York Times* carrying the news shown here:

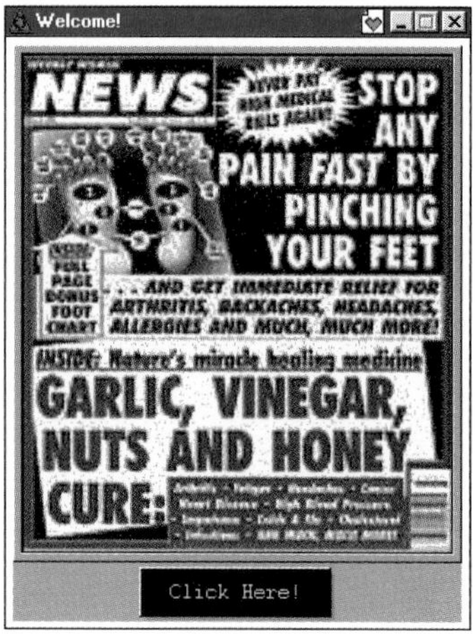

WHERE TO NEXT?

Man does not live by news alone. There's also sports and entertainment, which is up next. If you want to know who's leading the league in hitting, or which movie is likely to score big at the box office, AOL is the place to go.

CHAPTER 9

Your Ticket to Sports and Entertainment

INCLUDES

- Checking scores
- Player statistics
- Movie reviews
- Online TV listings
- Popular music CDs
- Video games

FAST FORWARD

CHECK THE SCOREBOARD ➤ *pp. 183–184*

To find out how your favorite team is doing, use the following steps:

1. Click News & Scores in the Sports channel window or in the Today in Sports window that is displayed when you first go to the channel.
2. Click the Scoreboard button.
3. Click the sport you want.
4. Double-click any score for a summary of that game.

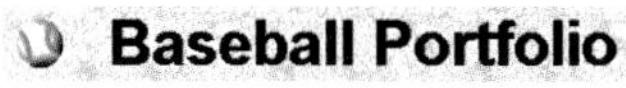

CREATE A PLAYER PORTFOLIO ➤ *pp. 184–185*

With AOL, it's easy to follow your favorite baseball and basketball stars on a daily basis. Just create a player portfolio that automatically tracks their performance. Here's how:

1. Double-click the STATS Pro Sports Center folder in the Sports Channel window.
2. Click Pro Baseball Center or Pro Basketball Center, then click Player Portfolio.
3. Choose Create Team and follow the instructions.
4. When you're done, click Save Team.

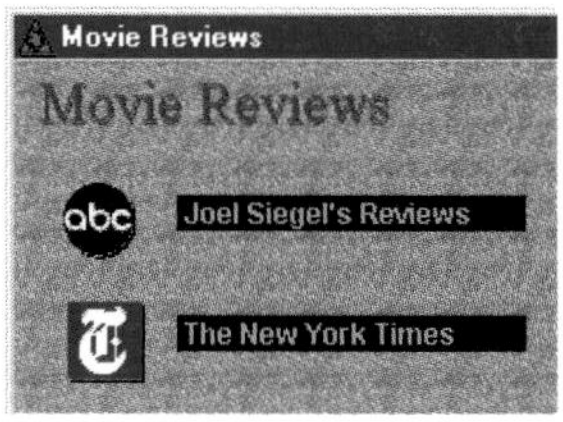

READ A MOVIE REVIEW ➤ *pp. 188–189*

1. Click Entertainment in the Channels window.
2. Click Movies, then click Movie Reviews.
3. Select one of the options, such as Entertainment Weekly.
4. Locate the review you want on the list and double-click to view it.

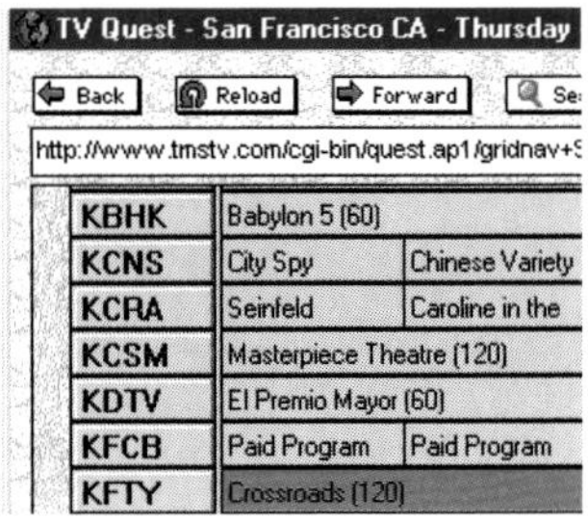

FIND OUT WHAT'S ON TV ➤ *pp. 191–192*

For online television listings, do the following:

1. Click Television in the Entertainment channel window.
2. Click TV Listings to go to the TV Quest window.
3. Click What's On TV, which takes you to the TV Quest site for AOL users on the World Wide Web.
4. Select your city and click Continue to see what's on in your area.

GET THE LOWDOWN ON A NEW CD ➤ *pp. 193–194*

1. Click MusicSpace in the Channels window.
2. Select the category for the recording artist you're interested in.
3. Double-click the name of the artist.
4. Double-click the item about the new compact disc.

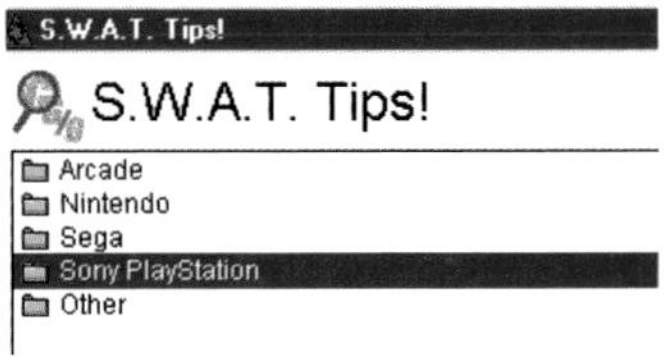

FIND CHEAT CODES FOR VIDEO GAMES ➤ *pp.194–196*

Many video games have secret codes that let you give your characters added power and protection. The game makers don't tell you these cheat codes, but you can find them through AOL. One way is to visit the S.W.A.T Tips section of GamePro Online. Another is to check out game-oriented newsgroups on the Internet. You'll find direct links to such newsgroups in the Games channel.

When you stop to think of it, sports and entertainment play an enormous role in the lives of most people. And there's no way you can keep up with everything—or can you? AOL lets you find information fast on anything from the latest blockbuster movies to the summer Olympics. There's news, features, gossip, and statistics in abundance, all easily accessible. And best of all—no commercials. That makes it ideal for busy people.

SPORTS

There are lots of ways to get sports news. The morning paper is loaded with stories about yesterday's events. Sports channels on television provide regular updates. But if you want to know what's happening right now, the best place to go is AOL. It's almost like being at the game, only you don't have to park or stand up for the national anthem. When you go to AOL's Sports channel, the first thing you see is the Today in Sports window, which gives you quick access to some of the top stories of the hour. It appears in front of the main channel window, like this:

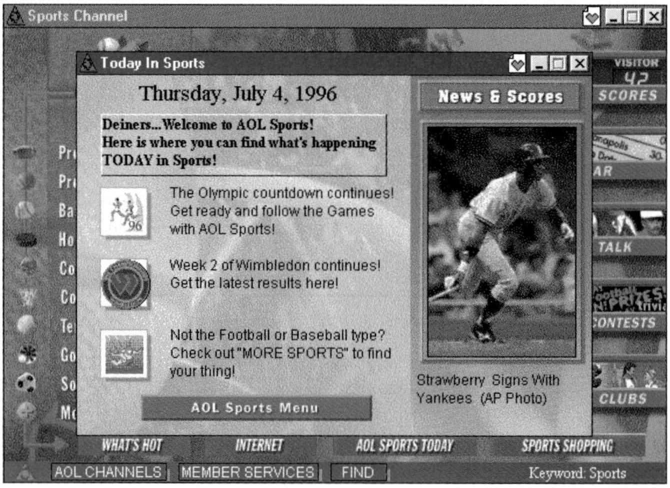

To display the channel window, either close the Today in Sports window, or click AOL Sports Menu.

Keeping Score the Easy Way

Results of professional and major college events are put on AOL practically in real time. In fact, you can even follow games while they're in progress. There are a couple of ways to get scores. Here's the most straightforward:

1. Click News & Scores in the Today in Sports window or the Sports channel window.
2. Click the Scoreboard button.
3. Click the sport you want.
4. Double-click any score to view a summary.

Another, more elegant presentation is available for major sports from Stats, Inc. For example, let's see how the San Francisco Giants are faring against San Diego today. Follow these steps:

1. Click Baseball on the Sports channel.
2. Click News and Scores.
3. Double-click NL Scoreboard to see line scores for the day's games, like this:

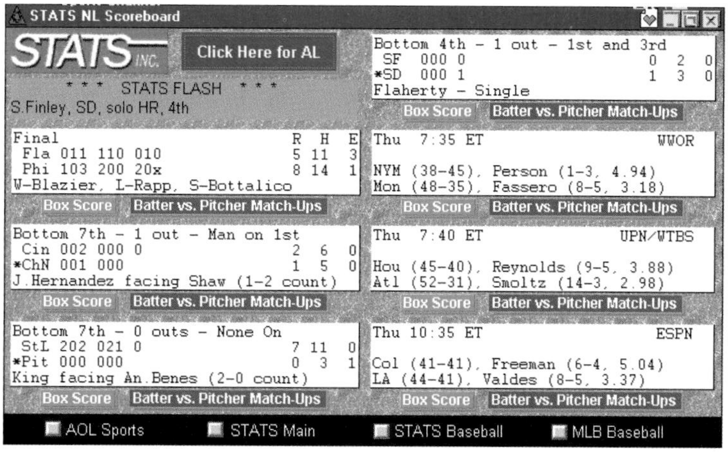

I see that the Giants are already behind. Oh well, it's been that kind of season.

The Stats, Inc., scoreboard is updated dynamically pitch-by-pitch, which means you can leave it on your screen and watch the events unfold.

Find Out Fast Who's First and Who's Worst

Scores are just the beginning. You can also see team and individual statistics, league leaders, standings, and schedules for every major sport. A major provider of statistics on AOL is Stats, Inc., a sports information and statistical analysis company. And they're the ones to turn to when you want stats fast. Double-click the STATS Pro Sports Center folder in the Sports channel window to access the Stats, Inc., window, shown here:

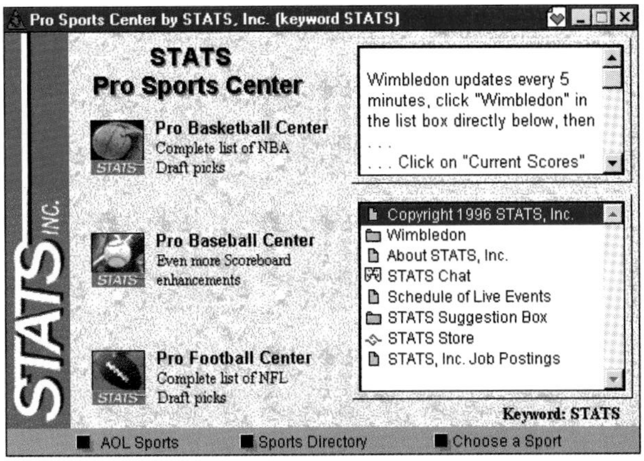

Follow Your Favorite Players

Stats, Inc., lets you easily follow the performance of your favorite baseball and basketball players throughout the season with Player Portfolios. These are sort of like fantasy league teams, only you're not competing with anyone else. They're great for busy people who get eye strain going from box score to box score every morning. To create a portfolio, use the following steps:

1. Click Pro Baseball Center or Pro Basketball Center in the Stats, Inc., window.
2. Click Player Portfolio.
3. Choose Create Team and follow the instructions.
4. When you've finished, click Save Team.

habits & strategies

If you belong to a fantasy baseball or basketball league, use the portfolio to keep track of your fantasy team. You'll know at the end of each day how you're doing, and whether you ought to follow the advice of the guys at the office and change your lineup.

You can add or delete players from your team at any time and you can have as many teams as you like.

You'll Know More About These Guys Than Their Mothers Do

Thanks to the number crunchers at Stats, Inc., you'll be eating statistics for breakfast when you check out your portfolio. Want to know how your players did today? How about yesterday? During the past week? Or maybe you'd like averages for the season to date. No problem, all those statistical breakdowns are available instantaneously. Are computers great or what?

And for Pro Football Fanatics... AOL offers Grandstand Fantasy Football during the National Football League season. This is an actual fantasy league in which you compete against other AOL members. If your team is good enough, you could win autographed collectables from top NFL players, T-shirts and free online time. But you've got to be a serious fan to play, because unlike the Stats, Inc. profiles, which are free, this costs money ($29.95 for the 1996 season). If you're interested, click Pro Football in the Sports channel window, then double-click the Grandstand Fantasy Football folder.

The Real Inside Scoop

Want a real insider's view of sports? Look no further. AOL features regular journals written by some top pro athletes in football, baseball, and other sports, as well as online columns by some of America's top sports writers. To access them, double-click the Athletes & Experts Online folder in the Sports channel window, then choose the athlete or expert you want. Here's a journal entry from champion cyclist Leigh Donovan:

Special Treatment for Special Events

AOL isn't just for everyday sports news. Special areas are created for major events. As I write this, for example, there are areas devoted exclusively to Wimbledon tennis, the Tour de France bicycle race, and the summer Olympics. All three are quite impressive, with up-to-date news and graphics and lots of background information. The Olympics area features detailed facts on all the nations sending athletes to Atlanta. There's same-day coverage of the Tour de France. And in the Wimbledon area you can treat yourself to some historical photos, such as this one:

You Won't Find This in the Newspaper

Most daily newspapers are pretty stuffy in that they don't think wrestling is a real sport. They argue that it's fixed. Of course it's fixed, but millions of people follow it anyway and they want to know how Rowdy Roddy Piper and Jake "The Snake" Roberts are planning to dismember their next opponents. As a matter of fact, the World Wrestling Federation area is one of the most sophisticated places on AOL. It has news, message boards, a chat room, photos, sounds, video—even live online appearances of some of the biggest, baddest boys in the business. From the following window I see that Brian Pillman is going to be online live tonight (hope he's not mad).

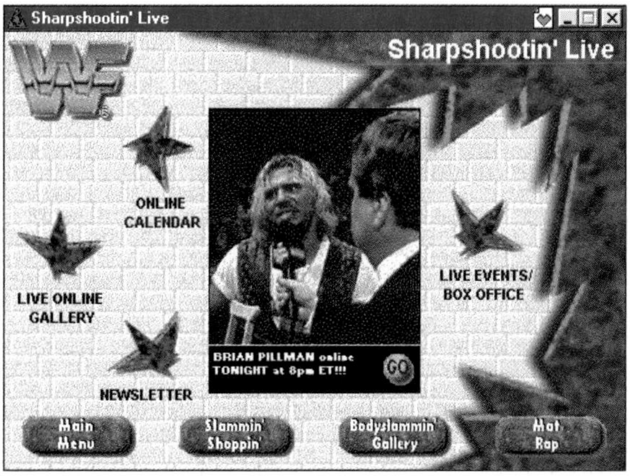

SHORTCUT

Many Internet sites can be accessed directly from the windows for individual sports. In fact, most of the resources listed in the tennis, golf, and soccer areas are on the Web. Any listing with a blue "W" before it is a Web site.

Meanwhile, Out on the Internet

While AOL's sports menu is robust, there's an abundance of sports-related stuff on the Internet, and it's easy to find. AOL even maintains special World Wide Web pages that direct you to sports in cyberspace. To access the main AOL Sports page on the Web, use the following steps:

1. Click the Internet button in the Sports channel window.
2. Double-click AOL Sports on the Web in the list at the right side of the window.
3. Double-click the Sports Pages hyperlink to display the following window:

ENTERTAINMENT

So you're a busy person. You still need to unwind once in a while by going to the movies, camping in front of a TV sitcom, or reading a good book. That's where AOL's Entertainment channel comes in. It tells you when and where the latest flicks are playing and whether they're worth going to see. You'll also find television listings for your area, and best-seller lists to help you decide what to read.

You Want Reviews, They Got Reviews

I don't know about you, but I love to read movie reviews. They can pump up a good film so that I can't wait to see it, or they can convince me not to waste my money on a stinker. Normally, you have limited access to reviews—the one in your newspaper and maybe one or two on TV. With AOL, however, the possibilities are plentiful. Just do the following:

1. Click Entertainment in the Channels window.
2. Click Movies, then click Movie Reviews.
3. Choose from among a top-notch group of reviewers from the *New York Times*, the *Chicago Tribune*, *Entertainment Weekly*, *Variety*, and other publications. Here, for example, is *EW*'s review of Disney's "The Hunchback of Notre Dame."

REVIEW: The Hunchback of Notre Dame
MOVIES
TOWERING ACHIEVEMENT
Disney reaches new heights with 'The Hunchback Of Notre Dame,' in which the most unlikely of animated heroes struggles valiantly to get over the hump.
By Owen Gleiberman
When it was announced that Disney would produce an animated musical version of THE HUNCHBACK OF NOTRE DAME (Walt Disney, G), there were doubts, even jokes, about transforming Victor Hugo's classic tale, with its famously misshapen hero, into a
Photo courtesy of Disney
Entertainment
BEAUTY AND THE BEAST: Esmeralda and Quasimodo

Here's a tip: If you want a review of a recent movie that's no longer in theaters, try searching back issues of *Entertainment Weekly*. You'll find the magazine among the resources listed in the Entertainment channel.

For complete biographical information on Hollywood stars, past and present, check out the CineMedia site on the World Wide Web. To get there, double-click CineMedia from the list of resources in the Movies window.

Hollywood History at Your Fingertips

By clicking Old Favorites in the Movie Reviews window, you'll get access to a database of films going back to the 1920s. You can search for movies by title, director, or year of release, or search for stars to list the movies they were in. It's great for those of us who either can't remember the name of the film or the name of the actor. There's a synopsis of each movie along with credits and any interesting sidelights.

Sights and Sounds of the Silver Screen

Because AOL is a multimedia online experience, it brings more to the party than just printed reviews. You can also get photos, videos, sound bites—even screensavers featuring the latest box-office blockbusters. Want to see a picture of the White House exploding in "Independence Day"? How about a short action clip of Jim Carrey in "The Cable Guy"? Just double-click the Photos of the Stars folder in the Movies window, which will take you to the photo area for *Critics Choice,* a multimedia syndicate that publishes entertainment news and reviews. There you can download a multitude of multimedia fragments, including this shot of a San Francisco cable car blowing up in "The Rock":

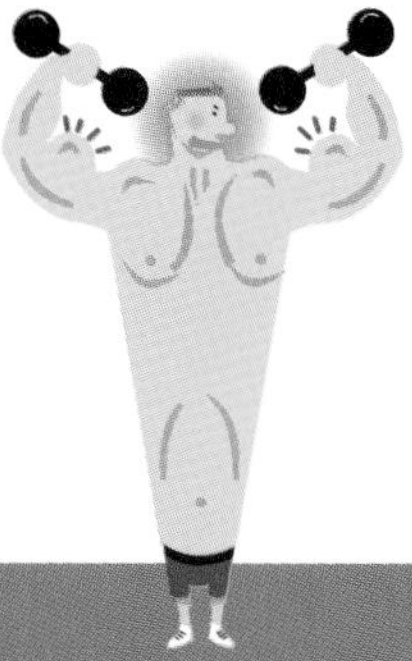

definition

Screensaver: *A software program that automatically runs when you're not using your computer. It prevents damage to the monitor caused by having the same image displayed for prolonged periods. Movie screensavers typically feature images or short sequences showing main stars or themes.*

Nationwide Theater Listings

How many times have you rummaged through the daily paper looking for the elusive movie theater listings? There's a much easier way, believe me. Here's what you do:

1. Click Movies in the Entertainment window.
2. Click Local Movie Listings, which takes you to Movielink on the World Wide Web.
3. Click Search by Theater, enter your zip code, and press ENTER to see a listing of theaters in your area.
4. Click a given theater to see the day's schedule, such as the one shown here:

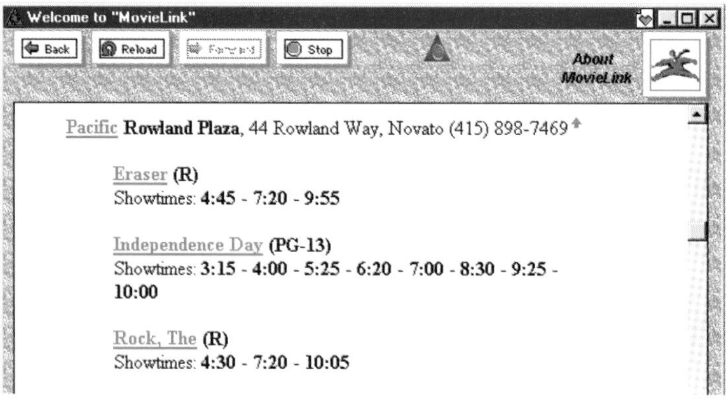

Check Out What's New in Video Stores

Can't wait for the big movie you missed in the theater to make it into the video store? Check out the weekly listing of new home video releases. You'll find it by clicking Home Videos in the Movies window.

An Online TV Guide

At first blush, it seems a little funny that you would use your computer to find out what's on television. But then again, why not? If you want the most up-to-date information of any kind, you're likely to find it online. And AOL delivers with TV Quest, a service that lets you view TV listings anywhere in the country. Start with the following steps:

1. Click Television in the Entertainment channel window.
2. Click TV Listings to go to the TV Quest window.
3. Click What's On TV.
4. Choose your city and click Continue.
5. Use the Channel Down, Channel Up, Earlier, and Later buttons to modify the listing, or click the menu button and set your own criteria.

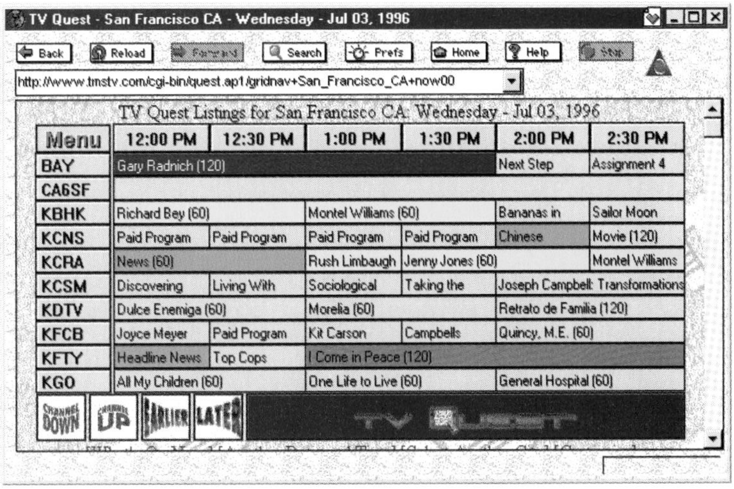

Find Your Favorite Program Fast

In addition to showing what's on TV at any given time, TV Quest lets you search for specific shows, movies, and sports events—just click

In the next few years, online services and the Internet will start to become available on high-resolution computer/televisions that sit right in your family room. You'll be able to view TV listings on AOL, then go straight to a program using a remote control.

the appropriate search link at the bottom of the listings window. Just to see what would happen, I searched for "I Love Lucy" and found that if I wanted to, I could watch 28 episodes in a single week!

Beam Me Up, Scotty!

One of the most popular of all destinations in AOL is the Star Trek Club—a forum devoted to the popular television series of the same name. Whether you're old enough to have been a fan of the original TV series or are a "Next Generation" lover, you'll find yourself right at home on this virtual USS Enterprise. You'll find the Star Trek Club in the index on the main Entertainment window. After double-clicking to the club's window, shown here, you can beam yourself into a chat room full of Trekkies by clicking The Bridge.

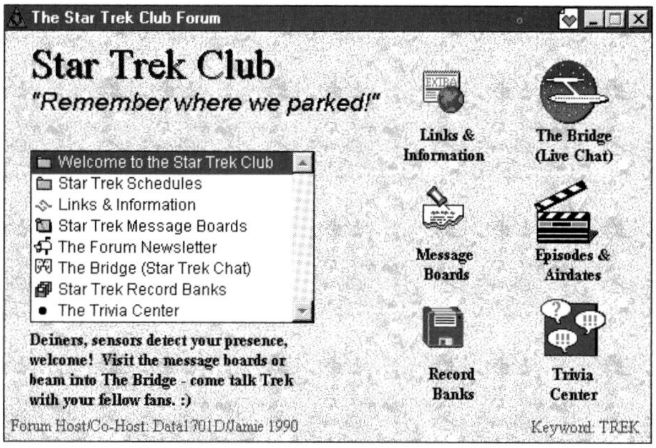

"Star Trek" isn't the only TV show to have it's own area on AOL. "Frasier," "Friends," "Mad About You," "Melrose Place," and "The X Files" all have online forums for fans.

Whatever Happened to Books?

Although AOL is chock-full of information on movies and television, it's a little harder to find information about books. I guess that reflects the general attitude of society toward reading. But at least you're reading *America Online for Busy People*, right? Anyway, if you want to see what's up in the world of literature, the best way is to go to the Learning & Culture channel rather than the Entertainment channel. There, click Books to access book reviews as well as best-seller lists for fiction and nonfiction.

MUSICSPACE

Music may be a universal language, but everyone has their own musical tastes. Fortunately, the MusicSpace channel caters to all kinds of interests. It features areas for rock, country, classical, jazz, R&B, pop, alternative—even music from other countries. This is great for busy people, because it gives you ready access to information about your favorite kinds of music, both on AOL and the Internet. There are also message boards and chat rooms for each type of music, so you can argue with other members over such things as whether Metallica's long-awaited CD "Load" was worth the wait. To learn about the latest popular CDs, click New Releases, which will display this window:

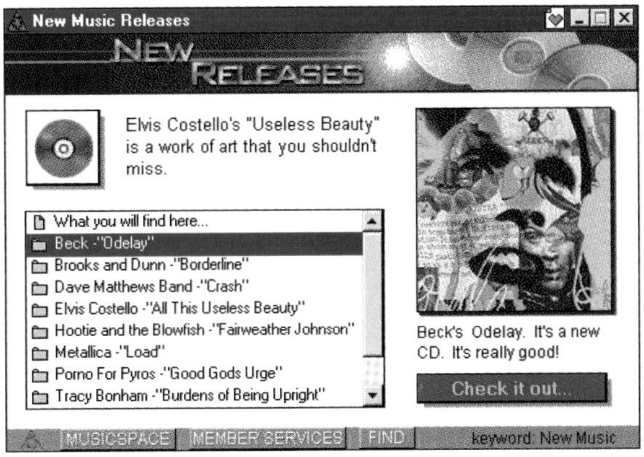

From Janet Jackson to Alan Jackson

AOL maintains areas for many recording artists, so you can find biographies, fan clubs, and notes on their CDs all in one place. Say you'd like information on the latest album by Alan Jackson, a red-hot country singer. Follow these steps:

1. Click Country in the MusicSpace channel.
2. Double-click Jackson's name in the list of artists to display Jackson's AOL window.
3. Click "Alan Jackson Biography—Who I Am" to display the following window:

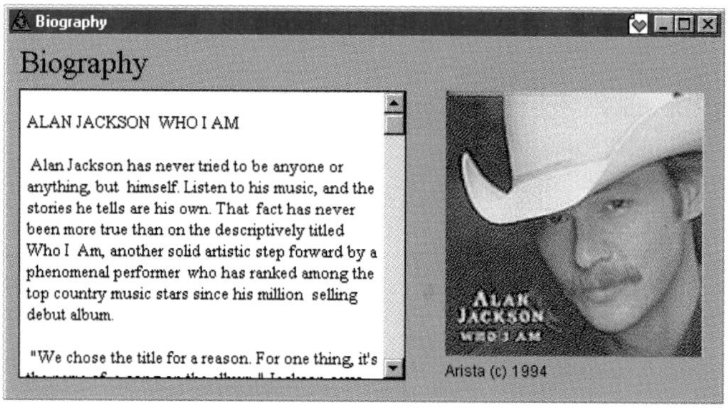

"Who I Am" is the title of the CD. There's a picture of the cover of the disc, along with a commentary about the album, including quotes from Jackson himself. These sorts of high-tech liner notes are available for many CDs in MusicSpace. In many cases, short sound clips from CDs are available for downloading.

THE "LONG STRANGE TRIP" CONTINUES

Not even the death of lead singer and guru Jerry Garcia seems to have fazed fans of the Grateful Dead. The band no longer performs, but its legion of camp followers still flock to the Grateful Dead forum to exchange memories and insights into the band that rocked the world for more than a quarter of a century. The forum contains chat rooms, message boards, and schedules for the Grateful Dead Hour, a weekly radio show heard in dozens of cities around the country. The easiest way to access the forum is with a keyword, which, appropriately enough, is *dead*.

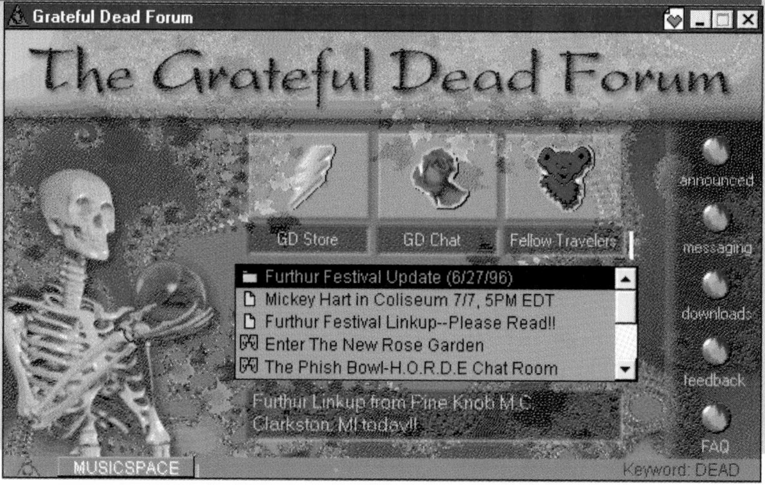

GAMES

Want to get your kids interested in computers? One sure-fire way is to turn them on to the Games channel. Whether they like arcade-type action, role-playing adventures, or sports games, they'll find stuff here to keep them in front of the computer for hours. In fact, it may ruin your busy schedule, because when you need the PC, junior will be using it. Anyway, here are some of things you'll find on the Games channel:

- Hundreds of shareware games that you can download
- Links to video game sites and newsgroups on the World Wide Web
- Clues and secret codes that let you play tough games like an expert
- Some pretty good games from AOL, including the new Air Warrior, a multiplayer, interactive online game. Here's the window for it:

Top Secrets You Can Have Free

From watching my son play video games, I know that to get the most out of them, you need to know certain secret codes that give your characters added power and protection. Game makers seldom tell you about these codes, even though they're built into the games. Here are a couple of good ways to find them:

- Check out GamePro Online (keyword: *Gamepro*), the AOL version of one of the best magazines on video games. It features candid reviews of all the latest games, features on the hottest technology, and the aforementioned comprehensive area called S.W.A.T. Tips, which gives you codes and clues for many popular games.

- Go to video game–oriented Internet newsgroups—where experienced gamers share some of the best clues and codes. It's gotten to the point that codes for top games start showing up in newsgroups almost before the game is out. To access game-oriented newsgroups, click the Forums button in any of the category windows of the Games channel. The newsgroups are listed with other resources.

WHAT'S NEXT?

Now that you've had your fill of sports and entertainment, it's time to get serious. In the next chapter, you'll see how to get expert financial advice, keep track of your investments—even do your own market research. Hurry, I think I heard the opening bell on the stock exchange.

CHAPTER 10

Personal Finance Made Easy

INCLUDES

- Stock quotes
- Personal portfolios
- Market research
- Mutual funds
- Finance forums
- Business on the Internet

FAST FORWARD

GET A CURRENT STOCK QUOTE ➤ *pp. 202–203*

AOL updates stock quotations throughout the trading day. Here's how to find the current price of a stock:

1. Click the Stocks & Portfolios button on the toolbar.
2. Enter the ticker symbol of the company whose stock price you want.
3. Click Get Quote or press ENTER.

CREATE A PORTFOLIO ➤ *pp. 203–205*

To keep track of the stocks and mutual funds you own, put them in virtual portfolios. To create one, use these steps:

1. Click the Stocks & Portfolios button on the toolbar.
2. Click Portfolios, then choose Create Portfolio.
3. Give the new portfolio a name and click OK.
4. Select the new portfolio in the Portfolio Summary list.
5. Click Add Item and fill in the box with the ticker symbol of the stock or fund, the number of shares, and the purchase price. Then click OK.

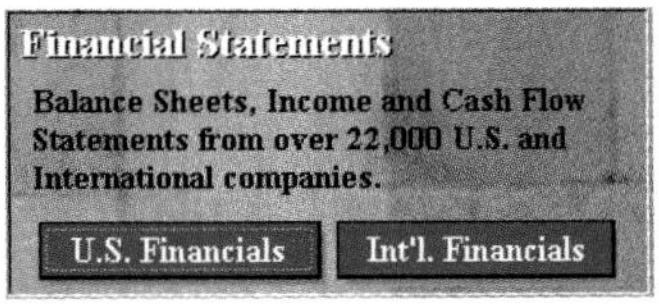

CHECK A COMPANY'S EARNINGS ➤ *pp. 208–210*

Want to know how a company is faring before you buy its stock? Do the following:

1. Click Company Research in the Personal Finance channel window.
2. Click Financial Statements, then click U.S. Financials.
3. Type in the company name or its ticker symbol, then click Search.
4. Double-click the name of the company to see its financial results.

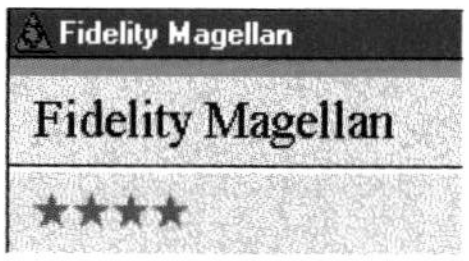

SEE HOW A MUTUAL FUND IS RATED ➤ *pp. 212–213*

1. Click the List Alphabetically button in the Personal Finance channel window.
2. Double-click the Morningstar Stock & Fund Reports folder in the Personal Finance channel window.
3. Click Mutual Funds, then click the Search button.
4. Enter the name of the fund and click Search or press ENTER.
5. Double-click the name of the fund to see a rundown on it. The rating will be at the top.

GET ADVICE FROM FOOLS ➤ *p. 214*

One of the most popular areas on AOL is The Motley Fool, a financial forum that goes on the theory that an individual investor can do just as well as a Wall Street pro. There are several ways to access the Motley Fool, including using the keyword *fool.* But you won't feel like a fool once you get there. The area is loaded with solid advice, plus message boards where you can exchange observations about the world of finance with other members.

FIND A CORPORATION'S INTERNET SITE ➤ *pp. 215–216*

Thousands of businesses now have home pages on the World Wide Web. To locate a company in cyberspace, use these steps:

1. Double-click the Hoover's Company Profiles folder in the Personal Finance channel window. (If you don't see the folder, click the List Alphabetically button.)
2. Select Business on the Web.
3. Click Corporate Web Sites and locate the company in the alphabetical listings.
4. Double-click the name of the company to launch the AOL Web browser and go directly to the site.

If you're like most busy people, personal financial matters are extremely important to you. You want to handle your money wisely, make sound investments, and guarantee financial security for your children and for yourself when you get to retirement age. But the world of finance is complex and rough. How do you know if you're making the right moves? You can go out and find a financial advisor, but there's an easier way—let AOL give you a hand. In this chapter, you'll discover resources in the Personal Finance channel that can turn you into a financial wizard.

QUOTES AND PORTFOLIOS

During the trading day, AOL updates stock quotes every 15 minutes. That's because under financial disclosure laws, quotes can't be released to the public until 15 minutes after they're posted by the stock exchange.

With AOL, you can quickly view the current trading activity of a stock or mutual fund by using the following steps:

1. Click the Stocks & Portfolios button on the toolbar to open the Quotes & Portfolios window.
2. Enter the ticker symbol of the company or fund.
3. Click Get Quote or press ENTER. As quick as you can say "Sell" the window will be loaded with all the pertinent information about your investment, as in the example using IBM, shown in Figure 10.1.

Finding Ticker Symbols

Suppose you don't know the ticker symbol (the letters that the market uses to identify the company or mutual fund). No problem. Click Lookup in the Quotes & Portfolios window, type in the first few letters of the name, then click Search by Company. You'll be presented with a list that matches your criteria, along with their ticker symbols.

Creating a Portfolio

If you own stocks or mutual funds, chances are you're constantly wondering how they're doing. More importantly, you're always trying

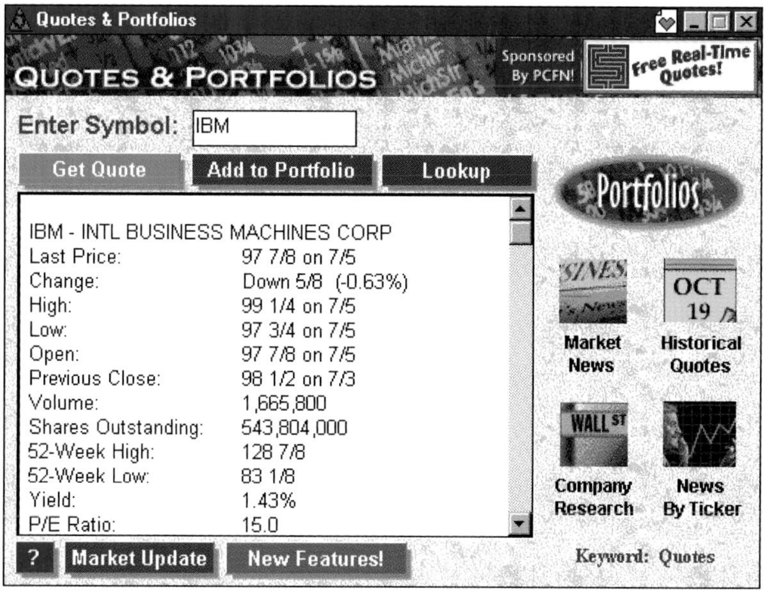

Figure 10.1 Quotes & Portfolios window

to figure out how much money you've made or lost in the market. In the past, you had to wait for the morning paper to find out how your investments performed, and you needed a calculator to tally up your gains and losses. But not anymore. Just put your holdings in virtual portfolios and let AOL take care of everything. You can have up to 20 portfolios per screen name, with up to 100 items in each portfolio. Here's how to create a portfolio:

1. In the Quotes & Portfolios window, click Portfolios to display the Portfolio Summary window, shown here:

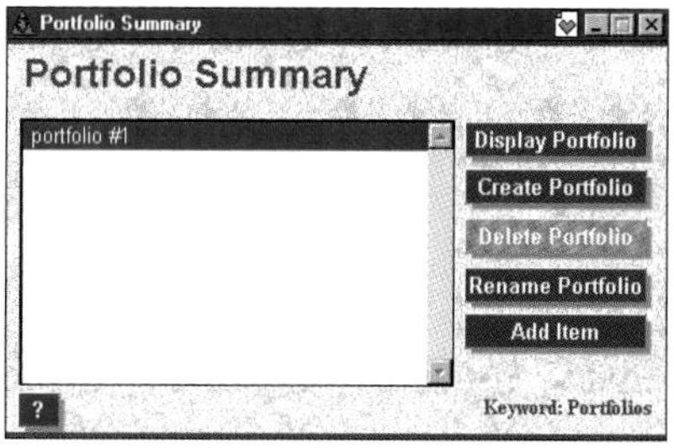

2. You'll notice there's a default portfolio called portfolio #1, which you can use if you want (or you can change its name using the Rename Portfolio button). To start a new portfolio, click Create Portfolio.
3. Give your new portfolio a name and click OK.
4. Select the new portfolio.
5. Click Add item, then enter the ticker symbol of a stock or mutual fund, the number of shares, and purchase price (leave the share number and price boxes blank if you're just tracking a stock and don't own it).
6. Click OK. You'll receive a confirmation that the stock or fund has been added to the portfolio.

habits & strategies

Take advantage of the ability to have multiple portfolios. Use one for stocks you own, another for stocks you're following closely, and yet another for your mutual funds.

Adding More Items

If you want to put multiple items in your new portfolio, repeat steps 5 and 6 for each additional item. You can also add to a portfolio later by entering the ticker symbol of an item in the Quotes & Portfolios window and clicking Add to Profile. Then select the profile you want to use, enter the number of shares and the purchase price, and click OK.

Viewing Your Portfolio

Any time you want to see how your stocks are doing, click Portfolios in the Quotes & Portfolios window and double-click the name of the portfolio you want. A window like the following one will be displayed:

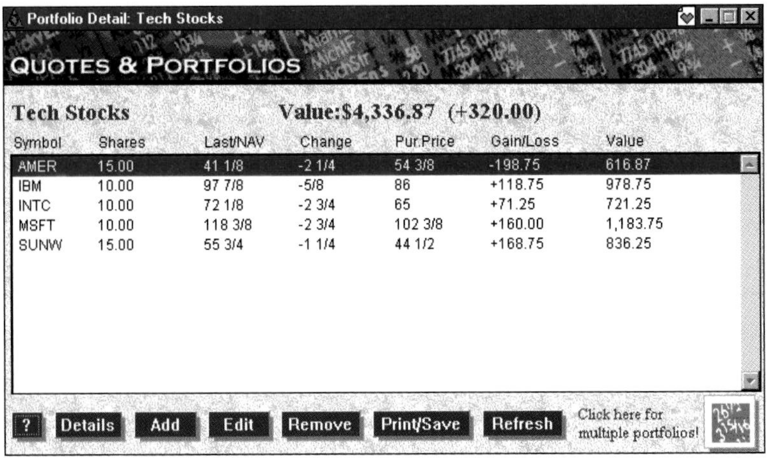

Symbol	Shares	Last/NAV	Change	Pur.Price	Gain/Loss	Value
AMER	15.00	41 1/8	-2 1/4	54 3/8	-198.75	616.87
IBM	10.00	97 7/8	-5/8	86	+118.75	978.75
INTC	10.00	72 1/8	-2 3/4	65	+71.25	721.25
MSFT	10.00	118 3/8	-2 3/4	102 3/8	+160.00	1,183.75
SUNW	15.00	55 3/4	-1 1/4	44 1/2	+168.75	836.25

As you can see in this sample stock portfolio, the gain or loss for each issue is shown, along with the value of the holding. And at the top you'll find totals for the entire portfolio. Looks like I'm still ahead despite a rotten day yesterday (the Dow Jones industrial average fell more than 100 points). My mock investments, top to bottom, are America Online, IBM, Intel, Microsoft, and Sun Microsystems. By the way, you can view details of any stock in your portfolio by clicking Details. And if you leave the portfolio open on your screen, you can see updated prices any time by clicking Refresh. (Be careful, though, because you'll also be racking up AOL connect time, which can get expensive.)

CAUTION

Trading stocks online is fast, efficient, and relatively inexpensive, but it also can be hazardous to your financial health. For all intents and purposes, you become your own broker when you do this, so make sure you're up to speed on the companies and industries in which you're trading.

Trading Stocks Online

With AOL, you can actually buy and sell stocks online. At this writing, several discount brokerages were available, including PC Financial Network (a service of Donaldson, Lufkin & Jenrette Securities Corp.; E*Trade Securities, Inc.; and Quick & Reilly. Trades can be placed any time day or night—which is a lot more convenient than hunting down a stock broker. And the commissions for trades typically are less with a discount broker than if you use a full-service investment house. PC Financial Network even lets you see what it's like to trade online before you commit yourself. Here's how:

1. Double-click PC Financial Network: Brokerage from the list of folders in the Personal Finance channel window. (If you don't see the folder, click List Alphabetically.)
2. Click Try Our Online Demo, then click Try the Practice Account Now.
3. Click Trading to practice buying and selling. You also can click Accounts to access detailed information about your investments. For example, you could instantly view the balances of all your holdings, as shown in Figure 10.2.

MARKET RESEARCH, AOL STYLE

There's no secret to solid investing, but it does take work. You need to thoroughly research every stock you buy. And AOL gives you

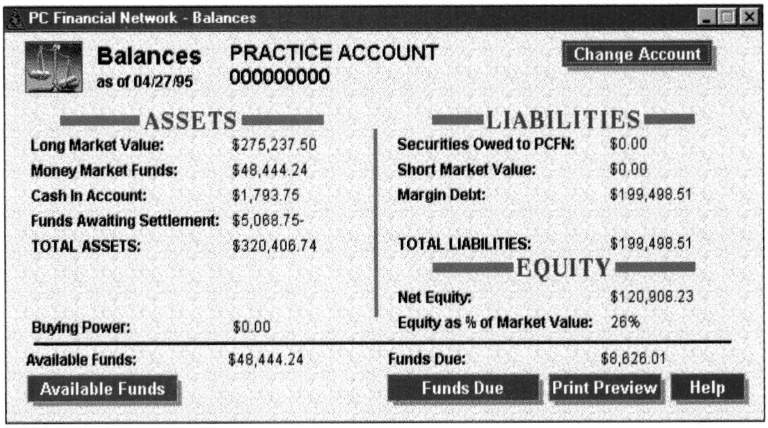

Figure 10.2 PC Financial Network-Balances window

habits & strategies

Daily financial news about the stock market and individual companies can greatly affect your investments. Make it a habit to check the Business section of Today's News in AOL before deciding to buy or sell.

the tools to do it. In fact, you have access to some of the same tools used by professional brokers and analysts. With them, you can

- Track past performance of a stock
- Look into the company's history
- View the company's financial results
- Check analysts' earning expectations.

The place to start is the Company Research window, shown in Figure 10.3, which you get to by clicking Company Research in the Personal Finance channel window.

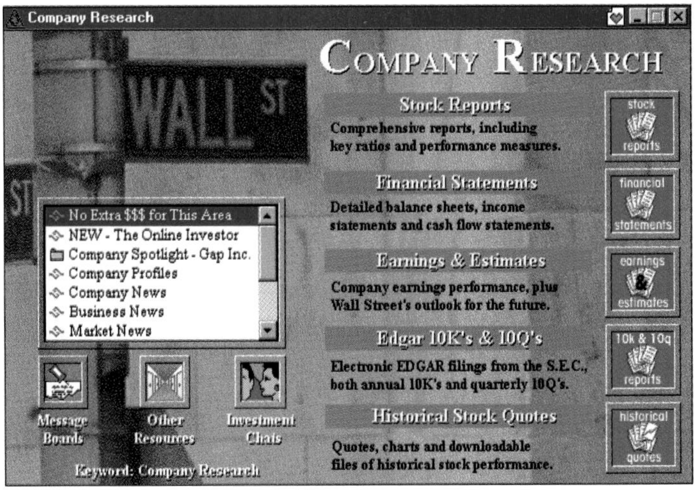

Figure 10.3 Company Research window

Viewing a Stock Chart

Past performance is no guarantee of future results, especially when it comes to Wall Street. However, it's often possible to spot trends based on stock charts. To create a chart of a publicly traded stock, do the following:

1. Click Historical Quotes in the Company Research window.
2. Enter the ticker symbol or name of the company you want.
3. Select a time period for your chart (daily for a month, weekly for a year, or monthly for three years), or specify your own parameters by clicking Custom).
4. If you want to include trading volume in the chart, or show a moving-average or how the stock compares to the Standard & Poor's 500, click Preferences and make your choices.
5. Click Graph to create and display the chart. To illustrate, I created a straight forward chart showing the closing prices of Microsoft Corp. over three years (see Figure 10.4).

If you'd rather see raw data than a chart, click Quotes instead of Graph. The information will include not only closing prices, but also the volume plus the high and low for each date.

Checking a Company's Financials

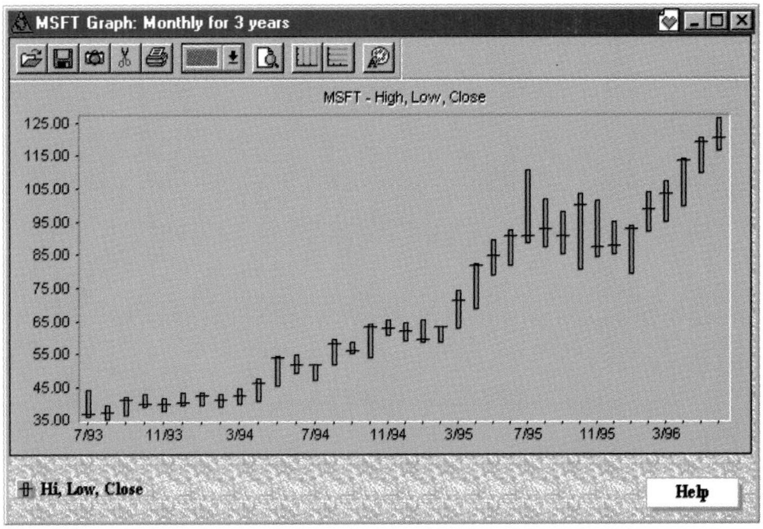

Figure 10.4 Sample stock chart

habits & strategies

Historical stock data generated in AOL can be used in other programs. You can save stock charts as images, while tables of quotes can be saved and later imported into spreadsheet programs and financial software such as Quicken.

There are several ways to look into the recent financial history of a public company. The easiest is as follows:

1. In the Company Research Window, click Financial Statements.
2. Click U.S. Financials, then enter the ticker symbol or name of the company and click Search.
3. Double-click the name of the company from the list of search results (there may be other companies with similar names).

This will provide you with annual income figures and balance sheets for the company, along with detailed information on liabilities and cash flow. If you just want basic revenue and earnings data, however, try doing this:

1. Click Stock Reports in the Company Research Window, then select Search the Stock Reports.
2. Enter the name of the company or its ticker symbol and click Search.
3. Double-click the name of the company to display the information. In addition to stuff on the stock, you'll find financial data, including earnings for the past four quarters—which can tell you a lot about how the company is doing. Here, for instance, is the quarterly data on General Motors:

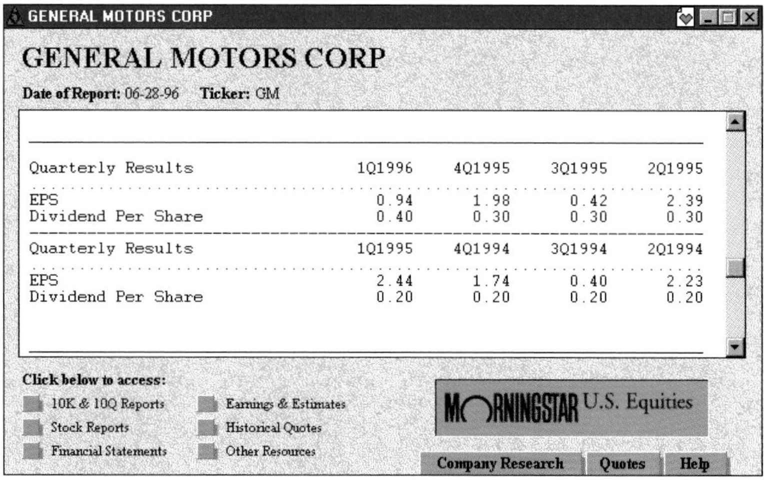

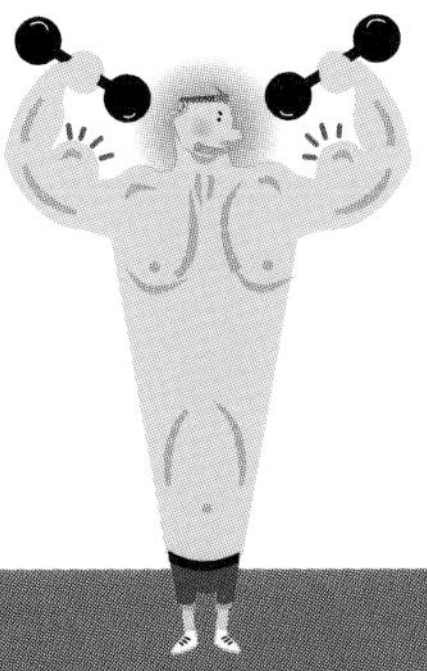

definition

EDGAR: *Stands for Electronic Data Gathering, Analysis, and Retrieval. It's operated by the Securities and Exchange Commission, which oversees U.S. corporations.*

Government Data Is Good, But. . .

AOL offers direct access to EDGAR, the federal government's electronic filing system for documents that public companies must release. These include 10Ks (annual reports) and 10Qs (quarterly earnings). To access EDGAR, click the button for 10K and 10Q reports in the Company Research window. But if you expect to find up-to-date information, forget it. EDGAR is typically several months behind, so the latest earnings report you're looking for may not be there.

How to Get Background Information

It often helps to know the history of a company, especially one that's gone through a reorganization or is currently in transition. For that the best place to go is Hoover's Company Profiles. These are smartly written capsule profiles of major corporations in many industries, complete with information about key officers and the company's products and competitive position. To access one of the profiles, use the following steps:

1. Double-click Company Profiles from the list of resources in the Company Research window.
2. Click Search Company Profiles and enter the name of the company or its ticker symbol. Then click Search.
3. Double-click the name of the company to display the profile, like the one shown here for Sun Microsystems:

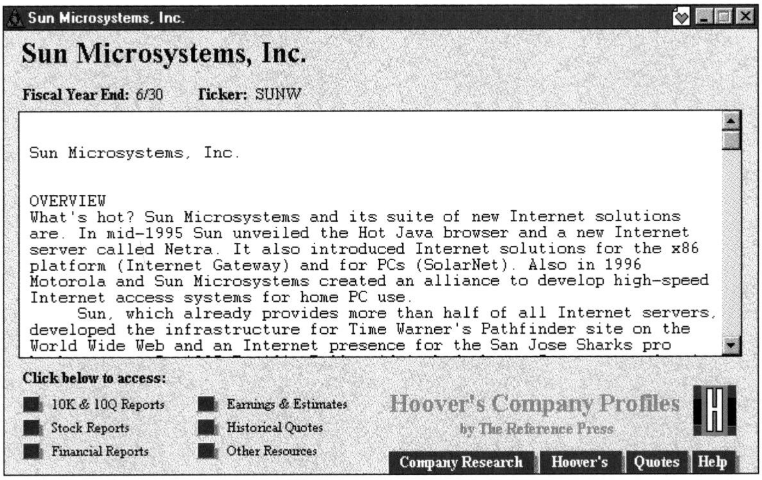

Great (and Not so Great) Expectations

Wall Street analysts make it their business to go out on a limb and predict per-share earnings for public companies. And with AOL, you're privy to such forecasts. To see the latest expectations for a public company, do this:

1. Click Earnings & Estimates in the Company Research Window.
2. Click Search Earnings & Estimates.
3. Type in the company's name or ticker symbol and click Search.
4. Double-click the name of the company to display the estimates from First Call, as in Figure 10.5, which shows quarterly estimates for Netscape Communications.

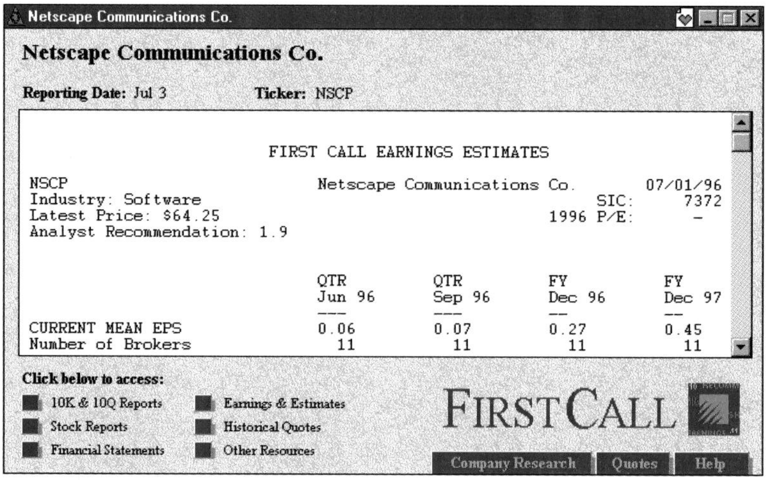

Figure10.5 Example Earnings & Estimates search

MUTUAL FUNDS

Americans are increasingly turning to mutual funds as a primary way to invest. And no wonder. Funds are less volatile and risky than stocks, so you can go to bed at night knowing you won't be wiped out in the morning. Many mutual fund companies now offer services on AOL. You can find out how individual funds are performing, and some

BRUSH UP ON FINANCIAL JARGON

If you're a new investor—or if you just want to broaden your knowledge— AOL has resources to give you a fundamental education on the ways of Wall Street. Two of the best places to go are the Wall Street Words dictionary, which you'll find among the resources in the Company Research window, and the PC Financial Network's Investment Lingo area, which you can reach with the keyword *Lingo*. Using either of these tools, you can easily find out what "return on equity" means (if you care).

providers even let account holders manage their own funds, buying and selling shares online. Reflecting the growing clout of mutual funds in the marketplace, AOL now has an entire area devoted to them. To access it, double-click the Mutual Fund Center folder in the Personal Finance channel window. You'll see the screen shown in Figure 10.6.

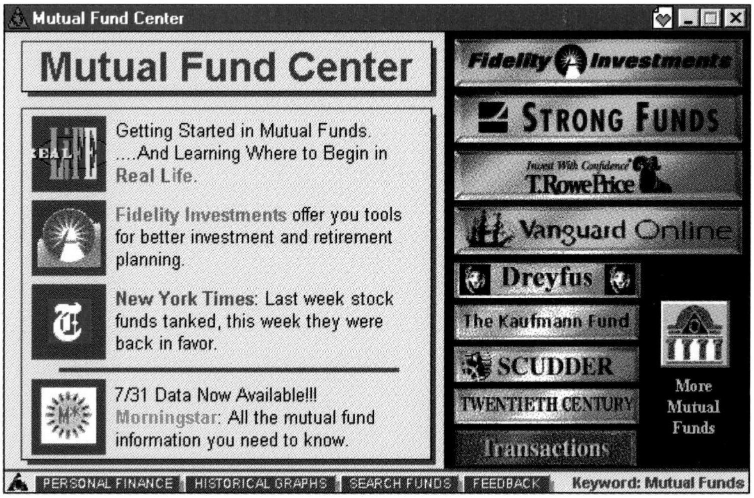

Figure 10.6 Mutual Fund Center window

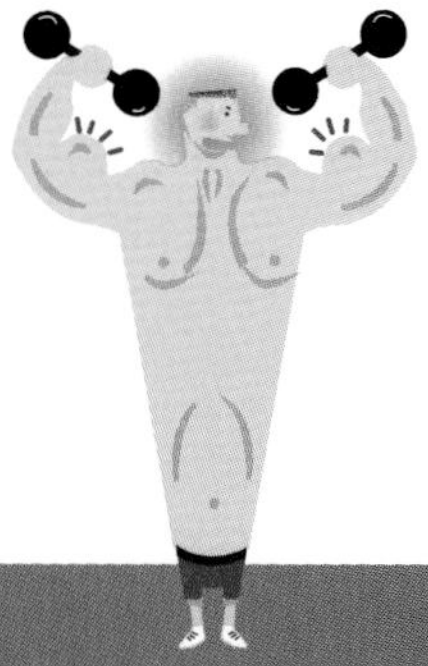

definition

Mutual fund: *A collection of stocks, bonds, or other securities managed by a professional investment firm. When you buy shares in a mutual fund, you're not pinning your hopes on a single security. Your gains and losses reflect the overall performance of the fund.*

Don't know much about mutual funds? Don't worry. In the Mutual Fund Center you'll find a plethora of information and advice about investing in them. For example, T. Rowe Price provides areas on Investment Fundamentals and Retirement Planning, and Vanguard offers something called Vanguard Online University. It includes three free courses: Fundamentals of Mutual Funds, Retirement Investing Seminar, and Advanced Fund Investing. Each course includes study materials (which you can download), a recommended reading list, and a final exam.

Rating the Mutual Funds

Although you can learn how different funds are performing from the providers themselves, it's not a bad idea to get an outside opinion on just how strong each fund is. For that you should use Morningstar, an independent company that tracks and evaluates some 6,800 mutual funds. Morningstar is generally considered the top company in its field and it happens to have a sizable area on AOL. To access it, double-click the Morningstar Stock & Fund Reports folder in the Personal Finance channel window (click List Alphabetically if you don't see it). Then click Mutual Funds to display the window shown in Figure 10.7.

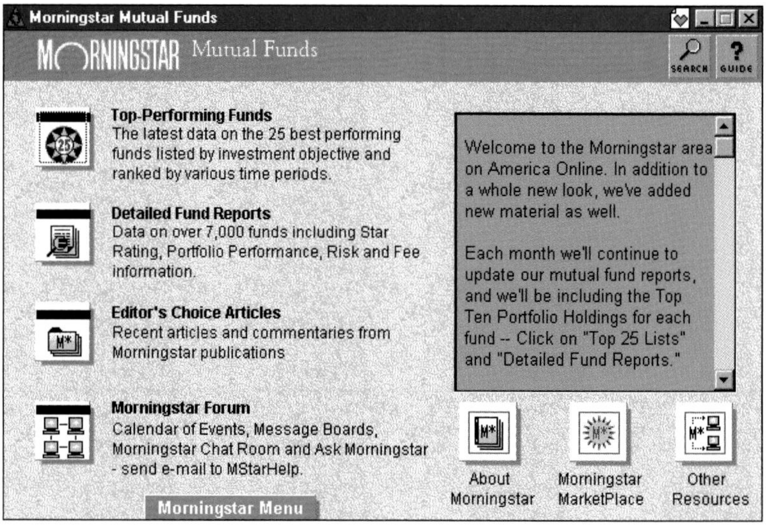

Figure 10.7 Morningstar Mutual Funds window

Okay, now do the following:

1. Click the Search button at the top-right side of the window.
2. Enter the name of the fund you want and click Search.
3. Double-click the name of the fund in the Search Results window to display the information on the fund, as in the example shown in Figure 10.8:

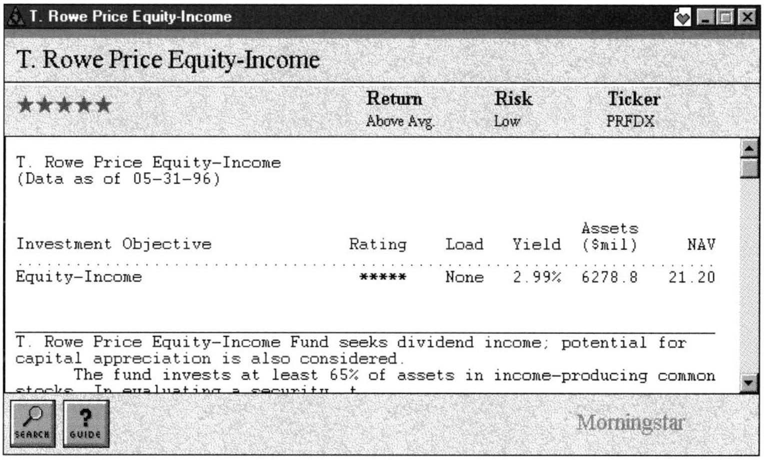

Figure 10.8 Example search results for a mutual fund

habits & strategies

To see how a mutual fund is doing on a daily basis, look it up the same way you would find a stock quote. Click the Stocks & Portfolios button on the toolbar, enter the ticker symbol for the fund, and click Get Quote. If you don't know the symbol, use Lookup or find it through Morningstar.

Hey, from the looks of things, my fund is a highly rated (five-star), better-than-average performer. Not too shabby.

FINANCE FORUMS

Wouldn't it be nice if there were somewhere you could go for friendly advice on how to manage your money? A place you could ask questions and get answers to questions about investing, taxes, and day-to-day finances. Well, there are such places, and you'll find them among the forums in AOL's Personal Finance channel (to access them, use the keyword *pf forum*). Following is a look at a couple of the best.

These Guys Are No Fools

One of the most interesting and entertaining areas anywhere on AOL is the Motley Fool forum. Started by two young brothers, Motley Fool is named for a line in Shakespeare's "As You Like it." Motley fools used humor to impart knowledge, and they could tell the king the truth without being punished. The philosophy of the latter-day Fool is that individual investors can do just as well as seasoned professionals. Motley Fool's message boards, where you can share investing strategies and observations with other members, are among the most active on AOL. Last time I looked, more than 300,000 messages had been posted on its message boards. (Wall Street takes these "Foolish" message boards seriously: they've even been credited with moving individual stocks higher and lower.) Here's a look at the Fool's main window, which can be reached in a number of ways, including using the keyword *fool*:

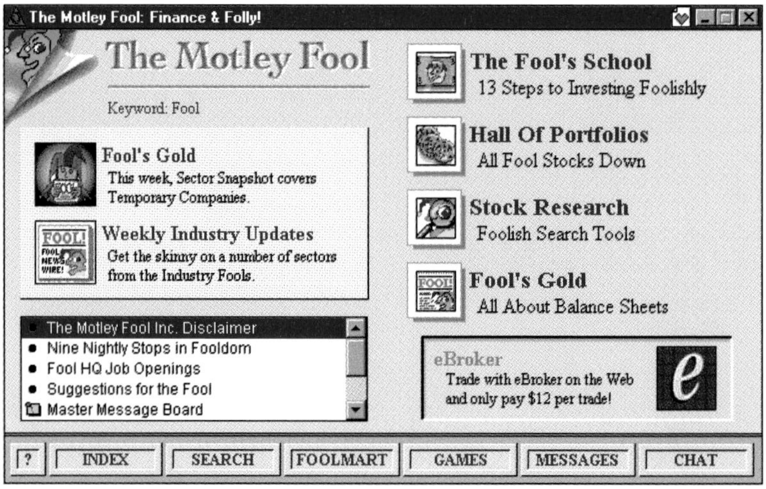

Getting Help with Your Taxes

Preparing your income taxes can be the most perplexing, frustrating experience in the world. The tax regulations are so complicated you'd think nobody could understand them—not even the government that wrote them. If you've had it up to here with forms and formulas,

Official tax forms are formatted in Adobe Acrobat, a technology that lets you make printouts that look exactly like the original. If you plan to download tax forms, you'll also need to download and install the Acrobat Reader software, which can be found along with the forms in the Tax Forum.

it's time to visit The Tax Forum. Here you'll find an impressive list of resources to help you through the income tax jungle, including

- The Ernst & Young Tax Guide
- Federal tax forms you can download and print out
- Tax shareware to help you calculate how much money you won't have when Uncle Sam is finished with you

And if you're really stumped, you can send questions to the Internal Revenue Service by e-mail. Just click the Ask the I.R.S. folder in the Tax Forum, click the Ask the I.R.S. button, and then double-click the category your question applies to. The following form will appear:

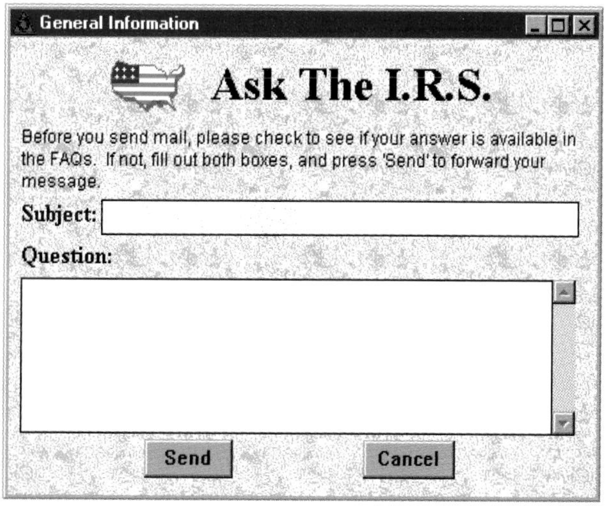

Fill it out and click Send to transmit it to the Tax Man. You'll receive a reply by e-mail.

BUSINESS ON THE INTERNET

The Internet may have begun as a tool of scholars and the government, but oh how it's changed. Today, the World Wide Web is primarily a business medium, featuring thousands of home pages for companies big and small. These sites provide consumer information about products and services, as well as news about employment opportunities. The question is, how can you find your way around this huge virtual business community? The answer is, use the resources on

AOL to guide you. In particular, take advantage of Hoover's Business on the Web area, which you can reach with these steps:

1. Double-click the Hoover's Company Profiles folder in the Personal Finance channel window. (You may have to click List Alphabetically to see it.)
2. Click Business on the Web to display the following window:

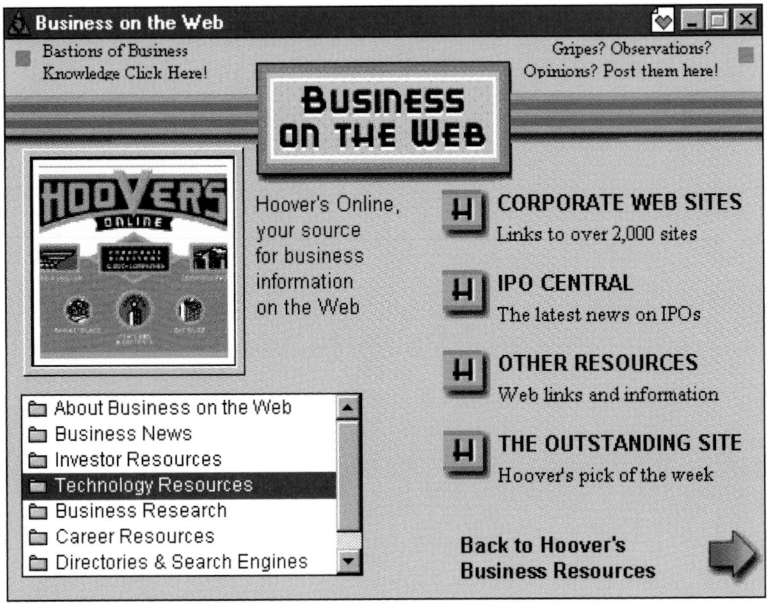

This is one of the most comprehensive online guides to business on the Internet I've seen. Especially useful is the list of more than 2,000 corporate Web sites, which are arranged alphabetically. Double-click any listing to automatically launch the AOL Web browser and go directly to the site.

OKAY, WHAT'S NEXT?

A little online knowledge, that's what. First, you'll get an introduction to the Reference Desk channel, with its high-tech, electronic encyclopedias, dictionaries, and other materials. Then I'll show you how to use AOL's educational resources to get help with homework, plan for college—even change careers. So hold onto your mouse.

PRIORITY!
MEMO:
FIRST CLASS
OVERNIGHT
RUSH!

CHAPTER

11

A World of Knowledge at Your Fingertips

INCLUDES

- Electronic encyclopedias
- Other reference works
- Online telephone books
- Internet resources
- Help with homework
- Finding a college

FAST FORWARD

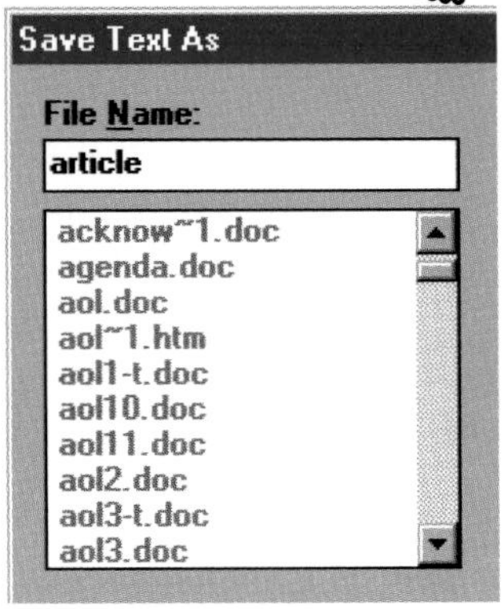

SAVE A REFERENCE ARTICLE ➤ *pp. 223–224*

In a public library you have to find a copy machine to save reference materials for use later. With AOL, you can print the article out by clicking the Print button on the toolbar or saving it to your hard disk. Most articles on AOL can be saved simply by choosing Save As from the File menu and following the same procedures you'd use to save any Windows document. The copy will be stored in a text format that you can use with any word processor.

IMPROVE YOUR WRITING ➤ *pp. 228–229*

The Reference Desk channel includes an area called Writer's Resources. Here you'll find tools to help you polish your prose, including an extensive thesaurus, an online book of quotations, and several grammar guides, including the *Elements of Style,* the classic that's been used in classrooms since 1918.

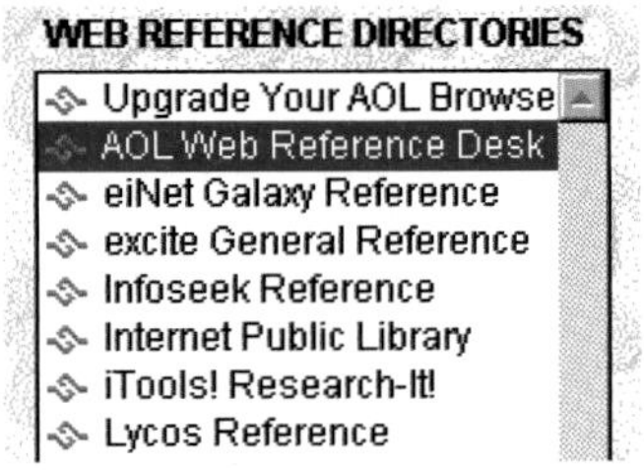

TAKE ADVANTAGE OF THE INTERNET ➤ *pp.230–231*

In addition to its own shelf of reference materials, AOL makes it easy to find all kinds of resources on the World Wide Web. Just click Internet Tools in the Reference Desk channel window for links to reference directories from major Internet search services such as Yahoo, Lycos, and Infoseek. AOL even has an Internet reference directory of its own called the AOL Web Reference Desk.

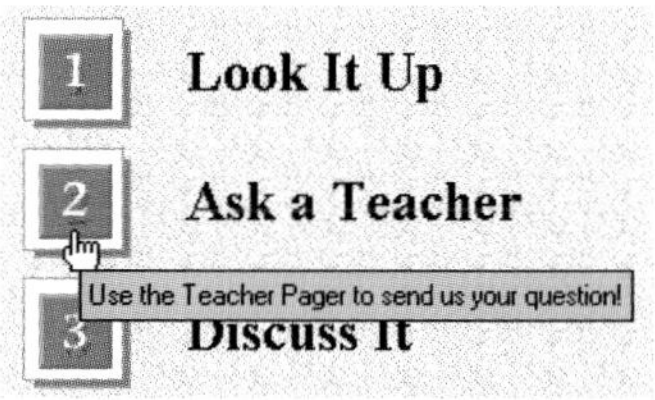

STUMPED BY HOMEWORK? ASK A TEACHER ➤ *pp. 231–235*

When all else fails, you can e-mail questions about schoolwork to AOL's army of volunteer teachers, and one of them will get back to you within a couple of days. Just do the following:

1. In the Learning & Culture channel window select Homework Help.
2. Choose Homework Help for Kids (ages twelve and under) or Homework Help for Teens.
3. Click Ask a Teacher and enter your question in the box.
4. Send the question by clicking the appropriate subject.

GET INFORMATION ON COLLEGES ➤ *pp. 235–236*

When it comes time to choose a college, a good place to start is the College Handbook, which contains information on tuition, admission requirements, and majors for more than 3,000 colleges and universities. To access the handbook, do the following:

1. Choose Student Center in the Learning & Culture channel window.
2. Click the button labeled Sr. High Center.
3. Double-click the College Board folder, then click College Handbook.

If knowledge is power, you're going to feel mighty powerful when you finish this chapter. First you'll explore the Reference Desk channel, where AOL keeps encyclopedias, dictionaries, and other reference materials. Then it's on to the Learning & Culture channel, the place to go for help with your child's schoolwork, or to plan for a career. As always, AOL enhances its own content with lots of links to sites on the World Wide Web. The bottom line is that this chapter is going to be an educational experience.

THE REFERENCE DESK

Until just a few years ago, if you wanted the kind of information available in the Reference Desk channel, you had to go to the public library. But AOL is better than the library. For one thing, it's open 24 hours a day, seven days a week. And you don't have to get in your car and drive to it. Best of all, you don't have to worry about overdue books.

Electronic Encyclopedias

The computer age has just about done away with printed encyclopedias. And no wonder. What's the point of buying two dozen heavy books when you can get the same information right on your PC. With AOL, in fact, you have a choice of three general-purpose encyclopedias—Compton's Living Encyclopedia, the Columbia Concise Encyclopedia, and the Grolier Multimedia Encyclopedia, which is shown here:

The best part about online encyclopedias is that the publishers continually update them, so you'll always have timely information. In contrast, printed encyclopedias and even those on CD-ROMs go out of date pretty quickly.

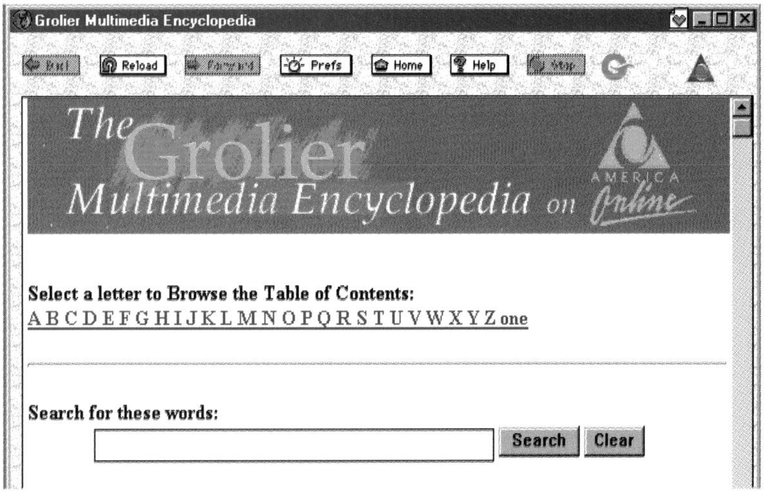

The Grolier encyclopedia may be the best of the lot. It contains over 31,000 articles, 5,000 pictures, and 400 maps. But what's really impressive is its interactive capability. It's formatted for the World Wide Web, so you can use hyperlinks in a text article to jump to another article on a related subject.

Searching Is a Snap

Searching a printed encyclopedia is a real chore. You have to look up your subject in a huge index, then find the article in another massive volume. With AOL, on the other hand, you can quickly search an encyclopedia—and many other sources in the Reference Desk channel—using the same basic techniques described in Chapter 8 for finding news stories. You can join words and phrases with "and," use "or" to expand your search, and use "not" to eliminate items you don't want.

Saving an Article

Here's another advantage the AOL Reference Desk has over a public library: When you want to copy something from an online encyclopedia or other reference work, you don't have to find a vacant copy machine and fish through your pockets for change. Just print out the article (click the Print button on the toolbar while the article is onscreen), or save it on your computer's hard disk. To save the contents of a text box on

habits & strategies

Don't limit your research to just the main reference works. Many magazines on AOL also can be searched, and some of them, such as Scientific American, can be excellent resources for students. You'll find a folder in the Reference Desk channel window featuring a partial list of searchable periodicals.

AOL, just choose Save As from the File menu and follow the same procedure you'd use to save any word processing document.

What About Stuff on the Internet? I'm glad you asked. You can save an article from a reference work on the World Wide Web using the Save As command, but it will be stored in Web format and won't look too good when you open it up in a word processor. Here's a better way:

SHORTCUT

Use the CTRL key in combination with other keys to manipulate text without taking your hands off the keyboard. While holding down CTRL, press C to copy a selection or A to copy an entire article. Then press CTRL-V to paste the text somewhere else.

1. With the article onscreen, use the mouse to select the text of the article, then choose Copy from the Edit menu.
2. Choose New from the File menu to display a blank text window like the one shown here:

3. Choose Paste from the Edit menu to insert the text in the window.
4. Choose Save As from the File menu and save the file. It will be saved in text format.

Copying to a Word Processor

If you like, you can copy text from any AOL or Web-based reference work directly into a document you've created with a word processor. Just copy the text as in step 1 above, then launch your word processing program and open the document in which you want to insert the material. Place the insertion point where you want the text to go and choose Paste from the word processor's Edit menu.

Other Basic Reference Works

Encyclopedias are just the start of AOL's online reference library. You'll also find all kinds of other guides and manuals in the Reference Desk channel. To view a list of them, click the List Alphabetically button in the channel window. To access an item on the list, double-click it. Let's take a look at some of the most interesting reference resources (in my humble opinion).

The New York Public Library Desk Reference

Drawing from the resources of one of the world's great libraries, this is sort of a combination encyclopedia-almanac (just the thing to help you brush up for a big game of Trivial Pursuit or Jeopardy). It's organized into more than two dozen categories and features downloadable illustrations, tables, maps, and lists. And of course you can search for specific topics. The best part about this online library, which is shown below, is that you don't have to go all the way to New York to use it.

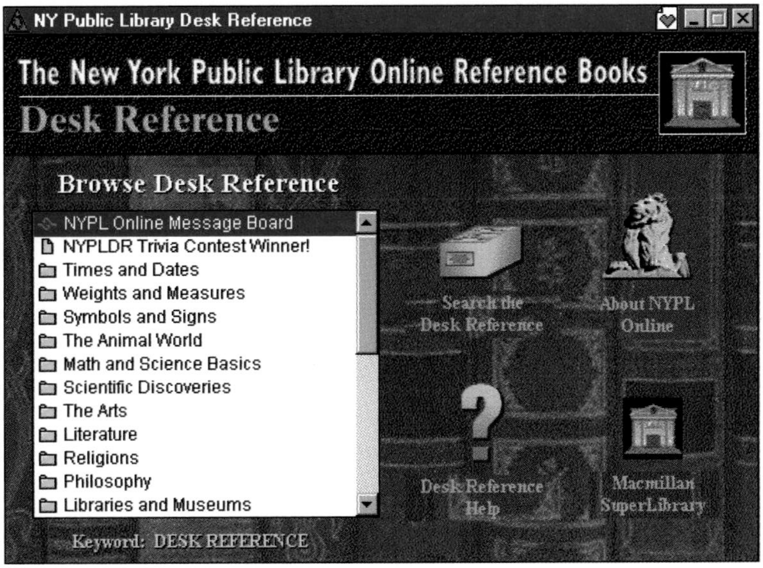

A Guide to Drugs (the Legal Kind)

Ever wonder about possible side effects of a prescription drug you're taking? Or whether it's a bad idea to take one drug along with another? You could ask the pharmacist at the local drug store, but there's a much quicker way—check out the *Consumer Reports Complete Drug Reference* online. You can search it to find info on over-the-counter as well as prescription drugs.

Free Online Medical Information

Got a medical question you've been itching to ask someone? Well, wait no longer. With Physician on Call, you can get answers from health-care professionals. This service, from Columbia/HCA Healthcare Corp., isn't designed to answer questions about emergencies or provide diagnoses. But it's great as an up-to-the-minute online medical guide. E-mail your question and within four days you get a reply from a health-care professional—at no charge! To access this free service, shown below, use the keyword *Columbia.net*, then click the Physician On Call button.

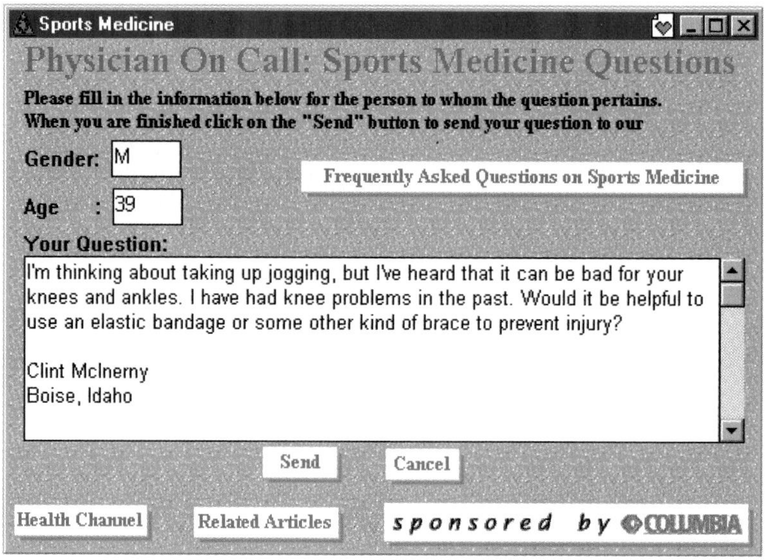

Who Needs a Lawyer?

The Nolo Self-Help Law Center even has an area set aside for lawyer jokes, such as this one: What's the difference between God and a lawyer? God doesn't think he's a lawyer.

At one time or another, almost everyone consults a lawyer. However, you may save yourself a fee by getting answers to some legal questions using online reference materials from Nolo Press, a leading publisher of self-help law books. Two of the guides are especially helpful—*Nolo's Little Law Book* and *Nolo's Pocket Guide to Family Law.*

The Political Process Explained

The American political process is one of the marvels of the modern world (some people marvel at how smoothly it works, while others marvel that it works at all). Anyway, if you have a question involving U.S. politics, check out the Student's Election Handbook, shown here:

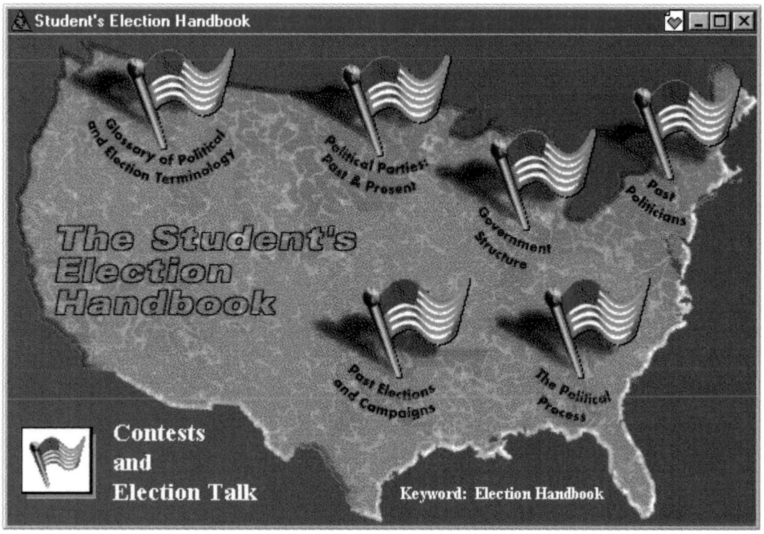

In addition to facts about past elections, you can avail yourself of all kinds of information about U.S. politics. It's almost like taking civics again, which is probably not a bad idea since most of us didn't pay attention in high school.

habits & strategies

Don't get rid of your printed dictionary. Unless you're already online, it's probably faster to look something up in a book than it is to sign on to AOL and find it in an online dictionary.

A Way with Words

As a writer, I always keep a dictionary handy. When I'm signed on to AOL, however, I don't ever reach for it because there's a great one in the Reference Desk channel. It's the *Merriam Webster Collegiate Dictionary,* which contains more than 160,000 entries. And its faster and more useful than my printed dictionary. Not only can you search for words, you also can find all entries in the dictionary that mention a particular word.

Other Online Dictionaries

In addition to the standard dictionary, AOL offers a medical dictionary, a dictionary just for kids, and a computer-and-Internet dictionary. There's also the *Dictionary of Cultural Literacy,* a storehouse of definitions covering everything from mythology and folklore to popular expressions. Do you know, for instance, where the phrase "the real McCoy" came from? According to the *Dictionary of Cultural Literacy,* it refers to a prizefighter named McCoy, who had so many imitators that no one was sure who the real one was. To access this treasure trove of popular wisdom, click List Alphabetically in the Reference Desk channel window, then double-click the dictionary in the list of resources. It will look like this:

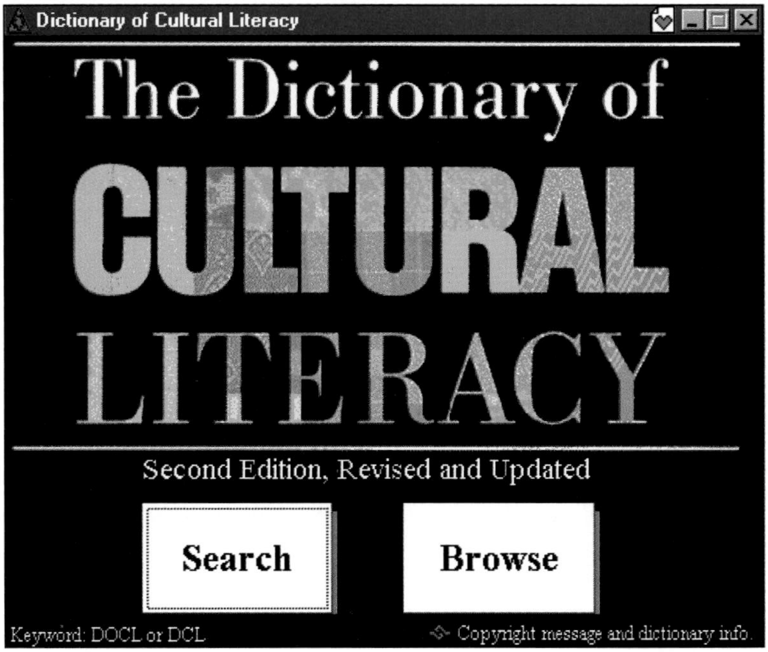

How to Write Well

Can't find just the right word to express yourself? Or maybe you're unclear about whether to use "who" or "whom." No problem. Just click the Writer's Resources button in the Reference Desk channel window for a choice of online reference guides for the grammatically challenged. These include:

- A thesaurus with more than 130,000 synonyms, antonyms, and related and contrasted words, as well as idioms. It's similar to but better than the thesaurus in most word processing programs.

- *Elements of Style*, the 1918 classic grammar manual by William Strunk that is still used today in high schools and colleges.
- An online book of quotations with a wide range of entries, including an entire section on the wit and wisdom of comedian Stephen Wright ("It doesn't matter what temperature the room is, it's always room temperature").

Find Somebody Fast

Need a phone number or an address? You could call directory assistance or thumb through an enormous telephone book filled with tiny type. Or you could take advantage of AOL's online directories, with which you can locate millions of people and businesses across the country (not that you'd want to). Click Phone & Addresses in the Reference Desk channel window to display the window shown below with all your options:

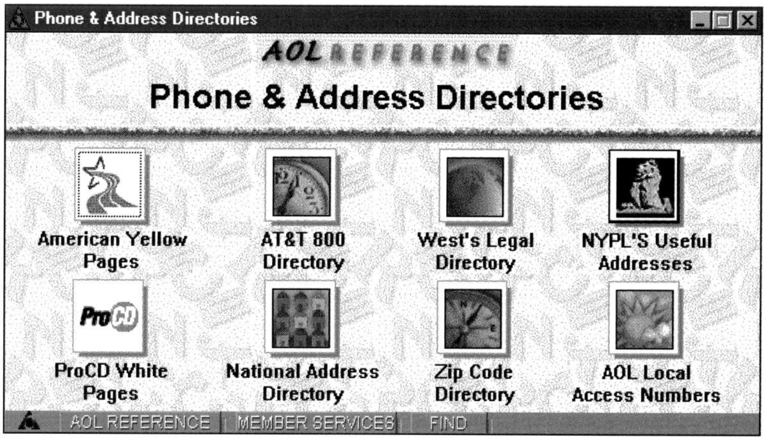

This Is One Big Telephone Book

If you need a telephone number, look no further than the ProCD White Pages. This online directory is like having a phone book in your computer. Actually, it's like having thousands of phone books, because it contains some 100 million residential phone numbers, as well as 15 million business numbers. The folks at ProCD say that if you stacked up the phone books necessary to hold all these numbers, the stack

habits & strategies

Using the phone directories on AOL can save you money. That's because most telephone companies now charge for directory assistance calls. In many cases, it's cheaper to sign on to AOL and quickly find a number online than it is to call an operator.

would be 42 stories high. The online phone directory has a couple of key advantages over regular phone books:

- You can search by full name, or just last name, and you can search a city or an entire state (would you believe there are 44 Einsteins in California?). This could come in handy if you're into geneology and want to track down long-lost relatives.
- In addition to a phone number, in many cases you also get an address complete with ZIP code—something you don't find in most phone books.

The Mother of All Reference Libraries

Besides its own resources, AOL offers direct access to the enormous reference resources of the World Wide Web. For example, you can search through the plays of Shakespeare at a Web site at the University of Sydney in Australia. Or find a passage in the King James version of the Bible using a site at the University of Virginia. There's even a terrific site at the University of Wisconsin, shown here, that holds the lyrics to thousands of popular songs:

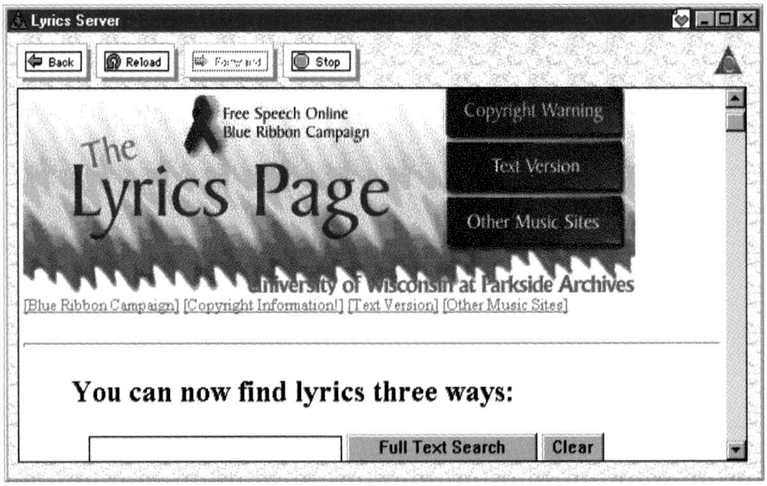

You'll find the Web sites mentioned above and many others among the resources in the Reference Desk channel window. Click List Alphabetically to view a list of them.

Search the Web for Reference Materials

To really "drill down" into the reference resources available on the Web, you should use the reference directories of the major Internet search services, such as Yahoo. AOL has made this easy to do by collecting a number of links to major directories. They're listed in the Internet Tools window, shown below, which you can display by clicking Internet Tools in the Reference Desk channel window.

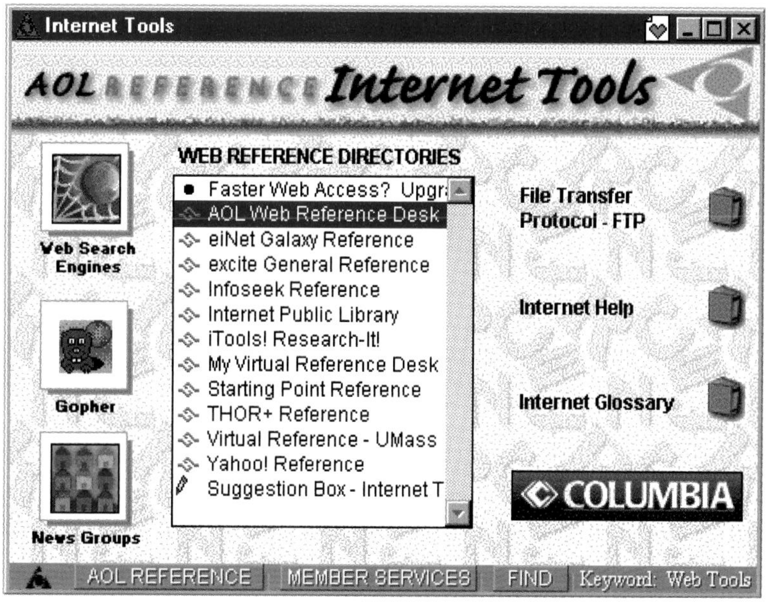

You'll notice that AOL itself has a directory called the AOL Web Reference Desk. This is a Web page that includes links to a wide range of materials covering everything from religion to government.

YOUR ONLINE EDUCATION CENTER

If you're like most busy parents, sometimes you don't have either the time or the energy to sit down with your child in the evening and pore over homework. Especially when it comes to subjects like math, where you might not be much help even if you tried. Don't despair, however. Nobody's going to flunk as long as AOL is around. There are several ways to utilize AOL as a school-away-from-school. You can

- Obtain real-time assistance in chat rooms dedicated to particular subjects, such as math and English.
- Use academic message boards to get advice from other members.
- Send questions by e-mail and get answers from professional teachers.

By the way, all this stuff is free, which is really amazing when you consider the cost of private schooling these days.

To get academic assistance online, click Homework Help in the Learning & Culture channel. You can then choose Homework Help for Kids, which is for elementary and middle school children, or Homework Help for Teens, for high school and college students. (You'll also see a button for the Academic Assistance Center—which coordinates the online educational activities.)

Open for Discussion

Once you've clicked into one of the Homework Help areas, choose Discuss It from the main menu to display a screen like the one shown here:

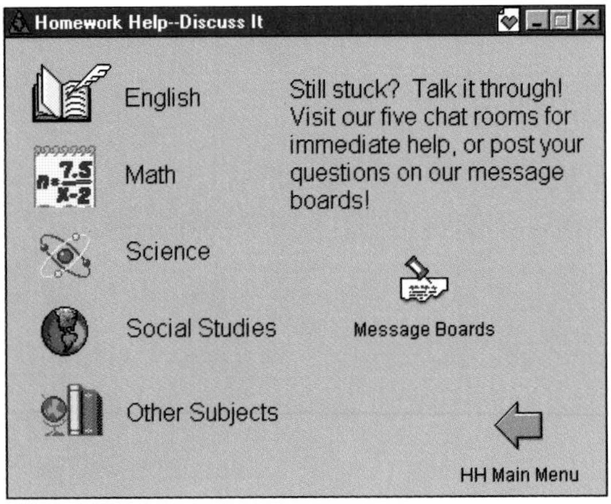

As you can see, there are five chat rooms—four dedicated to subject areas, and a fifth room on Other Subjects, which is also the main tutoring

The subject chat rooms are open in the afternoon and at night. The main tutoring room is open all the time, although there may not be a teacher there in the early morning hours.

room. The rooms are staffed by volunteer teachers, and other members also participate. It's like being in a regular classroom, only you can sip a Coke while you work. The teachers are there to help students understand problems, but not to actually do homework for them.

Using Message Boards

In the preceding illustration, you'll notice there's an option that takes you to message boards. Going this route, you can post questions and field responses from other members (and teachers). It's not as immediate as chat rooms, but the answers you get can be more thorough. The message boards for kids are divided into general subjects, while the boards for teens cover a wide range of topics, as you can see here:

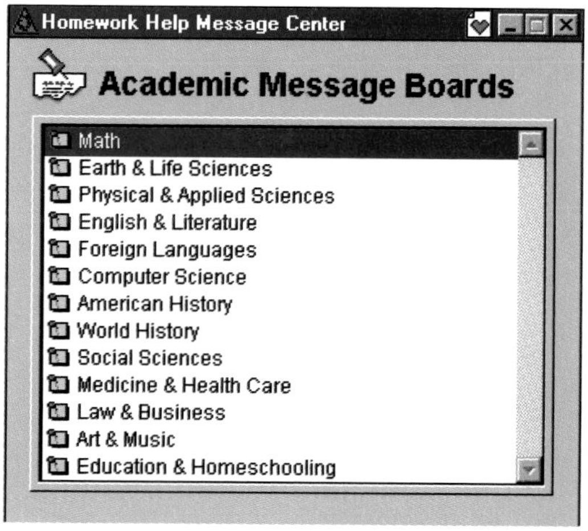

habits & strategies

The Academic Assistance Center receives more than 3,000 Teacher Pager queries every day. With that kind of volume, they ask that you use the Pager only in cases where you can't find the information elsewhere. So scour the resources in the Reference Desk channel before using this option.

Paging a Teacher

If you don't need an answer right away, you can e-mail your question to AOL's Academic Assistance Center. It will be given to a volunteer teacher in the proper field, who will give you an answer by e-mail, usually within 48 hours.

Check Out the Knowledge Database

The Academic Assistance Center has taken answers to Teacher Pager questions and made them available in a Knowledge Database. This is a good place to check before using other options, such as Teacher Pager.

If your question is a common one, it may already have been answered. The database is fully searchable. To access it, do the following:

1. Click Student Center in the Learning & Culture channel window.
2. Double-click the Academic Assistance Center folder.
3. Click Assistance by Subject.
4. Click Knowledge Database. This displays the following dialog box:

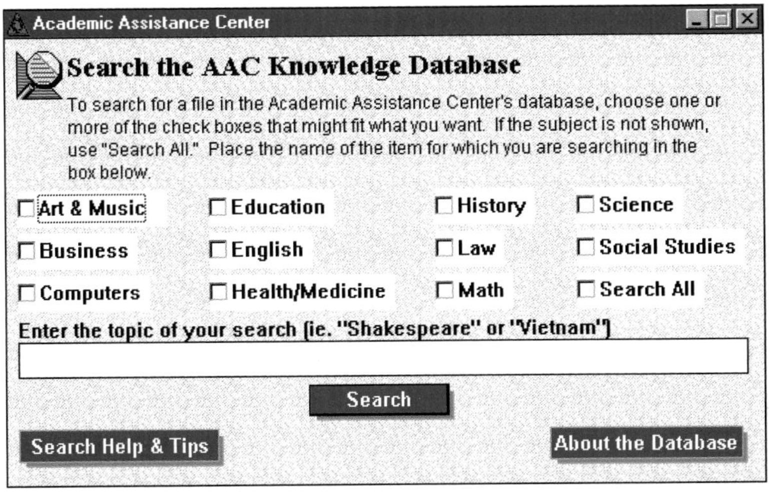

FOR YOUNG CHILDREN, THERE'S KIDS ONLY

If you have preteenage children, consider using the Kids Only channel. There you'll find the same Homework Help for Kids that's available in the Learning & Culture channel. You'll also find other learning areas, leisure time activities, and games for the younger set. And the circus is always in town with Ringling Online. If Kids Only seems to be enough, you can close off the rest of AOL to your child. Just choose Parental Control from the Members menu, then click Block All But Kids Only.

How to Get Personalized Tutoring

Suppose your child is really struggling in algebra. Maybe it's time for some one-on-one help. To sign up for online tutoring, do the following:

1. Click Homework Help in the Learning & Culture channel window.
2. Choose the Academic Assistance Center.
3. Click Tutoring Center.
4. Select the message board folder on the right labeled Sign Up for Tutoring.
5. Choose a subject and post a message requesting dates and times that are best for you. A teacher will get back to you by e-mail with instructions on where and when to meet online.

PLANNING FOR THE FUTURE

What's the best college for you? How much does it cost to go? How and when should you apply? AOL can help you with these and other questions as you embark on the road to higher education. A good place to start is the area for the College Board. To get there, use these steps:

1. Click Student Center in the Learning & Culture channel window, then click the button labeled Sr. High Center to view a list of resources.
2. Double-click College Board to display the window shown here:

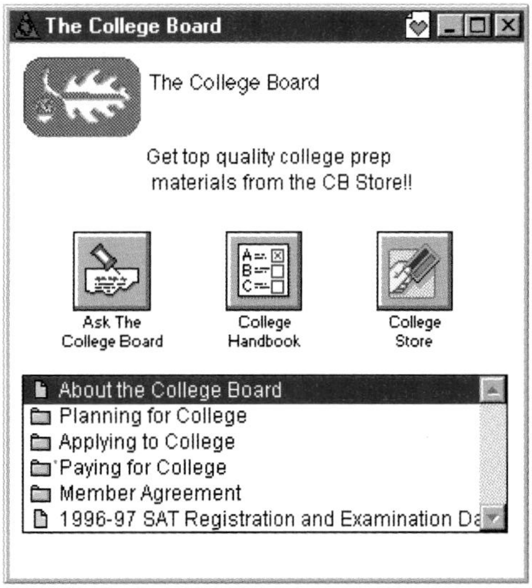

habits & strategies

Need financial help with college? The Senior High Center includes several good sources of information about scholarships, grants, fellowships, and other kinds of funding. Double-click the Financial Aid/Grant Info folder for news about current programs, as well as a library of financial aid directories and booklets.

From here you can access the College Handbook, which contains descriptions of more than 3,200 colleges and universities. For each school you can learn about majors that are offered, admission information, athletics, and student activities. For instance, if you look up "Harvard," you'll discover that in 1996 annual tuition and fees came to $20,444; estimated expenses including books, supplies, and personal expenditures, excluding transportation, were $1,975; and room and board was $6,710. Whoa!

Career Guidance

Looking for a career change? Or perhaps a move to sunnier climate? Why not check out the electronic Help Wanted ads on AOL to get a feel for what kind of opportunities are out there. There are actually two databases of classified ads for employment—Help Wanted-USA and E-Span. Help Wanted-USA is the bigger one, publishing more than 10,000 ads each week for jobs all over the country—and even overseas! You can search both databases using keywords, including job type and location, or by using job codes. In a test search using Help Wanted-USA, I found 312 job listings for software engineers in California. (I think I'm in the wrong profession.) Anyway, to access the Help Wanted ads:

1. Click Careers in the Learning & Culture window.
2. Click the Job Listings button.
3. Click Career Center's Help Wanted ads to display the following window:

WHAT'S NEXT?

After all this research and studying, I think it's time for a break, don't you? Good, because in the following chapter, you're going to learn how to use AOL to plan your next vacation or weekend getaway. I'll also show you how to shop till you drop online. Just make sure to have your credit card handy.

CHAPTER 12

Travel and Shopping—The Really Fun Stuff

INCLUDES

- Making airline reservations
- Using online travel guides
- Perusing restaurant reviews
- Touring digital cities
- Exploring the International channel
- Shopping

FAST FORWARD

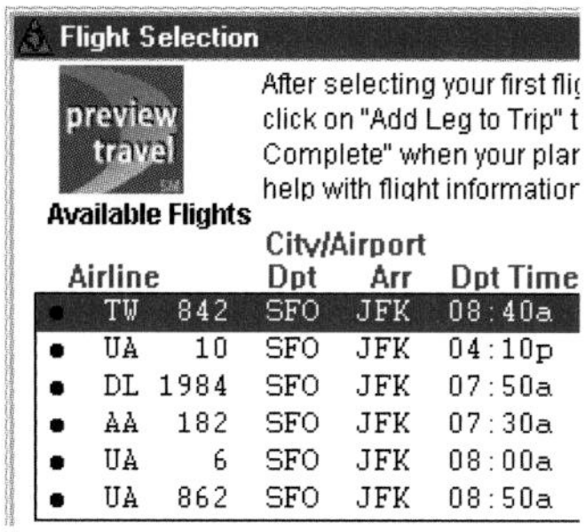

BOOK YOUR FLIGHT ➤ *pp. 242–244*

You can use AOL to reserve and purchase your own airline tickets. It's easy! Just follow these steps:

1. Click Preview Travel in the Travel channel window, then click Click Here for Reservations.
2. Fill out the registration information and indicate your travel preferences.
3. After you save your Travel Profile, click Begin Trip Planning and proceed to find flights that go where you want to go, when you want to go.
4. When you've completed your round-trip itinerary, click Accept and enter your credit card information.
5. Click Purchase Ticket.

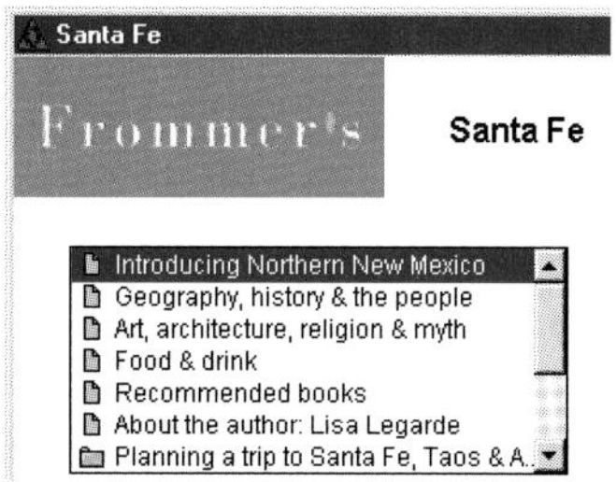

USE AOL'S ONLINE TRAVEL GUIDES ➤ *pp. 245–249*

Looking for information about hotels, restaurants, or sightseeing in a popular vacation spot? To check out some of the best travel guides available, double-click American Express Travel Center in the Travel channel window. You can peruse each guide individually or use the Search All Sources button to search them all.

TOUR A DIGITAL CITY ➤ *pp. 249–251*

These days you don't have to live in a city to know what's going on there. With its new Digital City channel, AOL is turning major metropolitan areas into virtual online communities, for which you can find the latest local news and information on weather, sports, and cultural activities. You can also use localized classified ads to find a job or buy or sell houses, cars, and other merchandise. Just go to the Digital City channel and click a geographic region to find cities that have been digitized.

READ AN ENGLISH NEWSPAPER ➤ *pp. 251–252*

No, not a newspaper in English, one from England!

1. Click World of AOL in the International channel window.
2. Click U.K. and then click Today's News.
3. Choose any of the available newspapers, including the *Daily Mirror* and the *Independent*.

BUY SOMETHING ONLINE ➤ *pp. 252–255*

Feel like shopping? Then head to AOL's Marketplace for some new clothes, perhaps, or maybe some nice chocolates. Here's how to make a purchase online:

1. Browse through the Marketplace channel using either the category folders or an alphabetical list of vendors.
2. If you find something you want to buy, select Click Here to Order and fill in the ordering information for the item, which will then be placed in an electronic Shopping Cart.
3. Click Checkout and enter your credit card information.
4. Click Complete This Order to finish the online purchase.

What do busy people do when they aren't busy working? They're busy having fun, that's what. And since you've worked so hard while reading this book, it's time to do just that. In this final chapter, you'll learn how the Travel, Digital City, and International channels can help you plan for your next vacation (or even make a business trip more enjoyable). Then you'll finish up in the Marketplace, an extensive and secure online shopping area in which you can buy anything from a teddy bear to a computer modem.

DO-IT-YOURSELF TRAVEL RESERVATIONS

Preview Travel handles reservations for more than 700 airlines worldwide. AOL users pay no extra charges to reserve flights online. Preview Travel also plans to offer hotel and car reservations sometime in late 1996.

Before you can go anywhere exotic, you have to make airplane reservations. First you have to call a travel agent and go through a laundry list of questions about when and where you want to fly. And then you have to wait while the agent tries to find the best price for you. But guess what—the agent is using a computer to look through a database of available flights. And you can do the same thing yourself, using America Online's Preview Travel feature. In other words, you can be your own travel agent.

Setting Up a Personal Travel Profile

To use Preview Travel, click Preview Travel in the Travel Channel window. Then click Click Here for Reservations to enter the online reservation system. If this is your first visit to the area, you'll be asked to agree to Preview Travel's terms of service. After reading the terms, click Accept Terms to continue. You'll then be asked to provide registration information and travel preferences, including

- Your mailing address
- The airlines on which you prefer to fly

- The class of service you want—coach, business class, or first class
- Your seat preference—aisle, window, and so forth
- Any special meal requests—kosher or low-cholesterol, for instance

Building a List of Available Flights

After completing this personal Travel Profile, click Begin Trip Planning. You'll be led through a series of questions to find flights and book your reservations. You'll be asked for the number of passengers in your traveling party, your destination, and the date and time you want to depart. Then, in just a few seconds, you'll see a list of available flights, as in this example for a trip from San Francisco to Seattle:

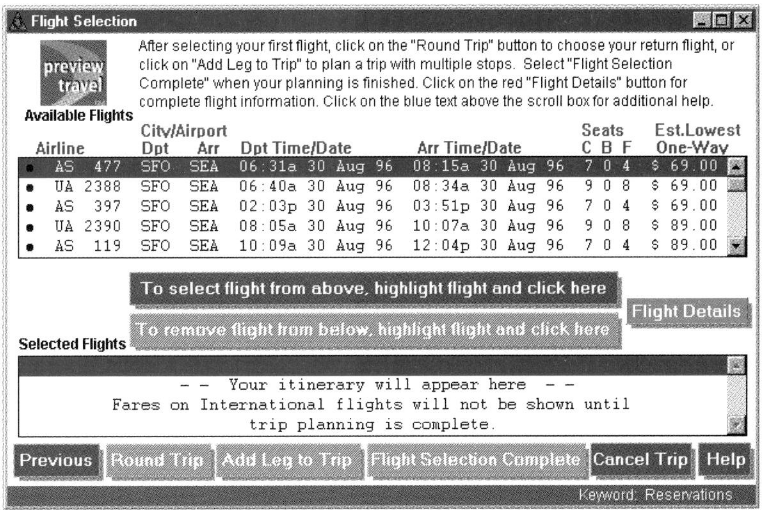

CAUTION

There's often a huge difference between restricted and unrestricted airfares. Be sure to familiarize yourself with any restrictions before booking a low-cost flight. You can do so by clicking View Fare Rules in the Fare Display window.

Select the flight you want, then click Round Trip and repeat the flight selection process for your return trip. After you click the Flight Selection Complete button, you'll see a Fare Display window containing the lowest available fare for the flights you've chosen, as well as the lowest unrestricted fare. Make your choice, and the next window will display your complete itinerary, as well as the total airfare. Here's what the round-trip itinerary for the trip from San Francisco to Seattle looks like for one person:

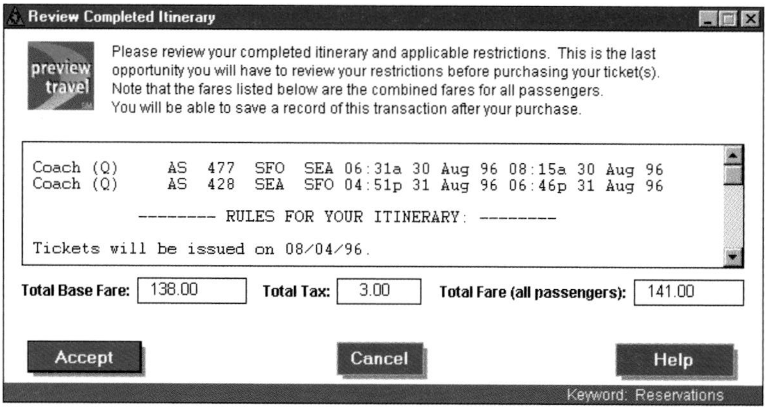

Buying Your Ticket

Okay, now you're at the point where you have to fish or cut bait—in other words, it's time to purchase the tickets. (You can't just reserve flights on Preview Travel and pay for them later.) If you decide to book the flight, click Accept and enter your credit card information. Then click Purchase Ticket. Your flight will be automatically booked, and the tickets will be sent to you at no extra charge by second-day air service.

You can also use the ExpressNet Travel feature from American Express to reserve airline tickets, hotel rooms, and rental cars on AOL. But there's a catch—you must have an American Express card.

Changing Your Mind

You can change or cancel a reservation at any step of the process until you actually buy the ticket. But once you've made the purchase, the only way to make a change is to call the airline directly.

Don't Forget the Rental Car

You can fly to another city, but you're probably going to need a car once you get there. And renting a car can be an even bigger pain than making an airline reservation. Fortunately, Avis has a World Wide Web site linked directly to AOL. You can access a rental location anywhere in the world and book a reservation by e-mail in a matter of minutes. To use the Avis online system, click Preview Travel in the Travel channel window and then click the Avis Galaxy button to display the following window:

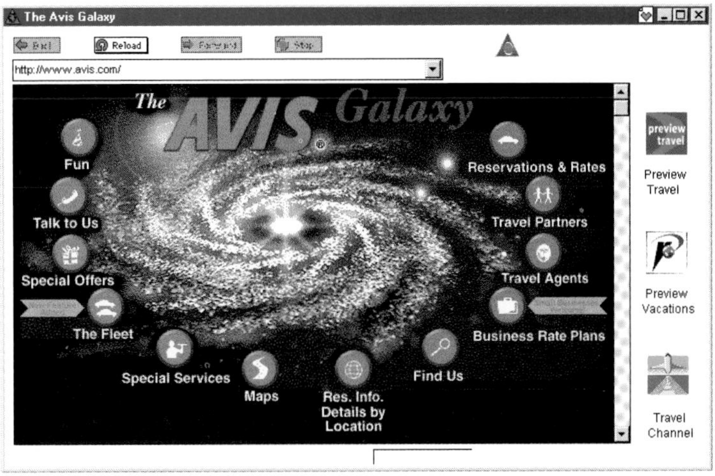

ONLINE TRAVEL GUIDES

Suppose you're going to Tokyo on a business trip and need to find a hotel. Or maybe it's time for a vacation, and you want to line up some good restaurants and sight-seeing in Santa Fe. Well, forget brochures and guidebooks; AOL has some of the best travel resources available anywhere. There are online versions of the top travel guides, including Frommer's City Guides, Fodor's Worldview, and the Zagat restaurant and hotel surveys. To reach these, double-click the American Express Travel Center folder in the Travel channel window. You'll see the Travel Info & Reservations window, shown here:

habits & strategies

AOL has members who have been just about everywhere. So check out the Message Boards in the Travel forum, which you'll find in the Travel channel window. You'll find discussions on every possible destination, from Alaska to Zanzibar.

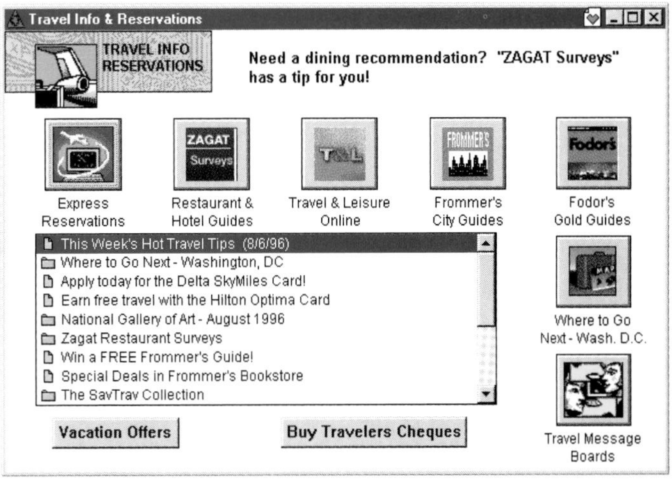

You can peruse each of the travel guides individually, just as you might browse through printed publications. Suppose, for instance, that you're planning a trip to New Mexico. To see what the city of Sante Fe has to offer, do this:

1. In the Travel Info & Reservations window, click Frommer's City Guide. You'll see a window with buttons for different world regions.
2. Double-click the Santa Fe folder to display the following window:

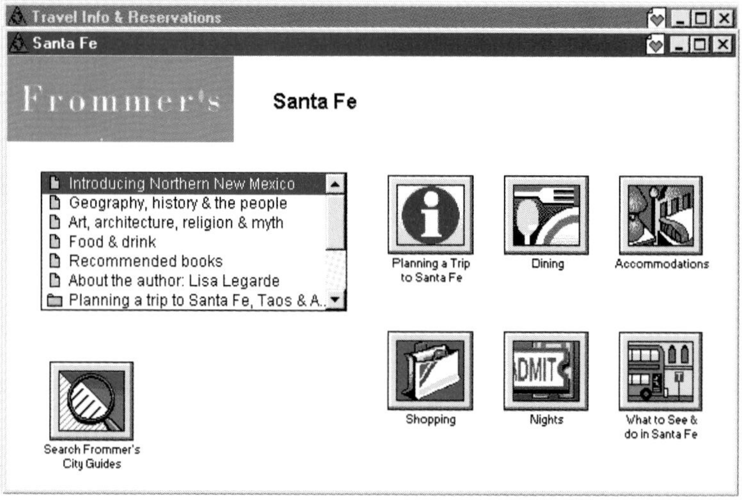

Create Your Own Trip Planner

If you're traveling to major cities, either in the United States or abroad, you can create your own travel guide by using Fodor's Gold Guides' Personal Trip Planner. A series of checklists lets you indicate your destination and exactly what you want in the way of hotels, restaurants, and other travel information. When you're finished, your choices are used to generate a personalized guide that you can print out for easy reading or to take with you on your trip. To use this handy feature, click Fodor's Gold Guides in the Travel Info & Reservations window, and then click Personal Trip Planner to get started.

Where Shall We Eat Tonight?

The restaurant guides on AOL aren't just for folks who travel. They're also great for finding good places to eat right in your own area. Let's say you live in New York City and you want to find the place that makes the best hamburgers. Here's what you do:

1. In the ExpressNet Travel window, click Zagat Surveys.
2. Select the button for restaurant surveys.
3. Double-click the New York City folder.
4. Double-click By Cuisine.
5. Double-click Hamburgers for a list of the hamburger restaurants listed as New York's best by the diners surveyed by Zagat. And here it is:

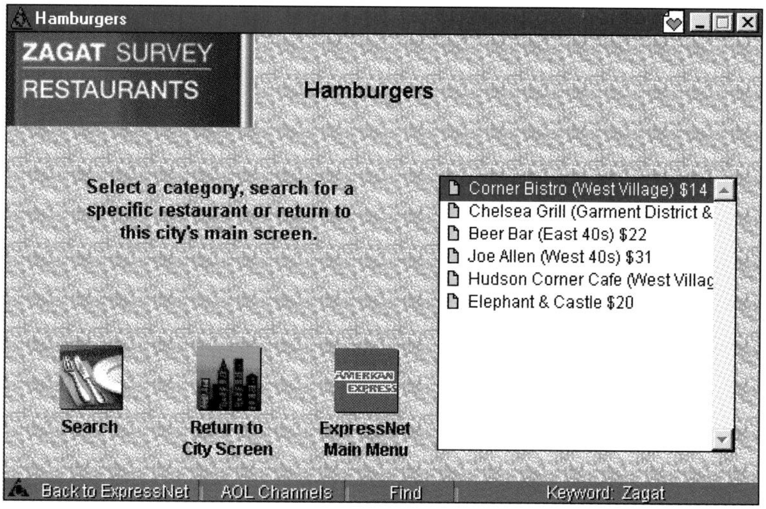

It's a Zoo Out There

When you're traveling on business, life can consist mainly of hotels and restaurants. But when you're on vacation, you want to take advantage of the other things an area has to offer. A good way to explore the possibilities is with Travel America Online, which you can access by double-clicking the TAO: Travel America Online folder in the Travel channel window. This is a collection of forums that present information from official state travel and tourism agencies, convention and visitors bureaus, and local attractions. You can scope out what's happening in a dozen states and 20 cities, including New Orleans, which, as you can see, is pretty proud of its Audubon Zoo:

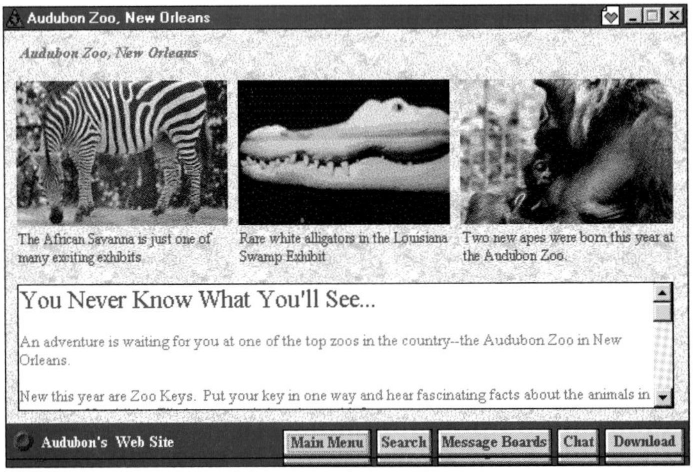

Travel Information on the Internet

Considering the global nature of the World Wide Web, it's not surprising that it has become an enormous network for travel resources. AOL provides links to many of them—just double-click the AOL Travel Web Sites folder in the Travel channel window. One of the most comprehensive sites is the Travel Channel Online Network, shown here:

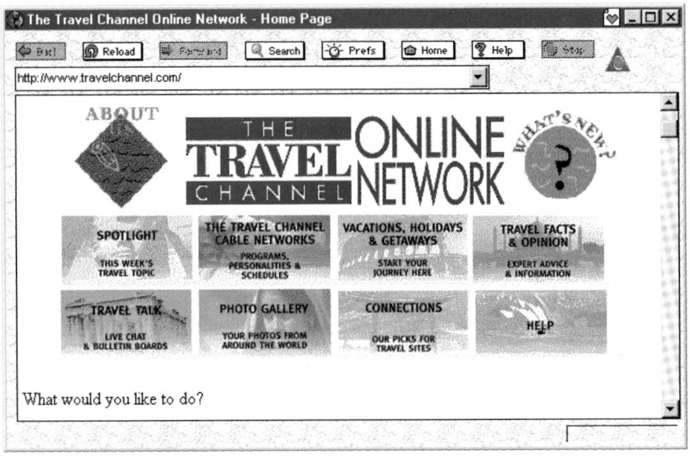

The site includes a searchable database of 26,000 Web pages of travel information. If you can't find a vacation here, you might as well just stay home.

LOOKING FOR A BED-AND-BREAKFAST?

Over the past few years, an increasing number of travelers have sought out the intimate atmosphere of bed-and-breakfast inns rather than cooping themselves up in big hotels. And in some remote areas, B&B's are the only places to stay. The problem has been how to find them, but AOL has the answer—an online guide to over 14,000 inns around the world—including five in Skagway, Alaska. Check it out by double-clicking the Bed & Breakfast Guides by Lanier folder in the Travel channel window.

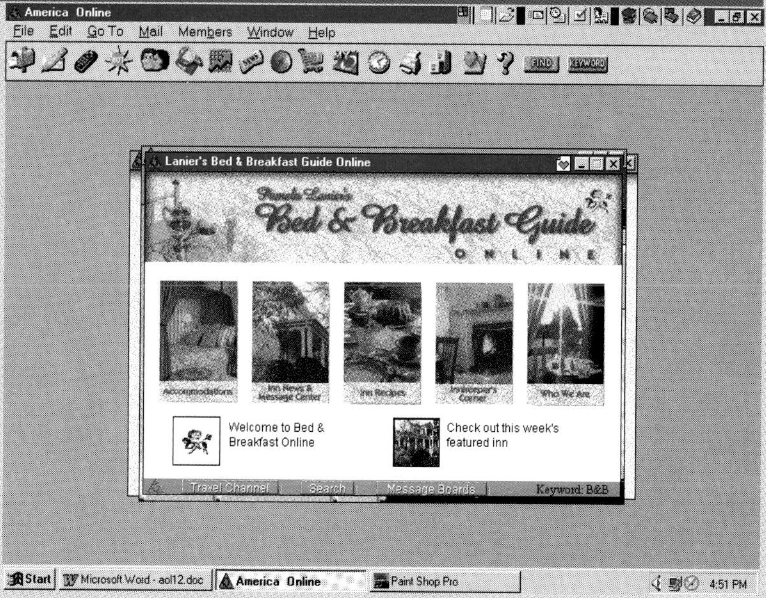

DIGITAL CITIES

Let's say you grew up in San Francisco but you now live in Boston. Wouldn't it be great to be able to click your mouse and be transported—in spirit, at least—back to the City by the Bay? Or perhaps you've been offered a job in Washington, D.C. Wouldn't it be terrific if you could look for a new home before you even got there? Welcome to Digital City, an ambitious new AOL project that creates online virtual communities. As of this writing, digital cities have been created for San Francisco, Boston, and Washington, with 20 more U.S. metropolitan areas either under construction or planned for the near future. Here's the Digital City window for Washington, D.C.:

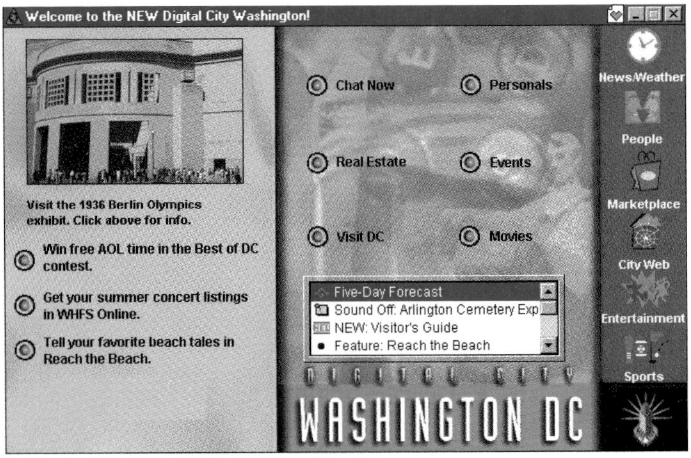

SHORTCUT

To view a list of digital cities, click the Find button on the AOL toolbar, type **Digital City** *in the search box, and click Search.*

It's Just Like Being There

Each digital city features breaking news, weather reports, and local sports news. There's also a calendar of events, restaurant information, an interactive classified advertising section in which you can find a job or buy or sell a home or a car, and a chat room in which you can trade banter about the local culture. You can even find out how bad the traffic is, as in the illustration shown here. Then you'll remember why you left the city in the first place. (Actually, this feature can be a real help if you live in the area.)

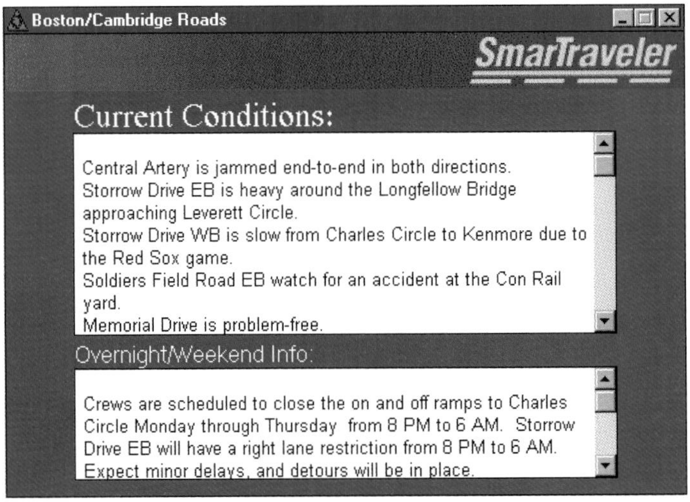

If Your City Isn't Here, Try the Web

Hundreds of cities across the country are now offering tourist information over the Internet. AOL provides links to many municipal Web sites in addition to its own Digital City areas. To access information about a specific city, follow these steps:

1. Click the button labeled Search a City in the main Digital City window.
2. Enter the name of the city you're interested in and click Search Digital City.
3. Double-click the name of the city. If your selection is a digital city, you'll see the AOL Digital City window for that city. If your selection isn't a digital city, you'll be connected to that city's Web site.

THE INTERNATIONAL CONNECTION

AOL Digital cities also are springing up on foreign shores—the United Kingdom cities of London, Edinburgh, and Glasgow are already represented. In addition to these international digital cities, AOL offers considerable coverage of the world through the International channel. In this channel you'll find news and information about nations you didn't even know existed. And places such as the United Kingdom, Germany, France, Canada, and Japan have their own areas, which you can access by clicking World of AOL in the International channel window. Figure 12.1 shows the window for AOL U.K., which looks like a variation of the main Channels window.

This Proves It's a Small World

Gazing at this window almost makes you feel as if you're sitting at a personal computer on a foggy evening in London. You can check out the latest rugby scores, read the headlines in the *Daily Mirror* ("Killer's 28-Year Reign of Terror"), or get updates from the London Stock Exchange.

habits & strategies

Want to read French news in French, or German news in German? No problem. Just go to the AOL U.K. window, click Today's News, and then double-click News in French or News in German.

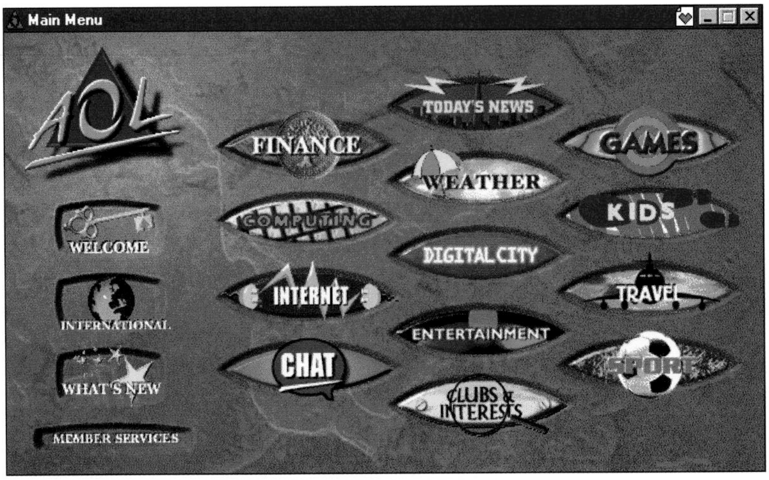

Figure 12.1 AOL U.K. window

ONLINE SHOPPING

If there's one thing people like as much as traveling, it's shopping—which brings us to the Marketplace, our final destination. (I saved this for last because if we'd done it first, you would have already spent all your money and lost interest in the rest of the book.) Seriously, though, in the Marketplace AOL offers a huge virtual shopping mall that's open 24 hours a day, every day.

Some people don't like to shop on the Internet because of the possibility that their credit card number will be stolen. But AOL is a closed computer system, so your financial information is just between you and the companies you deal with.

Where to Find Stuff: Everywhere

You've probably noticed that no matter where you go in AOL, somebody's trying to sell you something . For instance, when you check out the latest compact discs in the MusicSpace channel, you're given the tempting opportunity to buy them, as in the example shown in Figure 12.2.

If you'd rather do all your shopping in one area, however, you can find everything just by visiting the Marketplace. In this channel, merchandise and services are organized into categories, although you also have the option of viewing an alphabetical list of vendors. There's a lot to look at, believe me, with dozens of companies hawking everything from coffee to contact lenses.

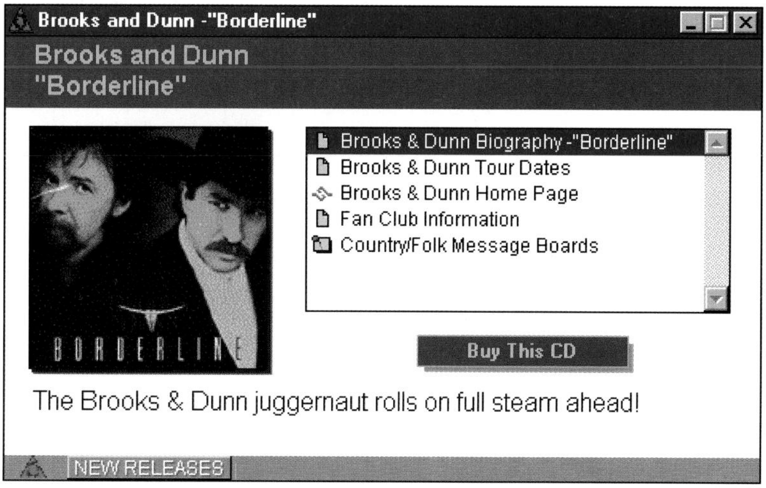

Figure 12.2 A buying option in the MusicSpace channel

CAUTION

Online shopping doesn't necessarily offer you the best deals. Even if the price looks right, you'll have to factor in shipping charges, which can make an item more expensive than if you just bought it in a store.

Buying Something

Go ahead, look around till you find something you want. Okay, that's enough—I haven't got all day. I'll tell you what—why don't I pick something out so you can see how the online shopping process works? I'll choose something everybody loves—chocolate; specifically, a 16-piece assortment of chocolate truffles from Godiva. To find it, I double-clicked the Food & Beverage folder in the Marketplace window, then I double-clicked Godiva Chocolatier, then I double-clicked Truffle Assortments, and finally I double-clicked the item itself. (That's a lot of double-clicking, but it was worth it.) The result is shown in Figure 12.3.

This is a standard dialog box for most merchandise on AOL. As you can see, it includes a photo of the item, a text box with a description of it, and buttons at the bottom that let you complete your purchase. Now, suppose that after looking at this box of chocolates and reading about it, you want to buy it. (Who wouldn't?) Select Click Here to Order, which takes you through a series of dialog boxes in which you enter ordering and shipping information for the item you want. (If you're buying clothes, this is where you'd tell them your size.) You can also fill out a gift card if you want.

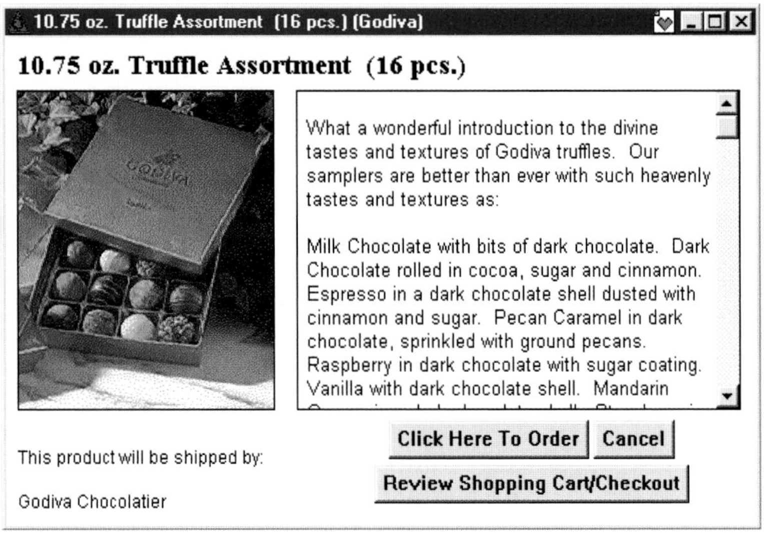

Figure 12.3 A buying option in the Marketplace channel

Going Through the Virtual Checkout Counter

When you have completed the ordering and shipping information dialog boxes, you'll come to a window that places the truffles into a virtual Shopping Cart. At this point, you can either click a button to do some more shopping and add more items to the cart or you can complete your purchase. (With the Shopping Cart, you can buy from different online stores and send stuff to multiple locations all at once.) For the sake of this discussion, let's go ahead and order the chocolates, using the following steps:

1. Click Checkout, fill in your credit card information, and then click Continue.
2. Fill out the shipping address, if necessary, and then click Continue.
3. Review the information in the Order Summary dialog box, as in the example shown here:

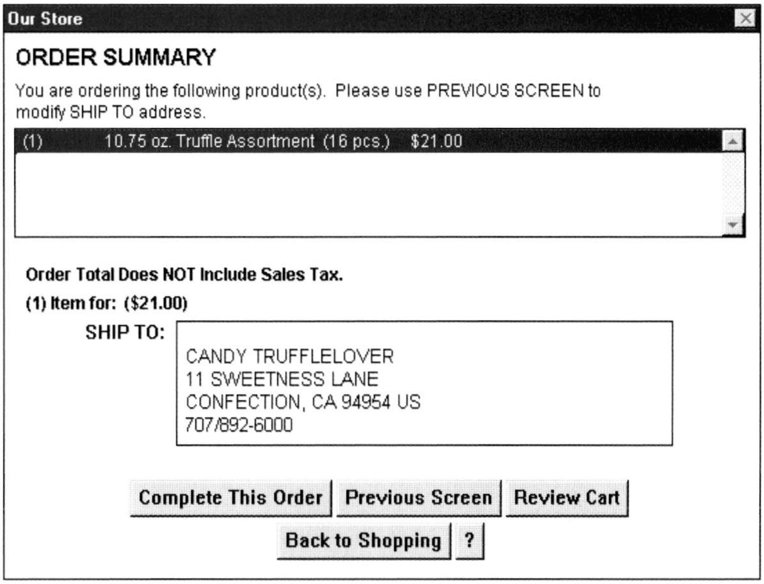

4. Click Complete This Order.

That's it—you'll soon be munching on truffles. And isn't that a lovely way to end this chapter?

WHAT'S NEXT?

Nothing. The book's finished. From now on, you're on your own. Well, not quite—if you turn the page, you'll find an appendix that lists some of AOL's most useful keywords. These will help you jump around from place to place in a jiffy. Good luck!

APPENDIX A

Keywords

This appendix is all about keywords—the easiest way to jump from place to place in America Online. I've included keywords for many of the features covered in the book, and lots of others that can make your travels around AOL faster and more efficient. Enjoy.

GENERAL PURPOSE

Keyword	Purpose
BILLING	Information about your account
BUDDY	Buddy lists
CANCEL	Cancel your account
DOWNLOAD 101	Downloading help
HELP	Member services
KEYWORD	Find a keyword
MEMBERS	Member directory
NAMES	Create or delete screen names
NEW	Latest features and services
PARENTAL CONTROL	Set or modify parental controls
PASSWORD	Change your password
PROFILE	Create or modify your member profile
QUESTIONS	One stop infoshop
SHORTHAND	Online shorthand, FOR INSTANCE: :) = SMILE
TOS	View AOL's terms of service
UPGRADE	Get the latest AOL software

THE INTERNET AND E-MAIL

Keyword	Purpose
AM GLOSSARY	Definitions of Internet terms
ANSWER MAN	Answers to Internet questions
MAILING LISTS	E-mail mailing lists directory
NEWSGROUPS	Internet newsgroup window
WEB	Launch the AOL Web browser

COMPUTERS AND SOFTWARE

Keyword	Purpose
CALENDAR	What's hot in PC forums
HOF	Downloading Hall of Fame
MAC	Apple Macintosh forums
MAGAZINE RACK	Computer magazines
NEWSBYTES	Newsbytes computer news
NEWSWIRE	Computer industry news
SOFTWARE	The software center
VIRUS	PC Virus Information Center
WIN	Windows forum
ZDNET	ZDNet from Ziff-Davis

NEWS

Keyword	Purpose
AIDS	News and information about AIDS
BUSINESS	Business News
CAMPAIGN 96	News about the presidential campaign
CQ	Congressional Quarterly
EDITORS CHOICE	Pictures of the week
NEWS SEARCH	News search database

ENTERTAINMENT

Keyword	Purpose
COMICS	Online comic books
CONCERTS	Concert tour information
COUNTRY	Country music
DAILY HOROSCOPE	What's in the stars
DEAD	Grateful Dead forum
HOME VIDEO	News about video releases
JAZZ	Jazz music
LABELS	Record companies
LOTTERY	State lottery results
MOVIE REVIEW DB	Movie reviews database
MOVIE REVIEWS	Movie reviews
MOVIES	The Movies window
MTV	MTV Online
NEW MOVIES	New movie releases
NEW MUSIC	The latest CD releases
RADIO	Radio forum
ROCK	Rock music
STAR TREK	Star Trek Club forum
TRIVIA FORUM	Trivia games
TV GUIDE	Online television listings

SPORTS

Keyword	Purpose
AUTO RACING	Auto racing news
BOATING	Boating and sailing
FOOTBALL	Pro football

Keyword	Purpose
GFF	Grandstand Fantasy Football
GS TRIVA	Sports trivia
HORSE	The Horse forum
NBA	Pro basketball
NCAA	College basketball
NHL	Pro hockey
SPORTS LIVE	Online chats with sports figures
SPORTS NEWS	The latest news and scores
STATS	Stats
WWF	World Wrestling Federation

PERSONAL FINANCE

Keyword	Purpose
COMPANY PROFILES	Information on corporations
COMPANY	Company research
EDGAR	Corporate financial reports
FOOL	Motley Fool forum
FUND	Morningstar Mutual Funds
HISTORICAL QUOTES	Historical stock and fund quotes
IRS	Internal Revenue Service
LINGO	Definitions of investment terms
MUTUAL FUNDS	Mutual Fund Center
PF SOFTWARE	Personal finance software center
PORTFOLIO	Your personal stock and fund portfolios
SBA	Small Business Administration
STRATEGIES	Business strategies forum
TAX	Income tax forum

REFERENCE AND EDUCATION

Keyword	Purpose
CAREER CENTER	AOL Career Center
COLLEGE BOARD	The College Board
COLLEGIATE	Merriam-Webster's Collegiate Dictionary
COLUMBIA	Columbia Encyclopedia
COMPUTER TERMS	Webster's Dictionary of Computer Terms
COURSES	Online study courses
DESK REFERENCE	NY Public Library Desk Reference
ELECTION HANDBOOK	Student Election Handbook
GROLIER'S	Grolier's Encyclopedia
HELP WANTED	Online help wanted ads
HOMEWORK	Homework Help
KIDS DICTIONARY	Merriam-Webster's Kids Dictionary
MEDICAL DICTIONARY	Merriam-Webster's Medical Dictionary
NOLO	Self help law center
PHONE DIRECTORY	Telephone directories
PLACES RATED	Places Rated Almanac
RSP	Scholarship and grant information
STUDENT CENTER	Student Center window
SUPERLIBRARY	MacMillan Information SuperLibrary
WHITE PAGES	ProCD National Telephone Directory
YELLOW PAGES	Business Yellow Pages
ZIP CODES	Zip Code Directory

TRAVEL

Keyword	Purpose
AAA	American Automobile Association
B&B	Bed and Breakfast listings
CRUISE CRITIC	Information on cruises
FROMMER	Guides to major cities
RESERVATIONS	Travel reservations
TRAVEL FORUM	AOL's travel forum
ZAGAT	Restaurant and hotel surveys

SHOPPING

Keyword	Purpose
AMEX	American ExpressNet
AOL STORE	America Online Store
AUTOVANTAGE	AutoVantage club for car buyers
BLOCKBUSTER	Blockbuster Music's online store
BOOKSTORE	Read USA's online bookstore
CLASSIFIEDS	AOL classified ads
EDDIE BAUER	Eddie Bauer outdoor clothes and gear
FAO SCHWARZ	F.A.O. Schwarz toy store
FEDEX	Federal Express Online
GIFT	Marketplace Gift Valet
GODIVA	Godiva chocolates
HALLMARK	Hallmark cards
HANES	One Hanes Place (Champion L'eggs, Playtex)
JCPENNEY	JCPenney
LENS	Lens Express contact lenses
NISSAN	Nissan cars and trucks
OFFICEMAX	OfficeMax office supplies

Keyword	Purpose
OMAHA	Omaha Steaks
PRICE	Price Online
SHARPER IMAGE	The Sharper Image
STARBUCKS	Starbucks coffee
TOWER	Tower Records
USPS	U.S. Postal Service

Index

A

D

E

G

H

I

J

K

L

M

N

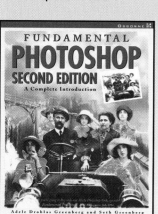

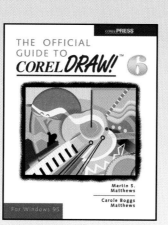